Justice For Cats
Caring for Your Cat & Starting a Shelter

Jessica Barbazon B.S.

Jessica Barbazon

iUniverse, Inc.
New York Bloomington

Justice For Cats

Caring for Your Cat & Starting a Shelter

Copyright © 2009 by Jessica Barbazon

All rights reserved. No part of this book may be used or reproduced by any means, graphic, electronic, or mechanical, including photocopying, recording, taping or by any information storage retrieval system without the written permission of the publisher except in the case of brief quotations embodied in critical articles and reviews.

iUniverse books may be ordered through booksellers or by contacting:

iUniverse
1663 Liberty Drive
Bloomington, IN 47403
www.iuniverse.com
1-800-Authors (1-800-288-4677)

Because of the dynamic nature of the Internet, any Web addresses or links contained in this book may have changed since publication and may no longer be valid. The views expressed in this work are solely those of the author and do not necessarily reflect the views of the publisher, and the publisher hereby disclaims any responsibility for them.

ISBN: 978-0-595-52480-8 (pbk)
ISBN: 978-0-595-51227-0 (cloth)
ISBN: 978-0-595-62533-8 (ebk)

Library of Congress Control Number: 2008939117

Printed in the United States of America

iUniverse Rev Date 1/29/09

Dedication

To cats in animal shelters
To cats who have lost their lives to coyotes
To cats abandoned by irresponsible guardians
To animals in research labs, suffering the horrors of vivisection
To all the cats I have rescued, for the great education and companionship

Contents

Dedication v

Introduction xiii

PART 1. BE AN ADVOCATE FOR CATS 1

CHAPTER 1   MAKE AMERICA A NO-KILL NATION NOW 1
    Current Methods of "Animal Control" Don't Work 2
    Story from an Abandoned Cat 3
    Killing is Not a Solution 4
    Time for Change 4
    No-Kill Shelters as "the Norm" will Reduce Abandonment 5
    Derogatory Language Needs to Change 6
    Same Money Reallocated 6
    Stop Investing in Methods for Killing 8
    Trap-Neuter-Return 9
    Mandatory Spay/Neuter Laws 10
    New Money Dedicated For Homeless Pets 11
    Media is the Key to Spread the Message 12
    Street Signs of Pride 16

CHAPTER 2   NEED FOR A NEW NO-KILL SHELTER 17
    My Concern for Animal Welfare 18
    Need for a Caring Shelter 22
    Beginning of the No-Kill Shelter 23
    Story of Callie, Austin, and Hemlock 25
    Daily Phone Calls to a Shelter 26

CHAPTER 3   CIRCUMSTANTIAL CAT RELINQUISH TOPICS 29
    Moving 30
        Traveling with Your Cat *30*
        Represent Cats Well to Other People When Moving or Traveling *32*
    Divorce 33
    Allergies 34
    Personal Health Problems 35
    Pregnancy 35

Newborn Baby... 36

Chapter 4   Litter Box Issues 39
Improper Elimination 39
Litter Box Etiquette 40
Proper Amount of Litter in the Box.................................... 41
Litter Options 42
Box Options.. 43
Short-Sided Box.. 43
Location of Litter Box... 44
Mood-stabilizing Medication for Litter Box Avoidance 44
Story of Butterscotch 45
Territory Issues Regarding Litter Box Evasion..................... 47
  Introducing New People 48
  Introducing Animals Together.. 48
  Unexpected Way that a New Animal Scent Gets in the Home........ 50

Chapter 5   Scratching and Claw Topics 51
Scratching... 51
Scratching Post Options.. 52
Build Your Own Post 53
Proper Scratching Location... 54
Deterring Methods When Cat Scratches Wrong Object...... 55
Training the Cat to Use the Post 55
Trimming Claws 56
Claw Sheath Option to Protect Furniture........................... 57
Declawing Reality.. 57
  Methods in Use for Declawing a Cat............................... 60
  Story from a Declawed Cat... 60
  Geographical Attitudes Vary about Declawing................ 61

Chapter 6   Helping Stray Cats.. 63
Strays... 63
Story of Jasmine.. 66
Rescuing a Needy Cat... 67
Spraying Urine.. 68
Females "In Heat" Behavior 69
Fighting 70
Story of Mr. T... 70
Trapping 70
Behavior Quirk from Some Feral Raised Cats..................... 72

Handling Ferals 72
    Catch the Cat in the Open Outdoors *73*
    Catch the Cat from Within the Pen *74*
    Housing Un-socialized Cats *75*

CHAPTER 7   CARING FOR THE CATS 77

Raising Young Orphans 77
    Maintaining Body Temperature *78*
    Formula Selection and Feeding *78*
    Wiping the Kitten for its Health *81*
    Teach the Kitten to Eat Canned and Dry Food *81*
    Litter Box Training *82*
Medical Exam 84
Giving a Bath 86
Cat Food 88
Story of Elijah 91
Better Cat Food Standards 96

CHAPTER 8   FELINE MEDICAL CONCERNS 97

Intestinal Parasites and Protozoans 97
    Hookworms and Roundworms *98*
    Tapeworms *99*
    Various Parasite Killers Available at Vets and Internet *100*
    Coccidiosis *100*
    Story of Arian *101*
Preventing Contagious Ailments 101
    Sanitation Policy *102*
    Chlamydia *103*
    Upper Respiratory Infection *104*
    Distemper (Panleukopenia) *105*
    Feline Infectious Peritonitis (FIP) *107*
    Feline Leukemia Virus (FeLV) & Feline Immunodeficiency Virus (FIV) 108
    Rabies *108*
Sterilization 109
    Health Benefits of Sterilization *110*
    How to Determine the Gender of the Cat *110*
How to Establish Whether a Cat is Already Sterilized 111
    A Spay for Females *112*
    A Neuter for Males *113*
    Sterilization through a Vaccine *114*

  Description of a Cryptorchid *115*
  Story of Owen *115*

CHAPTER 9 REASONS BY WHICH CATS COME UP MISSING 117
  Predators 117
  Coyotes: The Most Prominent and Prolific Predators 118
  Other Predators 123
  Research Labs 124
  School Dissection Labs 126
  Hit by Car 127
  Stolen by Human 127
  Leaving With a Visitor via the Vehicle 128
  Story of Garlin 128
  Getting Trapped in an Inanimate Object 130
  Story of Koshi 130
  Indoor Cat Escapes and is Terrified 131

CHAPTER 10 WAYS TO FIND A MISSING CAT 133
  Locate a Missing Cat 133
  Actions to Take Which Help Prevent Losing a Cat 135
  Collars 135
  Story of Oleander 136
  Microchips 137
  Story of Zipper 138
  Other Return Stories Because of Microchips 139

PART 2. PRACTICALITIES OF CREATING A SHELTER 141

CHAPTER 11 ESTABLISHING METHODS OF OPERATING A SHELTER 141
  Boundaries 141
  Donation with Taking in a Cat 142
  Get the Best Prices for Supplies and Services 143
  Determine the Cat Care Budget 144
  The Labor Force 145
    Foster Parents *145*
    Volunteers *146*
  Records for Each Cat 147
  Hoarding 148
  Where the Cats Will Reside in the Shelter 150
  Secret Location or Publicly Known Location 152

Chapter 12 Advertising Cats for Adoption 155
    Cat Breed Book 155
    Newspaper 157
    Internet 157
    Local Media 158
    Word-of-Mouth 158

Chapter 13 Adopting Out the Cats 159
    Adoption Process 160
    Adoption Counselors 160
    Understanding a Person's Character 161
    Components of a Good Adopter 162
    Never adopt out a Cat to Someone the Cat Dislikes 163
    Indoor Smoker and Indoor Cat Do Not Mix 163
    Cat Connection Specialist Expertise; Knowing the Cats Well 164
    Adoption Fee 165
    Adoption Form 166
    Requests for Free Cats – Don't do it 167
    Letting Go 167
    Have Pet Carriers for Adopted Cats 168
    Written Cat Care Information for Adopters 168
    Declawing Pamphlet 169

Chapter 14 Feline Lifestyles: Inside or Outside 171
    Inside Only 172
    Options for Indoor Cats to Enjoy Outdoor Air 174
    Inside and Outside 175
    Outside Only 176
    Bird Enthusiasts 177

Chapter 15 Black Cat Persecution in Society 179
    Halloween, Cults, Superstition and Black Cats 180
    Story of Hope 182
    Story of Orchid 183
    Story of Jack 184
    Story of a Black Stray at the Car Wash 186

Chapter 16 In the Event of Death: Feline or Human 189
    Grief Counseling 189
    Story of Nolan 191
    Story of Salmon 193

Story of Willow 196
Plan for the Cat after the Guardian Dies 197

PART 3. BUSINESS COMPONENTS 199

CHAPTER 17 STATE AND FEDERAL REQUIREMENTS TO OPERATE A SHELTER 199

Naming Your Shelter 199
Incorporating; Getting Non-Profit Status 201
Benefits of Obtaining 501 © 3 Status 203
Federal Tax Exemption 204
Forms Required 204
Public Charity or Private Foundation 205
Advance Ruling Period 206

CHAPTER 18 FUND-RAISING METHODS 207

Mail Campaign 207
Create a Mailing List and Letter 208
Local Business Support 211
Yard Sales 214
Thrift Store 214
Car Wash 214
Special Event Fundraiser 214
Grants 215

Epilogue 217

Appendix 219

What to Expect and How to Care for Your New Cat 219
State Contact Information for Incorporating 223

References 231

Introduction

The purpose of this book is to decrease the euthanasia numbers of our companion animals across the nation. More than four million pets are murdered every year because of an irresponsible person that was once in that animal's life, or some previous generation's life. Killing our feline friends is appalling, inhumane and unnecessary. There are superior alternatives to handle currently homeless pets.

I intend to motivate people into action. My personal experience of rescuing nearly six-hundred felines hopefully will inspire others to help cats. I am a good example that one person can truly make a difference. Concerned individuals can rescue one cat or start his or her own no-kill shelter. For those who cannot take in a cat, many ideas are described as to what a person can provide.

My mission began when I started rescuing every cat that crossed my path that was in need of a home and adopting from local kill shelters to save their lives, too. An earnest compulsion within me to rectify the injustice that many humans have committed against these intuitive, intelligent, affectionate companion animals prompted me to inquire about how to start a non-profit organization. I researched thoroughly to determine how to start a shelter, including those details in this book.

This book will benefit anyone who has a cat or wants to start a rescue shelter. It is especially created for those who want to start an animal haven. Every fact one will need to begin a non-profit organization is included. Cat guardians will learn answers to questions that have arisen about why his or her cat acts a certain way. Cat care topics are included, like how to properly train a cat to use a scratching post and how to travel with your cat. A reader will find this text to be astutely different from any other because of the new ideas presented.

The first portion of this manual pertains to being an advocate for the cats. My intention is to educate anyone who is concerned about the plight of homeless animals. Each person can participate in improving the lives of cats and reforming America into a no-kill nation. A completely new approach is elaborated on when it comes to animal control methods. Free sterilization needs to be available, and required, for all pets. Reallocate the spending of shelter money to include sterilization for cats in the community, instead of spending money on practices that do not address the source of the problem.

More no-kill shelters need to come into existence. Anyone needing to relinquish a cat to a shelter would feel better knowing that the cat will absolutely get to find an adoptive home. This will cause cat abandonment to decrease. By having street signs of pride, signs which will be erected on each street across the nation declaring the pets on this street are all sterilized, people will become alert for any abandoned cats that may show up on their street. Empowering individuals with knowledge about how he or she can change the world for a companion animal will encourage every person to take action.

All the issues that phone calls from the public present to a shelter to relinquish a cat are thoroughly detailed. The reasons people want to relinquish a cat are discussed. These topics are useful to individual cat guardians, as well, because any of these subjects, about behavior concerns could face all of us at some point.

Remedies to behavior problems are given, as I explain these topics in a method for counseling persons that call a shelter. Solutions to cat conduct dilemmas are presented which often allow guardians to realize they can keep their cat. The detrimental effects of declawing a cat are meticulously described. There is even a passage from the cat's point of view after having this gruesome procedure performed, which is a unique feature of this manual. Declawing often leads to problems such as the feline eliminating on furniture, either weeks after the bandages are removed or years later.

A protocol to follow for handling the cats and maintaining their health is incorporated. Ways to house the cats to keep them healthy are discussed. The topic of selecting a quality cat food is discussed. My adorable, spotted burnt-orange and white cat, Elijah, suffered from a common condition many cats encounter. He developed irritable-bowel type symptoms. A probiotic, such as Lactobacillus Acidophilus, was what his digestion system required for him to become a healthy cat again.

The section on finding a missing cat is useful for every cat caregiver. When a cat is missing, fear, concern, and anxiety consume the family that loves the cat. Having a valuable resource which provides answers to how the cat may have vanished is critical in this chaotic time. What is even more beneficial is having a resource to help one find his or her missing cat. Facts on coyotes, a cat's most prominent predator, are incorporated within the text along with ways to protect your cat.

The next part of the book is about the practicalities of creating a shelter. Before beginning a shelter, many decisions are required to be made. The methods by which to govern the rescue haven's relationship with the public are elaborated on to help one decide what will work for this particular shelter. Boundaries need to be established. Determining how many cats one can financially and physically care for properly is necessary.

Finding new homes is part of the rescue experience. Alternate methods of advertising help get cats into new homes. People need to be screened to ensure they are concerned about the cat's best interest. Cat connection specialists will pair the best-matched human family and cat. The facts on the horrors of Halloween are precisely detailed, which every cat guardian and shelter must know. Discussing where the cat will live, inside, outside or both is important when matching a suitable cat for the home environment that will be provided by the new guardian.

The final section of the book describes business components one will confront when starting and operating the shelter. Forming a corporation in your state begins the process. After the organization is formed, one can file for tax-exempt status through the Internal Revenue Service if desired. Modes to obtain funds for the organization are inserted in this division. For the aspiring creator of a non-profit organization, every state's contact information is included at the end of the book.

The book is meant to be used as a quick reference guide. Persons seeking to begin a no-kill cat refuge can utilize all of the details described within this manuscript. With this "how to" manual an ailurophile is given all the situations one will encounter with this endeavor. For cat guardians, any predicament that arises with your cat requiring some information, just grab this book. While operating a shelter or for a remedy for your cat, one can look in the table of contents for the page number of the section needed to answer any questions. Information in this manual is sometimes repeated in different chapters or sections because it is relevant to be included for full comprehension of each topic.

The terms guardian, caregiver, and caretaker are used interchangeably through the book. I do not approve of the word "owner" because I feel it keeps cats in a repressed state in society. Cats are individuals with distinct personalities who have been humankind's companion for thousands of years. They are not furniture, or some such owned item. It would be nice if in all parts of the law, they were recognized distinctly from objects.

This book will become a priceless asset on your bookshelf. Use this collection of data as a guide to any dilemmas your cat may present or for starting and operating your very own animal shelter. Years of hands-on experience with cats, is right at your fingertips. Moments of reading will infuse your mind with years of vast knowledge!

Chapter 1

Make America a No-Kill Nation Now

"What is right to be done cannot be done too soon." Jane Austen

America has a serious problem with the way it handles homeless pets. For decades many millions of domesticated, companion animals had been killed intentionally in Animal Control facilities. This method for controlling animal numbers continues today. Sterilization of cats is the key to becoming a no-kill nation. There are so many kittens born every year that there are not enough homes for them, but murdering them is not a humane way to solve the problem.

Each person is capable of taking action in some manner, to create change, for saving cats' lives. The only way lives can be saved is by starting with each home, each street, each community, and expanding this effort across the nation. With the movement of responsibility towards cats spreading, the number of animals being killed will drop drastically and it can happen rapidly.

We need to alter the thinking of mainstream animal control facilities into changing the way that shelters are operated. Killing four million pets annually in the United States is absolutely unacceptable! More cats are killed by animal control than any other cause. The media needs to be utilized to get the message out to every citizen about the plight of homeless animals. Homeless cats depend on humans to survive, hence the name, domesticated animals. Cats are our very special companions. We owe them that much, the right to a safe, long life.

Current Methods of "Animal Control" Don't Work

"Insanity: doing the same thing over and over again and expecting different results." Albert Einstein

The current method of rounding up stray and owner surrendered cats to kill them at government and privately funded shelters is absolutely wrong. This is not a solution. The killing just continues. It is unfathomable to me that citizens just sit around and tolerate this as an accepted form of "animal control." Many people love their pets, after all the pet industry is a multi-billion dollar industry. Why aren't animal lovers stepping up and demanding change? We must demand change.

The truth is we must demand change from ourselves first. Individuals who have not sterilized their pets, provided life-long homes, and those who have abandoned their pet have contributed to the problem. Due to these reasons, the animals have been reproducing exponentially. There are not enough homes able to provide care for all of them. This is how the problem began. It is so important that we all participate in fixing it (literally), since the quandary was created by us directly, by adding cats to the problem or indirectly by allowing it to continue.

Demanding change from your local shelters is also necessary. Tell them what you would like to see transformed, then ask what you can do to help them attain this status. Most shelters operate on limited budgets. They won't be able to make positive changes without some type of assistance and pressure. This is how the movement will begin, towards becoming a no-kill nation.

Animal control principally originated, for most places, to remove stray animals from someone's property. A dog on the loose certainly could be very dangerous to people and other animals, so someone was needed to remove it before harm was done. Any stray animal could, though rarely they do, harbor a zoonotic disease, like Rabies, therefore putting humans and other pets at risk. Due to necessity, counties issued a portion of their operating budget for animal removal. Now, what do they do with these animals?

There are no lines of citizens standing at the door to provide homes for the animals. The County does not want to spend money on food and care for any length of time. The animals can't speak and express that they don't want to be killed. But even if they could, would these people care? Every live being strives to survive. If the cat could just tell his story, perhaps someone would be sympathetic.

Story from an Abandoned Cat

"I was abandoned at the local fast-food hamburger joint when my mom moved. I was terrified. These big metal objects with rubber tires move quickly all over the place, some nearly crushing me. There is no food bowl or water bowl out here. No one calls my name anymore. I don't have a soft bed on which to sleep. I have no home. When water falls from the sky, my beautiful fur becomes wet and uncomfortable, not looking very nice any longer. Licking water from the ground when a puddle forms, though it is laced with oil residue, is my only water source. Not very tasty, I assure you.

An entirely new array of problems plagues me now. Fleas are all over my body, constantly biting me. I am so itchy. I am so hungry. I smell meat in the big, metal bin after darkness falls. Someone from inside the building carries the good-smelling food to it, not even acknowledging me. My only hope of a meal is to climb into the metal bin to find a piece of food. My mom used to put food in a bowl for me. Life was so nice back then.

One day a metal cage was placed here with some awesome smelling, real cat food. How nice! Then when I ate the food, a door slammed shut. I could not get out. This was a terrifying feeling. I was trapped in the hot sun for six hours before anyone came to pick me up. The feeling of thirst overwhelmed my dehydrated body.

The hot, steel trap was put into one of those metal things with rubber tires. I was driven to this place where I was put in another confining trap. There are other cats here. They are very scared, too. Now, as I am sitting here, I am watching a person go to the cages that are in front of mine, with a bottle and a needle. He sticks the needle into the cat then it is dead! This is horrible, why would someone want to kill cats? We are such nice creatures. What did we do wrong? I don't want to die. Please, don't kill me!

All I was doing at the hamburger restaurant was trying to get some food, is that so wrong that it is justified by death? My mom left me in the parking lot one day. I didn't know what to do or why she did this to me. Life has been so hard since that day, but this is truly the worst that it's been. I just can't watch this atrocity before me, a cat, probably just like me, abandoned, a total victim, being killed. There are three other cats in the line before me.

Why do you, humans, do this to us? You can abandon us for no reason, and kill us for no reason. Give me a chance to get a home again. I know someone will want me. I'm so nice and handsome. I would have never stayed at that parking lot, if I knew someone would want to kill me for it. I just thought my mom would come back for me. Every day I was full of hope that I would hear her voice call my name. I just want food, shelter, and love. Is that so bad?"

Killing is Not a Solution

Killing the homeless cats is convenient and cheap. Throw the bodies in the landfill and it's a done deal. What a simple solution to dispose of stray animals. Don't even blame the tight budgets that most districts face as the reason for using death as a solution. It does not need to cost any extra to embrace a life-respecting mission. If all the "shelters" would commit to the fact that killing is not an option for currently homeless animals, then those who operate these facilities could allow their minds to be open to other possibilities.

Most of the people either operating one of these facilities or working there do not like euthanasia as the solution. They would like the animals to get new homes, but this "practice" of killing has been accepted as the only method for controlling animal numbers. What I am suggesting is let's be completely open-minded on implementing new methods. The options are very feasible and will not extend their budget at all.

Simply spend the money on different resources with, "stop breeding" as the goal, instead of, "getting rid of and disposing of" as the goal. The fact is that "euthanasia" has become such an accepted term and "just the way it is" in dealing with homeless animals. Most people, especially from the government sector of animal control do not even consider anything else as "possible." Without additional resources, however, I am aware that all the killing can't stop immediately, but we can get the numbers down tremendously by making changes.

Fifteen years ago about sixteen million pets were killed across the country. Progress has been made due to a couple of reasons with regards to the number of pets euthanized. The implementation of sterilization projects along with encouraging the public to come and adopt homeless animals from the shelter has helped save lives. However, currently and for the last several years the number remains rather stagnant.

When referencing the number of euthanized animals, this includes cats and dogs. The number of four million is not exact because there is no established uniform reporting method and not all shelters participate. The number of cats killed exceeds that of dogs nationwide, overall. I encourage each person to help any animal that is in need. Implementing any or all of the ideas in this book promotes all pets to be saved.

Time for Change

"Man's mind stretched to a new idea never goes back to its original dimensions." Oliver Wendell Holmes

I am challenging every one of you to think in a new way. Can you handle that? For those persons that are already employed in animal welfare, this involves a whole new way of managing your facility with "life" being at its center. For individuals who are concerned about the plight of shelter animals, it is time to step up and take action.

Sterilization, along with educating the public about its importance and the plight of homeless animals are the methods by which becoming a no-kill nation can occur. There are many animal shelters, which have already implemented low-cost spay/neuter programs. I applaud those who are executing these programs because for each cat sterilized, literally thousands are being prevented from being born, humanely. Most refuges are aware that sterilization is the method by which to achieve positive change. The establishment of no-kill shelters is the main way to reform animal control.

> **Feline Fact**
>
> In four years, a breeding queen and her surviving offspring can produce well over two-thousand cats. This statistic takes into account the fact that only fifty-percent of the kittens survive into adulthood.

No-Kill Shelters as "the Norm" will Reduce Abandonment

By having no-kill shelters everywhere, this will cut down, yes down, on the number of strays. How can this be, you ask? The truth is that when pet guardians are in a desperate situation requiring them to give up their pet, abandonment can become the preferential choice.

- A guardian may choose abandonment over sure death at a common kill shelter, when a home has not been found for the pet and time has run out to continue searching for one.
- A person may rationalize that abandonment is the better option with hope that the cat, will simply live or better yet, a nice person will find it and take it into his/her home.
- Abandoning the cat increases the likelihood of having more cats living on the streets, for those that do survive.
- Multiply this act of abandonment many times over, for each community across the nation. For the cats that survive, numbers will increase through breeding creating serious exponential growth.

My point is that if people know for sure their cat will not be killed at a rescue haven, they will take it there. There will, unfortunately, always be some completely irresponsible people who will still abandon their cat, but by having no-kill shelters as the norm, this truly will reduce a majority of abandoned cats. This will eliminate so many of the homeless cats that Animal Control facilities spend many hours and lots of money trapping, transporting, and disposing of, in the end.

Derogatory Language Needs to Change

One thing that is simple to change is one particular word, commonly used by shelters. This term is "unwanted," when referring to all the pets that need a home. This word implies a very negative connotation. "Unwanted" implies something that is worthless, like trash. No one wants trash, do they? Cats are magnificent animals. These pets are wanted by someone, somewhere.

The person may just not have the financial or physical means to have the pet. For instance, I would love to save every cat's life. Financially and physically this would just not be possible, to have every cat. It is not that the pets are unwanted, because someone would love this particular cat. That person is not able to take the cat at this time. Please, shelter folks do not use this derogatory term any longer. Use the word "homeless" instead because the cat is currently without his own home. He needs a home and a loving family.

Same Money Reallocated

Staff spending needs to be reallocated, working towards a no-kill goal.

- Get rid of cleaning staff or receptionists and use more volunteers, perhaps.

- Reduce the number of Animal Control officers that trap and transport pets to be killed. This is a pertinent way to release funds designated towards salaries and reallocate it for increasing the number of sterilizations performed.

- The breeding animals must be addressed on a grand scale. There is a segment of the population that is extremely difficult to motivate to sterilize their pets, even with education. Free spay/neuter will work with some, but not others. Offering people $5 or some type of incentive that directly benefits them, while holding a Spay-a-thon perhaps, for each pet brought in, will promote pets to get spayed, drastically and quickly reducing homeless animal numbers. Allotting a portion of the budget in this manner could be immensely beneficial overall.

- Hire a full time veterinarian to work at the shelter performing sterilization surgeries every day.

- Another way would be to hire a couple of veterinarians on a part-time basis. These vets would remain in their own buildings. They would perform a certain number of sterilizations on a weekly basis.

- Reducing salaries is sometimes necessary to have enough money to get goals met. There are many cases of absolutely ridiculous pay for some of the people working in both private and government shelters. The executive director tends to be the one collecting an astoundingly enormous salary.

- Huge salaries to anyone, is very disturbing. Animal havens are created to help cats needing assistance and for the betterment of the community. When huge portions of the operating budgets are given to one or two people, it is a very sad situation for the animals.

Everyone should demand to know what the salaries being paid are, at your local facilities. Whether they will tell you personally or not, that's fine because, it is available in public records, at least as a whole for the organization. Government funded shelters usually have to release this information since they are funded by taxpayers. Privately supported animal havens are required to categorize and report their spending annually within the state and / or the Federal Government.

Increased inquiries about financial spending will let shelters know that citizens are concerned that the money is being spent on the animals. Most pet rescues are concerned about maintaining a good public image, to bring in donations, volunteers, and adopters. The community's support, or lack of, can make a big difference when a pet haven makes decisions on its budgets.

One must think in terms of getting animals sterilized, making that the ultimate goal. As an officer is out collecting strays, the animals are still reproducing, so by the time the officer comes back to this spot in the future, there are more kittens ready to be picked up again. So, however reducing staff in a way that allows, "human resources" money to be spent on sterilization instead, is the way one must think and apply it to your pet refuge.

Voucher programs allow citizens to pay an extremely reduced fee for sterilization of a pet. This method is a great way to encourage spays and neuters to occur. Convenience to guardians must be maximized with these programs. Allow vet clinics to issue them, when someone requests it, but there is even a superior way to support nonproliferation. Attempting to persuade as many vets as possible to offer a cheap price to everyone would be ideal. Many people's cooperation and empathy to the cause of sterilization is necessary, for it to make a serious impact on the number of homeless animals.

Veterinarians have a valid viewpoint on their objective to earn money. After being in college for many years while paying a lot of tuition money, they certainly want to make money after receiving their Degree. However, hopefully each veterinarian cares about animals. One would think that is why they went into this type of career, but please vets don't make sterilizations the procedure of huge profits. Jack up the price on something else if you must. Everyone in society needs to contribute to this cause in some form if we are truly going to become a no-kill nation. You are one of the few, in society, who can perform this surgery.

Stop Investing in Methods for Killing

Stop purchasing resources to perform euthanasia. These methods devised to "control companion animal populations" are despicable. Compassionate people from the new movement could never imagine using murder as a means of population control. Don't spend any resources, including labor and finances, on operating these torture chambers.

Pets are killed by one of a few common methods.

- Depletion of oxygen to the cat is one method employed. Hypoxia is a deficiency of oxygen reaching the tissues of the body. Lack of oxygen prevents cell functions that are necessary for life to continue.
- A direct decompression of nerve cells in the brain invokes loss of consciousness followed by death, essentially being knocked in the head.
- Injecting sodium pentobarbital into the pet is the most common method, basically causing a heart attack.
- Gas chambers involve putting the animals in a small chamber and pumping carbon monoxide in it.
- Decompression chambers suck the air out of a confining unit, where the pet is and deflates the helpless cats' lungs.
- Drowning
- Shooting

Enough already with such barbaric practices! What kind of cruel humans would employ such insanity, as killing their own companion animals, and with such agonizing methods? There is only one place these monstrous devices should exist and that is in a museum of ancient animal population control devices.

The display case could read as follows;

> "These heinous apparatus were created by humans to murder their own pets that were currently homeless. This was how they dealt with controlling population growth. The plastic trash bags on display were what the bodies of the dead animals were placed in before being tossed into the landfill along with all the rubbish, like empty bottles, used baby diapers, and rotten food. This is all the respect given to domesticated animals that helped humankind to survive for thousands of years."

Trap-Neuter-Return

Since abandoned cats are where much of the reproduction lies, we must address this population. The T-N-R programs are the ones that are going to bring the stagnant euthanasia numbers down. One of the main reasons so many pets are still being killed is because as animals are brought in and killed, more remain in the environment continuing to breed which replaces the ones who were hauled away. The breeding must stop.

Each territory that cats live in is equipped to sustain a certain number of cats. For instance, perhaps a territory is able to sustain seven cats and Animal Control removes four, the number will increase again, by breeding, until seven is reached. If all of the cats already there were sterilized and returned to their familiar environment, then no breeding could occur. Cats are territorial. Once a colony is established, they usually keep new ones from moving in to that location. This will allow the colony, or clowder, to maintain the territory which will eventually cease to exist as cats die off from natural causes.

Another major sector of reproduction is from "owned cats." Some guardians are extremely irresponsible. They don't get their cat sterilized. The disregarded cat produces many offspring, year after year. The surviving kittens are ignored who grow up to breed themselves or are brought to a county shelter. The result is more homeless cats brought into the world.

Across the country there are individuals and organizations that have T-N-R programs, trap-neuter-return, for feral cats. Cats are trapped, then taken to be spayed or neutered, given vaccines, Rabies at a minimum, de-wormed, sometimes tested for infectious diseases, like Feline Leukemia Virus (FeLV) and Feline Immunodeficiency Virus (FIV), often earmarked (by snipping off a small corner of one ear to indicate that this cat is already sterilized), and then returned to where it was trapped, since it knows this territory well. This method has been proven to manage numbers in the colony, by reducing the number of cats.

No kittens will be born into the colony. Someone should feed the cats daily. Eventually, each cat will die off naturally when his or her time comes. The colony will cease to exist through attrition. Any cats that become tame enough to find an adoptive home are handled in this manner.

Education of everyone in the community is of the utmost importance. Education is what has been lacking, judging by the euthanasia numbers. The government is mostly to blame for not educating, our often irresponsible, public. Clearly, by the number of animals being murdered for decades, there has been a serious problem, so where are the sterilization programs? Why don't we have mandatory sterilization of pets in every state? We need it. Let's work together to accomplish the establishment of this type of law in every state. Pets are dying every day. This is a law absolutely worth having.

Mandatory Spay/Neuter Laws

There will be opposition from backyard cat and dog breeders, wanting to make a dollar by promoting more pets to be born. Individual breeds are special and should be preserved. However, there are way too many people breeding pets, when so many are intentionally being killed at shelters. Here is a solution for the qualms of breeders.

Each state can offer a few permits, a certain number for each breed, for sale at a large fee. A few breeding pairs of cats and dogs will be allowed to remain unsterilized. Consequently, the heinously cruel puppy mills will be forced out of business. Any breeders should be closely monitored, which will cut down on cruelty and neglect. This compromise should satisfy everyone involved, at least to some degree, while getting homeless animal numbers down humanely. Make your concerns heard to your senators and members of Congress.

Violators need to go to jail, always. Please no $50 fine for this offense, of allowing pets to multiply, only for the offspring to be killed. Some would argue, is that justice to have jail time required? This is a serious problem that needs serious solutions. It is not fair that innocent pets should die because they had an irresponsible guardian. Where's the justice here? Only severe penalties will force people to obey. A slap on the wrist will not invoke change.

I have a way to fix the problem of pet overpopulation that does not involve any murder. This portion of my plan will require additional money to be designated to the animal welfare cause. Federal and/or individual state budgets must assign more financial support to this cause if we are to truly see the killing stop immediately.

New Money Dedicated For Homeless Pets

Since the government and the public are to blame, now is the time for restitution. The government should sponsor sterilizations. Allow and require every pet to get sterilized. The government can subsidize vets for the cost. Buy the supplies needed for these surgeries. Be sure every clinic has their supplies replaced for free. No pet should ever be turned away. Another option would be to hire veterinarians, making them government employees, to perform these surgeries all day. They could work from government funded Animal Control facilities or a separate building could be purchased. Now, what do we do with the cats sitting in cages at this time?

Our government needs to financially support cat sanctuaries. Fence in government owned land to house these cats. Remodel unused government buildings to house cats. Create many new jobs by refurbishing abandoned buildings in towns and cities across America for housing, as well. Use these places as adoption centers. The existing animal control facilities will become sanctuaries, and will offer cats for adoption, instead of being kill factories. This plan would cost more initially, but once places are established and the number of cats is reduced through sterilization programs, it won't remain as costly. Purchase or work closely with a pet food manufacturer, so food will come cheaply. The main expenses will consist of: food, veterinarians, cat care staff, medical supplies, and maintenance.

These sanctuaries will be embraced by the public. Urban areas will especially obtain the support of residents. Many people in metropolitan areas do not have a pet. They could spend time volunteering or just visit the sanctuary to experience a relaxing time with a loving, friendly cat to pet. This type of setting has already been proven to prosper in Tokyo, Japan. Since most people live in small apartments, they tend not to have a pet in Tokyo. There are places that people pay a fee to come and spend time playing with and petting cats. This could be a win-win situation in American cities. The animal gets to live and people can enjoy the company of a cat, while not having the expense and daily responsibilities of caring for one's own.

The government did not take action before the situation became completely out of control. The public can now support saving lives with their tax dollars instead of taking lives. It is better to spend tax dollars to save lives than to take lives.

Our precious domesticated cats are part of our society. They should be cared for as necessary, just as any other group that is in need, has already been allotted tax dollars in this society. Domesticated pets truly are dependent upon humans.

The government allots money for people who have made bad choices and need financial and medical help. The government also spends lots of money in foreign countries. Let's fix America's problems first. Pets are truly victims of circumstances, such as when they are abandoned. They had no choice in the matter. Any money put into budgets for animal control should be used to promote a better life, as it is for humans, not to take the life.

Once all of the cats have homes or die off naturally, the program can end. With every citizen doing something to contribute to getting strays off the streets, the problem will cease to exist. I am not in some fantasy utopia with these ideas. The mission is possible if everyone will cooperate. The government is needed to participate in this duty. Money is needed to support the sanctuaries. With education reaching the masses, the public should want to provide additional donations.

Media is the Key to Spread the Message

"Power is no blessing in itself, except when it is used to protect the innocent." Jonathan Swift

The media is the way everyone can be reached. It is such an underutilized resource. This must change. Citizens should not have to actively seek out information about the plight of homeless cats. This information should be infiltrated within the media that reaches people daily.

Our government may need to mandate the media to do their part. But, perhaps they will cooperate on their own. Offering tax breaks to those who mention animal welfare messages in their broadcasts is one way to encourage participation. Why should the government care about helping homeless pets? It is the right thing to do and this segment of the population has been wrongly treated and ignored for way too long.

Radio and television stations, print media like magazines and newspapers, local and national, are how we can make people aware of the pet overpopulation issue. At least once a day, these broadcast networks should be endorsing animal welfare topics. For example, Bob Barker on "The Price is Right," used his opportunity, being watched by millions, to tell people to have their pets spayed or neutered.

Bob Barker's action is a perfect example of media education. By Mr. Barker saying this message repetitively through the years, there is just no way to know how many lives he has saved. I would estimate millions due to the exponential growth statistics. Way to go Bob!

Other media moguls have used their fame to promote animal welfare. Oprah Winfrey recently used her power to reach millions of viewers watching her television show. She showed footage of horrendous puppy mills and mentioned the importance of sterilization. Ellen DeGeneres cares about cats and other animals and promotes kindness on her shows. Hopefully, more examples of what these influential people have done and are doing will become more common in the media.

Children need to be informed about the plight of homeless animals. Inclusion in public school curricula would be great. By the media attention, individual teachers could bring these topics up in classroom discussions, so that children can be made aware, should they not be hearing this ethical information from their parents. Most children watch TV and listen to the radio anyhow, so they are certain to hear about spay and neuter. They will begin to understand the idea of a no-kill nation. After all, today's children will be the ones operating the shelters in the future.

Those of you in charge of the media empires don't wait for a financially struggling shelter to offer to pay for "air time." Take it upon oneself to include some pet friendly terminology in the daily program. Cat rescues would love to pay for billboards and media air time, and some are able to, but why not let them save that money to feed more hungry pets? There are some facts and terminology that everyone should fully understand. Hey, media, let's get some information out there that will become part of everyone's knowledge.

- Euthanasia is the first word everyone needs to learn. What needs to be said about it is that it means to kill. The definition of euthanasia, according to Webster's Dictionary is, 'the act or practice of killing or permitting the death of hopelessly sick or injured individuals (as persons or domestic animals) in a relatively painless way for reasons of mercy. The truth is, across the nation, there is killing of very healthy animals due to lack of homes or places for them to go to live out their lives. The current conduct of shelters does not even fit under that definition.

- What happens to these homeless pets is murder, so we must acknowledge what is really occurring before it can be changed. Euthanasia sounds "kinder" than to murder or to kill. However, the result is the same, the innocent animal is dead. Call it what it is, don't sugarcoat the reality. We must get honest about the whole situation for current methods to change. People need to get mad and sad about these words and what is really happening. That's the only way to cause a change. Give people emotional turmoil, so they won't lie there, accepting murder any longer.

- About four million homeless pets are killed every year across the U.S.

- Sterilization is the next topic that must be mentioned. Explain that this medical procedure prevents cats from reproducing.
- A spay is for a female. It involves removing her reproductive anatomy.
- A neuter is for a male. This process involves removing his testicles, or reproductive parts.
- Females can get pregnant as young as five months old. This fact is not well-known. Countless numbers of people expressed to me they had no idea a female cat can get pregnant so young.
- Four months of age is the ideal time for this surgery. Most females have not yet come into "heat." The male's testicles have just dropped into place. Any cat that is older than this age, do not delay in getting them "fixed" because they are breeding factories.
- The gestation period of a cat would be good information to include. Females give birth about 63 days after breeding.
- As quickly as four days after queening, a female can come into heat and get bred again! This is another very unrecognized reality. The cycle just repeats and repeats.
- One queen can produce several litters each year, especially in warmer climates. With all the females in the litter able to get pregnant so young, one can see how the cat numbers will increase quickly.
- In just two years, sixty-eight cats can come from one breeding cat.

Everyone can do something to help the plight of homeless cats in his/her area. Absolutely everyone can make a difference. One's age, sex, race, economic standing does not matter in helping this cause. No one is excluded or has any excuse as to why he or she can't do something.

When one has the property and the means, adopt a cat, either a stray from the streets or from a shelter. Just imagine that one million people adopt a cat from their local shelter! This is a great way to support the plight of homeless cats. Give them a home. If you see a stray, but are not able to bring the cat home, do your own T-N-R. Every one sterilized will prevent hundreds or even thousands more from being born. When possible, get it to a no-kill shelter or try to find it a good home. When dealing with a feral, however, returning it (where it was caught) may be the best option.

Another great thing one can do is to feed a colony of feral cats. When one takes on this responsibility, it is critical that all the members of the colony get sterilized. It does not make sense to allow any breeding to occur.

For those who are not able to do anything hands-on with a cat, there are plenty of ways to help.

- Donate money to a no-kill group. Money can allow more cats to be rescued.

- Help a financially-challenged pet guardian:
Pay the bill for someone who can't afford to sterilize his/her pet or who rescues lots of strays. Buy some cat food for a person in need of help to properly buy everything his/her pet requires, so the person can continue to keep his or her cat.

- Buy or make cat beds for homeless cats. Knitting blankets can provide a warm bed for cats. Incorporating a high percentage of cedar chips into bedding will prevent harboring of fleas. Cedar chips by themselves, in a weather shelter, are fine as well.

- Nailing together some plywood for a weather shelter is a great way one can participate in helping homeless cats.

- Public service announcements in the media are a great option for someone to pursue. Purchase "air time" on a local radio or TV station to promote adoptions at your local shelter.

- Rent a billboard with the statistics of how quickly cats reproduce when they are not sterilized so that passersby can read it.

- Any person involved in an activity with other people can get them engaged. Realize the potential at schools, churches, clubs, or gyms. Use this opportunity to speak with others about helping a colony of cats or taking up donations to give to a no-kill shelter. Bake and garage sales are ways of accumulating additional funds to put towards your goal.

- Anytime you have several cat lovers, or ailurophiles, present think of ways each person can participate in a common goal. This situation presents an excellent occasion to organize how to provide for a feral colony. One person could trap and take the cat to the vets. Another person can be responsible for the daily feeding of the colony. Someone else may purchase the food or cover the vet bills.

- Volunteering at a no-kill shelter is another form of generosity towards the cats. One can spend time petting and caring for homeless cats.

- One could join in fund-raisers for a shelter, directly or indirectly. Directly would be by actually performing a function during the main event. Indirectly could be printing up flyers or offering some other type of service.

With all citizens focusing on this goal, many lives will be saved. Now that we have everyone aware of the plight of homeless cats and partaking in ending the suffering, we need to go one step further. From within my mind emerged an idea that I feel would dramatically induce pride into people.

Street Signs of Pride

Signs being placed on each street declaring that every animal has been sterilized are an awesome way to spark awareness and pride. "All animals spayed or neutered on this street," is what the sign would proclaim. This also serves as another form of education. Children might say, "Mommy, what does that sign mean?" Adults would realize sterilization is very important.

People on this street are monitoring their area carefully for homeless animals. This conveys a message to everyone that sterilizing and helping cats is an important cause. I would love to see this happen all across the nation.

People could make their own signs, when the county is not able to get some signs erected. Rural and urban areas need to participate. With citizens across the country taking part in this endeavor, this indicates that there is motivation among each community. Street by street is the only way such a massive mission can be accomplished, to sterilize homeless cats.

Each person's participation is the requirement to stop killing nearly 11,000 pets every single day and make this number zero. We need everybody's energy and thoughts to be focused on saving innocent lives. Let's be proactive in any way we are able, and it really can happen. The fact that I have personally rescued nearly six hundred cats demonstrates my point that one person can make a difference. If I motivate four million individuals to rescue one cat, look at the difference that could make. Now is the time!

Street Signs

All Pets Spayed or Neutered on this Street!

Chapter 2

Need for a No-Kill Shelter

"I am only one, but still I am one. I cannot do everything, but still I can do something; and because I cannot do everything, I will not refuse to do something I can do." Edward Everett Hale, American Orator and Statesman

    Rescuing cats in need of a home has always been a passion of mine. All of my life I have cared for cats. The animals always were and still are my best friends. I desired to assist more cats because there are many that need help. There are historical points through my life, which have guided me, to the aim of starting and operating a no-kill shelter for cats. After visiting local shelters to adopt cats to save some lives, I knew I must start a no-kill haven for cats. Cats deserve to have representatives who care about them.

    The interaction between staff and the public sets the whole public relations scene. The people working with cats at shelters are the only people potential adopters can talk to about the cats available for adoption. The shelter personnel must truly want to contribute to saving as many lives as possible.

    Offering homeless cats a place to go where they can live, without the option of intentional death inflicted by a human, was why I started the shelter. My shelter is absolutely no-kill and non-discriminating towards feral cats. Other local groups and many across the country kill feral cats. I hope to see the day that all shelters are no-kill for all cats. Cats are very much a part of society, coming here about four-hundred years ago with European settlers. They deserve humane treatment and care. Rounding up homeless cats and killing them is not humane, and is no way to treat any segment of the population!

My Concern for Animal Welfare

A great compulsion to restitute the inequity that some humans have committed against these glorious animals has always resided within me. It just seems natural that I would take on rescuing cats on a grand scale. I grew up on my grandparent's Dairy of Distinction recognized farm in upstate New York, near the St. Lawrence River.

It was on the farm where I developed a very close bond with animals. I raised and cared for many different animals including; cats, dairy cows (Holsteins), dogs, rabbits, guinea pigs, gerbils, horses, pigs, and a grumpy Muscovy duck as a child. I knew all the names of the 63 milking cows. Some were special friends of mine. Intuitive knowledge about cats, in particular, spawned inside of me, after spending lots of time caring for them.

As an adult, additional species can be included on my list that being; goats, sheep, chickens, Thoroughbred racehorses, bison, donkeys, ostriches, emus, rheas, beef cattle (Brahmans and Angus mostly), snails and King pigeons. I am quite familiar with each of these species, but have more knowledge of certain ones. After spending lots of time with, and having personally cared for all of these diverse species of animals, I have come to believe that the companion animals, cats and dogs, are very unique. This book is about the most fascinating species of animal, being that they are intuitive, intelligent, loyal, affectionate, graceful, reliable, perceptive, and our companion, cats.

As a child on the farm, I was always searching for new litters of kittens that were born in the haymow. We had some cats that would come in and out of the house as they pleased. In fact a very special cat, Fluff, who lived to be fourteen years of age, had a litter of kittens on the couch. There were many barn cats around the farm. Unfortunately, in the early nineteen-eighties in extremely rural New York, and obviously many other places, education about sterilization and proper care of cats, like vaccinations and de-worming was tremendously lacking. The cats were not sterilized. They did not have proper medical care. No one knew any different. However, they were fed and loved. Some lived long lives. Others did not.

The cats were my friends and playmates. This was a positive relationship for the cats and me. Being an only child, I adored their friendship. My mother worked all of the time, so I did not see her very much, but the cats were always there for me. It was brought to my attention that many animals in the world are mistreated.

My mother told me about animal experimentation that was performed in laboratories across the country for product testing and biomedical research. It was horrifying to me the things that any person could do to a cat or any other animal. How could this torture be legal? Scientists should not be allowed to commit such atrocities!

Honestly, much of what they do is heinous. Most of it does not provide any beneficial knowledge to anyone. There is a tiny segment of research that involves the promotion of animal health, such as a vaccine, which is not as cruel as the majority of animal research. I am not referring to any types that are not wickedly cruel or may benefit the animals themselves. Scientists obtain a very lucrative salary to torture innocent, voiceless animals, being sponsored by governmental agencies and private organizations. Think carefully about any causes you donate to because many nice-sounding charities contribute to torturing animals. If a citizen in society did any of the activity that some scientists are doing, they would go to jail!

How could cats, our dear friends, be allowed to be tormented in such a wicked manner, electrocuted, starved, portions of their skulls removed and their brains attached to a metal device in which to connect electrical devices to shock them and manipulate their movement, addicted to drugs, eyeballs removed, eyelids sewn shut, chemicals doused on the skin, bodies set on fire, and forced to inhale toxic substances? The knowledge of such brutality, especially at such a young age, greatly impacted my life!

My mission has always been to help cats. This was always foremost in my mind. When I was a bit older, the massive number of cats and dogs being killed in animal shelters across the nation became part of my knowledge.

Horses began to take a roll in my life. At the age of ten years old, riding Hunter-Jumper horses became a part of my routine. Professional English riding lessons taught me proper skills in this trade. Winning many ribbons in horse shows was a meaningful accomplishment. Upon turning twelve years old, we moved to North Central Florida. Taking riding lessons and competing in shows continued to be a part of my life. I began to gallop Thoroughbred racehorses at age sixteen, in the summer at the racetrack. My goal was to be finished with school so that I could make money and get on with my life.

Graduating high-school in three years, just turning seventeen, gave me the ability to work full-time galloping horses. Someone offered me a riding job on a farm in September, after I just completed my last class of high-school. I took it. One month later, a very bad riding accident was inflicted upon me.

A horse I was galloping tripped and fell down, rolling on top of me. I broke my back and cracked my Sacral-Iliac joint. To this very day, many problems continually plague me, including chronic pain from the injuries. My neck is often hurting due to degenerative disks from the accident. Sciatic nerve pain is tremendously painful when one of those decides to flare up. After completing several months of physical therapy sessions, then light duty work, I eventually began to ride again.

Soon, I realized galloping horses for a living is a dead end job, is very dangerous and extremely physically demanding. I worked in other portions of the horse industry, as well. A bit later, I obtained my Trainer's license after passing the nearly two-inch thick written test and the barn test at the racetrack. But a couple of years after my accident, I decided to go to college.

I earned three college degrees. The first college degree I earned was an Associate of Science in Accounting. I then went on to obtain an Associate of Arts degree. I continued on, receiving a Bachelor of Science in Computer Information Systems. While in college, I worked and took classes full-time.

My goal was to buy my own home with land, giving me the ability to rescue cats. One pet was already living with me. I soon found a tiny kitten in the road, literally. I brought him home, to my apartment.

Upon driving home for lunch one day there was a tiny kitten walking in the travel lane of a busy road. I could not believe it. I pulled off the road, waving at traffic to deter anyone from running over this kitten. Cars were traveling bumper to bumper, speeding along rapidly. They were going so fast that I could not get to the kitten. Every car missed her, but there was one more vehicle coming before I would be able to get out into the road to grab the kitten. It was a moving van, with wide tires. Unfortunately, it did not miss the kitten. Her eyes popped out of her head. It was horrifying for me and so sad!

I picked the tortoiseshell kitten up, moving her into the brush by the side of the road. Then I heard another kitten crying. The tiny feline was crying in the brush near a tree. I brought the precious bundle of fur home. This orphaned black and white tuxedo kitten was five weeks old. Cream Puff reminded me of a puffy little pastry, hence the decision for his name.

Cream Puff was a lucky DSH kitten the day I found him.

Several months later I heard a kitten crying in the laundry room of the apartment complex. I investigated, discovering a long-hair orange tabby kitten in a cage in the closet. The landlord said Animal Control would be coming to get him. I inquired to the landlord about me keeping him. They knew I already had two pets, which was the limit, but they agreed to let me keep him because I was a good tenant. The need for my own place was very evident now.

The concern of how to rescue another cat, when one crossed my path that needed help, worried me. With my own place, this would no longer be a relevant matter. This was an awesome feeling of freedom to not be concerned about someone else's rules.

Soon after acquiring my third pet, my first home with some property in a rural setting became a reality. This is when I really began rescuing a lot of cats. Working in horse training centers was still a part of my life.

These places often have plenty of cats that are not sterilized. The felines are in need of a home. At one complex, I rescued cats that were going to Animal Control. At another, which I lived near, I trapped many feral queens who recently gave birth to a litter of kittens along with individual felines that were abandoned. Over the period of about twelve years, from the time I had my own place and while operating the shelter, I rescued more than eighty (80) cats and kittens at this location. Most people were not aware that an obsessed cat rescuer monitored the area for abandoned cats. I took in the starving cats, if I found them before the coyotes ate them. In order to save more lives, I adopted several cats from local animal shelters that performed lots of killing. Cats were adopted for my birthday and at Christmas. Saving a feline life is the best present I could imagine!

Maintaining my population of cats became quite expensive. There were many more cats in my local area that needed to be rescued. I did not want to adopt the cats out because I was very attached to them and I would truly not know what will happen to the cat once it leaves my premises. That was scary for me. Would the cat really get a good home? Would the new guardian be committed to keep the cat, if they have to move? Did they think the decision of wanting a cat through well enough, so they will not decide to just abandon the cat later? All these thoughts ran through my mind. Eventually, I did adopt out cats into new homes with the establishment of screening procedures. Some time had passed now.

At this point I am married and have graduated from college with a Bachelor's degree. I just got my first job related to my field of study. However, I felt strongly compelled to start investigating how to start a non-profit organization. My desire was to help more cats.

> **A person only needs to be observant to find cats in need of help.**

Need for a Caring Shelter

Starting a non-profit organization would be the first step in attaining the mission of rescuing numerous needy cats. It seemed like the logical thing to do because when many cats are being rescued, there is usually a shelter at the forefront of the mission. I became aware of the current methods of operation of the local animal shelters. Volunteering or fostering cats for them was not the best way to help the most cats, I concluded.

Many pets are euthanized in the county I live in annually. Animal Control receives the most animals of any of the shelters. The result is that they kill the majority of them. In the year of 1996, more than 10,000 animals were euthanized. The privately run Humane society in the county also killed plenty, in the year of 1996, but not as many as Animal Control. They do not handle nearly as many there.

The statistics at Animal Control, in my area, have not changed a lot over the years. In 2003, there were 10,353 pets killed at Animal Control, out of more than 12,000 that were impounded that year. They have begun a wonderful low-cost spay/neuter program with a traveling bus to visit all areas of the county. With an increasing human population comes an increase of abandoned pets. Each pet sterilized prevents many more from being born, only to be abandoned.

I adopted cats from Animal Control and the privately funded shelter on several different occasions. By just going to these local facilities to save lives, I learned information that would later prompt me into starting my own shelter because the cats need someone that genuinely cares about their life. What impacted me most prominently was the attitude of the people working, at both of these shelters.

The staff was very rude and unhelpful. I was truly shocked! This was not an isolated incident, as I visited these locations on several occasions, witnessing the same treatment to other people there to adopt, as well as myself. This is no way to find homes for these unfortunate animals. Potential adopters that are spoken to rudely and given no assistance with questions are not likely to adopt.

Many people would just leave in disgust. Surely, they will spread the word to others in the community of their horrible experience. Animal rescue facilities certainly don't need more negative feelings being expanded into the community.

Many other people don't like going to these places for the same reasons as me. It is hard to be in such a sad environment knowing so many pets die here.

Personnel that act with such impropriety towards potential adopters are unacceptable. After all, these are the people that can save an animal's life. How must the animals be treated, if the humans that "are supposed to" be treated courteously, are treated like garbage? This type of interaction causes questions to arise in peoples' minds. Shelters need to be inviting, but most importantly show some concern about getting the cats out alive!

The apathy from the staff towards the animals is a main reason I decided against volunteering at one of these places, subsequently deciding to start my own rescue. The way they were conducting business was not acceptable. I did not feel whatsoever that these facilities were doing all that they could to get the cats adopted. I wholeheartedly disagree with euthanizing precious pets for lack of space. Another issue that was against my ideas of what is right was that of forcing a cat to live in a tiny cage. Who wants to live in a tiny cage?

Being helpful to people that want to give the cats a permanent home was a priority for me. A shelter's staff should always be courteous and helpful to potential adopters and persons that call on the telephone. Adoptions and donations will not increase with a bad reputation. Anytime a business has many paid staff or volunteers, it can become difficult to manage attitudes.

Over the years, these two local organizations have made improvements with their personnel. One shelter fired several volunteers, whom were some of the rudest people, surprisingly. The County run facility does employ some caring individuals now. Most of the staff that I know, act very professional. It is important for the person in charge of personnel be able to quickly recognize when interactions with the public become toxic. This supervisor must act quickly to remedy the situation. Promoting the mission of the shelter is what is important.

Beginning of the No-Kill Shelter

Needless to say, I began calling and researching, obtaining enough information to discover how to get on track in starting my non-profit organization. The non-profit organization was officially incorporated when I was twenty-five years old. It requires tremendous hard work and dedication to care for numerous cats, while answering all phone calls and counseling many people with cat issues. My compulsion was very strong to try to help change the plight of cats, due to humans' capricious attitude towards our cherished companion animal. Humans have been very irresponsible towards them, abandoning them when they become inconvenient.

I quit my job and began taking in cats from the public. This proved to be a full-time endeavor. There were no days off for me ever. I did not take any vacation for five years. It consumed my entire life, the cat care and the phone calls along with fundraising. The amount of phone calls that would pour in with requests to bring the cats to my shelter was surprising. Saving every cat possible was my goal. The phone continued to ring all day, every day.

Boundaries were not established for the phone call situation. I would answer the phone at 7:00 p.m. and beyond. I continued to return phone calls all evening, as well. My husband said I should just not answer the phone after 5:00 at night, but I just could not ignore the ringing. I thought I'll just have to call them back tomorrow. Perhaps there is a pending situation with a cat needing immediate attention.

The numerous hours I worked along with the emotional pressure of this business, as it is a life or death vocation became too intense. Attempting to help every cat can feel overwhelming. If I was not able to take the cat into this shelter, death would often be the cat's only other option. Without me taking the cat, some guardians would take the cat to Animal Control, where most do not come out alive. I developed a serious heart problem, accompanied by severe fatigue and low blood-pressure, at twenty-seven years old. My mission marched forward, to save lives, though.

One time, upon going to pick up some orphans, I was wearing a heart monitor. Many wires were attached to my chest to record my heartbeats. My feeble body could barely carry the crate of seven kittens. Once we all got home, I was their new mother! This was a very difficult period of time for me. These were not my only orphans. How to establish important boundaries before one begins to operate his or her shelter will be discussed later.

From dealing with numerous animal rescue agencies, operational methods which are and are not effective in assisting homeless pets have become clear. I must presume that this is just a microcosm of what is occurring at a national level, since the euthanasia rates are exorbitantly high. Many changes are needed.

Many people working in the field of animal rescue have greatly differing attitudes. Some people only like cats or dogs, but not the other species at all. Some citizens only participate to occupy their time, but not with genuine passion to make situations better for the animals. There are those with the attitude that feral cats should be killed, while others know that sterilization, and T-N-R (trap-neuter-return) programs are the best method to handle feral cats. Others will promote declawing of cats, while persons who love cats would never mutilate them. Some individuals believe in spaying very late-term pregnant cats, while others let the precious kittens get born. We need to try to set some of our differences aside, so there will not be a wasting of time arguing when we get together to make plans on a community level. Trust me it is difficult, but so counter-productive to argue amongst ourselves. This is why so many groups exist, though due to desiring to do what "they" feel is right. We all must focus on the mission of sterilization and the promotion of adopting and helping homeless pets to members of the community.

There is no greater gift than to save a cat's life! The cat can get out of the cage alive to have a wonderful life, perhaps for the first time ever. Rescued cats truly have gratitude toward their rescuer. They realize their life has drastically improved. One day soon before Christmas of 1996, I would adopt from the privately run Humane Society for the first time. I left with three cats that day.

Story of Callie, Austin, and Hemlock

One cat I adopted, Callie, was on the floor-level in her small cage. The papers on her cage stated she had been there for three months. The tri-colored beauty barely looked at me. She did not get up.

Callie was evidently depressed. She had clearly given up all hope of ever getting a new home. Day after day, she surely would watch people stroll through the room of cages. She was not at eye-level, probably not being noticed by many that walked through the room. She was a beautiful domestic short hair Calico about three years of age.

Callie became a happy cat with love and freedom!

It is very heart wrenching to walk into these kinds of places. Most of the animals present are going to be killed soon. It was hard to bring myself to even go to a kill shelter, but lives cannot be saved if I do not go there. Leaving with everyone is not possible, either. A choice has to be made on whom to adopt.

Callie was one that would be coming home with me that day. I could not imagine a cat being held in a tiny cage for three entire months. Swarms of empathy were spawned within me about the depression she must be feeling. Callie was a wonderful cat that lived with me for many years. She thoroughly enjoyed life. Two other cats were given the opportunity of life on this day.

Another cat demanded my attention on this day. Austin, a short hair gray and black mackerel tabby, was nine months old. This vocal, young cat wanted to get out of the cage. He was just begging for me to take him home. So, I did! One more feline got my recognition this winter day.

Austin, a DSH, was very grateful to get out of the cage at the shelter.

Hemlock was a beautiful domestic short hair. This sleek black and white tuxedo about 8 months old, desperately wanted some freedom. Needless to say, these three cats were the ones that left with me that day. I was elated to have saved these treasured felines. They were all wonderful cats.

Daily Phone Calls to a Shelter

The operation of a cat shelter includes being inundated with calls to take in cats that need placement. Most regions across the nation do not have enough organizations willing to provide cat care information or placement services to guardians in need of assistance. In order to help domestic felines, those who care for them must be given proper facts. Many of the issues that someone will call about, when he or she wants to give up the cat to a shelter can be remedied with proper advice about how to handle the situation.

I operate my shelter as a cat-care counseling service. It consumes lots of valuable time, but how else can the cat get proper care and remedies to problems if someone with the knowledge does not care enough to share it? For me, I started the shelter to help cats in whatever capacity, I could assist that cat.

One of the best ways to help a wonderful cat is by offering suggestions to a caregiver. These recommendations can help people to realize that keeping their cat is an option. Giving a guardian some ideas that he or she may not have thought of can make all the difference as to whether the person will keep the cat. The cat already has someone who loves it. Keeping the family together is ideal.

Much knowledge has been infused into my brain about these phenomenal animals. Cats are very often misunderstood. When a behavior occurs that humans find wrong, the truth remains that there is an instinctual or psychological reason for the behavior. Many people do not even consider there is an actual motive, and not one of intentional bad behavior, behind the conduct. A guardian is at wits end when he or she calls a shelter, to relinquish the cat.

For the best interest of the cat, one must be willing to ask questions about how the cat is behaving and the household itself. The goal is to get to the cause of the problem. I understand cats so well that after assessing a situation, a diagnosis can be made after asking some questions. Inquiries regarding what the cat is doing to "act up" will begin the process. Inquire about changes in the household, such as the addition of new persons or pets. This information will give a better understanding on the perspective of where the cat is coming from, in his instinctual odyssey. The more hands-on experience one gets with cats, the easier this task will become. A cat shelter should be a place that offers support to guardians, not simply a place to discard a pet that someone can't keep.

Another service that I provide is being a cat connection specialist. This title takes on a couple of different meanings to me. One is to know the cats, very well and match the correct adopter, with a well-matched cat. The meaning I am referring to, in this section, is connecting two people together with the purpose of getting a cat in a new home.

I take some extra time on a phone call to assist in placing a cat. There is not always space available at the shelter immediately to take in another cat. In these situations, I would take a description of the cat that needs to find a new home. I would explain to people that I will call them when space opens up and I can try to find a connection if one presents itself before space becomes available, with their permission for me to give out their phone number. This way when someone calls desiring a certain type of feline, if I don't have that cat, but know of one in need of a home, I can connect the two people.

Some people had expressed they don't have much time left before they must relinquish the cat somewhere. I thought this is a way that I can help a cat with nowhere to go, find a home with someone that really wants him or her. I have placed many cats through this method.

Chapter 3

Circumstantial Cat Relinquish Topics

"We can let circumstances rule us, or we can take charge and rule our lives from within." Earl Nightingale

When the cat must be given up, arrangements need to be made to get the cat a new home. One way to help the cat would be by accepting the cat into the shelter. However, no-kill shelters will not be able to take in every cat that needs help. The reason for not accepting every cat in need is lack of resources and the high number of cats that need placement.

Other ways to assist the cat, but do not involve taking the cat include giving the guardian information on what he or she can do to find the cat a good home. A caretaker can place an advertisement. Give details about what information to include in an advertisement. Explain how to screen people that respond to it. This is critically important. There are a couple of predominant reasons individuals want to relinquish his or her cat. Personal circumstances are the most common. Behavior issues are the next most frequent reason for guardians. Both situations can often be remedied to allow a caretaker to realize keeping the cat is a very viable option. First, I will discuss the circumstantial topics.

Moving

Moving into a different residence is the most recurrent situation callers will express. Apartment dwellers tend to call the most. The reason why some renters accept a new apartment that will not accept pets is beyond my comprehension. Sometimes it is because they can't afford the pet deposit required. Other times, it is pure lack of planning.

What it really boils down to is that the person does not have that much commitment to the cat. This is a sad situation, but the truth is that people love, and are committed to their cat at varying levels. True dedication means one does not even consider an apartment that does not accept cats. Do what is necessary to save up the pet deposit if finances are the concern.

Other moving situations involve a person that is relocating to a place a great distance away. Some people do not even consider that it is possible to travel with a cat. Ask the person when he or she calls, some questions about going to the new destination.

Obtaining critical information gives a better understanding of whether he or she would really like to keep the cat. Sometimes persons wishing to downsize their pet population think moving is a good excuse for that. When long distance relocation is occurring it is critical to tell someone that traveling with a cat is not difficult.

Questions to ask include the following;

- How long have you had the cat?
- Did you get the cat when she was a kitten?
- Have you ever traveled with your cat?
- Are there any behavior problems occurring with your cat?
- Do you have any other pets?
- Are the other pets moving with you?

Traveling with Your Cat

Pet supplies one already has will ensure a comfortable trip.

The provisions necessary are;

- Water bowl
- Bottle of water, preferably from cat's usual source
- Food bowl

- Cat food
- Litter box
- Litter
- Litter scoop
- Small plastic bags for excrement
- Safety collar with ID tag (kept on cat for duration of trip)
- Leash, not necessarily for walking, but for escape prevention by attaching to the cat's collar to assist another person within the car in holding the cat while someone else gets in or out. Never leave a leash attached to the collar while the cat is unattended!
- Medical records
- Pet carrier; A carrier is essential when one has a cat because it is the safest way to transport the cat. Going to the veterinarian is the main reason to own one. Having one for a natural disaster that could arise is essential. Carrying the cat in one's arm is just ridiculous, because the cat will be scared, just like everyone else. The cat could easily escape, and possibly be gone forever.
- Scratching apparatus, especially if traveling for more than a few days.
- Current photo of the cat; just in case the cat escapes, to show people or have flyers made immediately to display in the area.

Once the cat is safely in the vehicle, upon departure for the big journey, the cat can be turned loose in the vehicle. This is an optional decision, but if one does it, here are the actions to perform. The litter box should be placed on the floor. Set the cat in the litter box, so he will know it is available for his use. A stable food bowl can be placed somewhere else, so he can access it when he is hungry. When one stops to purchase gasoline for the vehicle this provides a good opportunity to give the cat some fresh water in a bowl. Since the vehicle is not moving, the cat can drink and is most likely to eat and use the litter box. A small amount of water can be left in the bowl at all times. Place a towel under the bowl to absorb any spillage. Extreme caution should be employed to ensure the cat does not escape when opening the door.

When traveling with another person take turns getting into or out of the mode of transportation as a safety measure to minimize escape risk. The cat being locked in his carrier until someone gets out of the vehicle is one way to handle the situation. The other person can then release the cat, so he can enjoy some water and relax. Once the other person returns, have the cat locked up again before opening the car's door. This method secures the precious cat's safety. A different method altogether may be required if your cat gets hysterical in the car.

For a cat that is not at all comfortable traveling, a very large carrier would be necessary. Get a crate that is big enough to place a small litter box inside with enough space for the cat to lie down, outside the litter box, of course, and for a food and water bowl (the type that would attach and hang on the door is ideal). Small amounts of water can be poured in, as needed, without opening the door. Keeping the cat in the crate for the journey may work best, even for well-behaved cats. Just let the caller know that there are options for traveling with his or her cat. The caller can decide which method is best.

Safety is an important factor. People have seat belts that hold them in the vehicle should a crash occur. Danger and risk exist for humans and cats in everything that one does, we can only try our best to handle each situation in the best way that we can. Having the cat in a carrier is probably the safest way for the cat to travel. Possibly the cat would remain in the carrier in a crash, whereas if the cat is loose and the window of the car or truck gets smashed out, the cat could easily escape.

Car seats for pets that allow the cat to see out the window are available for purchase. Some have specific harness attachments that keep the pet safely secured. Mentioning to a caller that these travel specific car seats exist, again, allows more options for the person to peruse.

Though this person was just considering giving up his or her cat, buying a car seat may seem far-fetched. However, pointing out that so many people travel with their pets, that companies have found it necessary to manufacture and market such items, should imply what a common event it is to take a pet on vacation and certainly to a new home.

Represent Cats Well to Other People When Moving or Traveling

Anyone with a cat should be aware of the message being sent to others as a cat guardian. Cats are very clean animals. It only takes someone going into a home with a cat, where the litter box is not being properly cared for, to give cats a bad reputation in society. A litter box that stinks is not being properly attended. A person walking into a home with litter box odor, upon entering, will conclude that a malodorous home is a consequence of a cat residing in the house. This is completely incorrect because the person is at fault for being a bad guardian, by not providing a clean, comfortable environment for the cat. This just spreads bad attitudes about cats in our society.

Upon moving into an apartment, one may wish to express to the landlord that the cat is a great indoor kitty and has no bad habits. A landlord is probably most concerned about his or her property not being damaged. Have your scratching apparatus for the cat. Express to the landlord the cat is sterilized and will not be encouraging cat fights or having litters of kittens. Some people have preconceived ideas about cats and in many cases people tend to remember bad experiences more than other types. By actively acknowledging these particular topics, all of the issues most landlords may have had unpleasant experiences with, are addressed and confirmed not to be a negative situation.

As a traveler, representing cats positively is important, too. When staying at a hotel with a cat, remove the used litter and excrement from the room. Put it in a trash can someplace outside the room. Pick up any litter that has fallen outside the box, onto the floor. If a mess is left along with lots of heavy, smelly trash for the housekeeping crew, they will tell management. Cats could subsequently get banned from the hotel and, again spread more bad attitudes about cats. Clearly, this has happened because some hotels will only allow dogs, but not cats! I am baffled by such backward thinking. Dogs frequently eliminate on the floor and have horrible body odor, when not bathed constantly. They have more potential to bring fleas and ticks into a hotel room because they have to go outdoors to go potty, even if wearing repellent for these nasty bugs. Canines are by far more detrimental guests than cats.

Caretaker Clause

Always be a responsible guardian and think how your actions can affect others' opinion about cats.

Divorce

Divorce is another cause that requires someone to move to a new residence. One spouse may be staying someplace temporarily, where the cat is not welcome. Looking at the big picture is what is paramount in this situation. This is just a few weeks out of many years the guardian and the cat will be together. Don't get wrapped up in the short-term. Try to see the plight in the long-term.

There are a couple of ways to handle a temporary living situation, while keeping the cat. Suggest boarding the cat at a cattery or an animal hospital as one option. Another method would be to buy a very large cage the cat could stay in, perhaps in the garage or wherever, for a few weeks. Someone may prefer to construct a small pen with lumber and wire. Mentioning all of the options is important so one can decide which is best in her situation. A benefit of making a pen at the residence is that the caretaker can spend lots of time, caring for the cat. These recommendations provide a method of handling the situation that will keep the guardian and cat together.

Allergies

Allergies are another common reason people will want to give up their cat. People are allergic to a glycoprotein, called Fel d1. It is present in the sebaceous glands of the skin, which is secreted into a hair follicle. This protein exists in the saliva, too. Tom cats shed more of it than neutered males or females. When a cat licks itself, the saliva is then spread to the fur. As fur falls off in the house the breathing problems can escalate for the human.

The allergen has another way of becoming present in an environment. Any living creature sheds old skin, which is replaced with new skin. This is called dander. It can harbor the protein which induces sensitivity in a few people.

Keeping your cat, while living with a cat allergy, is very possible. Bathing the cat is the best thing one can do to eliminate the actual allergen. Most cats are really not bad to bathe. This is one of those big myths, that cats hate a bath. However, some cats do hate a bath. Veterinarian offices offer bathing services, if one is not able or does not want to do it. Mudd is a large, Maine Coon cat and is a good example of a long-hair cat, an allergy suffering guardian may want to have bathed frequently.

Mudd is a beautiful Maine Coon.

Carpet and upholstery can make the problem even worse, as hair and dust stick to them. Dust mites thrive in these fabrics. Vacuum your home frequently to get hair and dust mites out of there. Get rid of all carpet, if possible. Most people are not aware of the allergen, (most think it is the hair itself) not realizing the benefits of bathing the cat. Some potential adopters that have visited my facility, with cat allergies, tell me their body can tolerate a cat with short fur, but not with long fur. The truth behind this situation is the amount of saliva present on the cat's fur. When the cat grooms itself, a cat with long fur just has more surface area available to leave saliva. However, there are a couple of breeds with long-hair and some short-hair breeds which are considered to be hypoallergenic (not non-allergenic).

These different breeds of cats trigger less reaction for people with cat allergies, for alternate reasons. The Siberian is a long-hair breed, but it produces much less Fel d1 than other breeds. The curly-hair La Perm, Devon Rex, and Cornish Rex are missing a certain layer of hair and barely shed at all. The La Perm comes in long or short hair varieties. The Devon and Cornish Rex are short-hair breeds. The Sphynx has no hair, other than a peach fuzz type of fur, barely visible on its body. They don't really shed, though they should be wiped down, to remove oil from the skin. The Russian Blue is a short-hair breed. Some breeders claim they are hypoallergenic, while others claim they are not.

Restricting the cat to certain areas of the house or moving the cat outside some of the time, if this is a safe option, can help relieve the problem. For instance, keeping the cat out of the bedroom where the allergic person sleeps can promote a peaceful home. These suggestions can often keep a family together.

Personal Health Problems

Personal health problems of an alternate nature can provoke caretakers to relinquish their cat. Persons of any age can develop ailments that become worse with time. Caring for the cat is no longer possible. An injury to the guardian can make caring for the cat an impossible task any longer. Senior citizens may need to move into an assisted-living facility. Bringing the cat there may not be an option. All of these factors contribute to calls the no-kill shelter will receive.

Pregnancy

Women that become pregnant definitely make up a bulk of the phone calls. Many doctors give the incorrect information to pregnant women when it comes to the sporozoan, Toxoplasmosis. This affliction affects the central nervous system of the fetus. Doctors often tell a woman if she has a cat, the baby will definitely get toxoplasmosis. This is so wrong! Women get scared, automatically wanting to get rid of the cat.

Cats are the least common way that a person can catch this parasite. Unfortunately, the most commonly talked about transmission method is that of cats giving this infliction to humans. It is so rare for that to occur. Our obstetricians need a wake-up call. Doctors need to quit presenting cats as some kind of death sentence to a fetus!

People become infected with Toxoplasmosis through numerous situations. People most often become infected from handling raw meat. Yes, the meat we eat! Eating undercooked meat is another very typical method of transmission. Pork is known to be the biggest culprit for the delivery of Toxoplasmosis. Working with the soil is yet another very mainstream mode for a person to come in direct contact with the protozoan. Persons that like to care for flowerbeds and gardens are particularly at risk. People handling soil should minimize exposure by wearing gloves and thoroughly washing hands.

A cat can get Toxoplasmosis by different methods. Toxoplasmosis can be picked up from the ground, if the cat goes outside. Another way for infection to transpire is from the cat eating a tainted animal, like a rat that has the infective stage present in its (the rat) body. Feeding a cat raw meat is a practice that can cause the cat to become infected. An indoor only cat would not conceivably pose any risk, unless you feed it raw human-grade meat that was infected. Rarely a cat will get it, however. Oocysts are egg-like entities of this sporozoan that pass in the feces of a contaminated cat. This is how transmission to a person could be possible.

The person would truly need to have extremely poor hygiene to catch it from cat feces. It is transmissible only after feces remains in the litter box for twenty-four hours or longer because the oocysts need between two and five days to mature into infective forms of the organism. A woman would then need to be certain to get lots of feces on her hands. To be sure to catch this ailment, don't wash your hands. Go eat some finger foods.

Someone who wants to take every precaution should wear disposable rubber gloves to clean the litter box. Another person living in the home could pick out the box while one remains pregnant. Don't allow feces to remain in the box for twenty-four hours. Leaving a litter box unattended for so many hours constitutes improper litter box care for a cat, anyhow.

Newborn Baby

Households with new babies are yet another source of callers wanting to renounce their cat. Most often the situation will involve the fact that the new mother, who once treated her cat as her child, now feels she has "a better child." The new mother no longer wants to take care of the cat. The cat has been replaced. Consequently, he will need to find a new home.

When a child is older, like any age between about two to four years old, sometimes it is in the best interest of the cat to find a new home. Children of this age range do not usually comprehend how to properly behave with a fragile animal. The child can hurt the cat. The child may chase the cat or pull its tail. Understandably, the cat becomes upset, anxious, and fearful. A cat that lives indoors always may have the worst possible scenario, not being able to escape the child's loud screaming and torment.

Making the cat its own space can help the cat. In every home, a cat should have a place it can escape from other members of the family. However, in small apartments or other small homes, with many small children, this is not always possible. Though certainly not a top choice of a cat resort, the top of the refrigerator provides an option that all households could make available, but the noise, of screaming children, is still inescapable.

This location is high, not being accessible by anyone except for the cat. As a cat rescue agency, always keep the cat's best interest a priority. Assess the situation in the best possible manner and if that particular cat ideally should get out of this particular home, then do your best to find space to take in this cat. Prioritizing a situation of urgency over the order of a call was how I handled deciding who should come to the shelter, when choices had to be made.

Chapter 4

Litter Box Issues

"Time spent with cats is never wasted." Sigmund Freud

The most notorious behavior problem is litter box avoidance. This prominent topic can often be resolved, when people are given the proper information on how to address the dilemma. When it comes to calls with regards to relinquishing a cat, everyone will not be completely honest about the particular situation. My skills have developed as sharp as a Swiss Army knife for identifying devious situations very quickly, getting to the truth of what is happening. The importance of getting to the whole truth cannot be stressed enough.

I have counseled many people as to what to do to correct the problem. Once given information, those seeking assistance feel empowered with the knowledge, becoming less stressed about the situation. After utilizing the information, in many cases, the issue is resolved. People frequently will keep their cat. Many people don't want to relinquish their cat, but feel they have no choice because they are not aware this problem can be remedied.

Improper Elimination

Improper elimination is the most common behavioral reason that a cat is relinquished by its guardian. This can mean the cat is relieving itself outside the litter box or "spraying." Spraying urine is when a cat backs up to an object and while wriggling his or her tail from side to side sprays urine upright on the object. Spraying is most often a behavioral issue.

Urinating and/or defecating outside the box could indicate a medical problem or it could be behavioral. Always take the cat to be examined by a veterinarian when a change in behavior occurs. A serious illness could be the cause of the cat's new action. Obtaining the proper treatment for the cat or simply ruling out a medical cause is important.

The solution to the problem could be very simple and solvable, like with proper litter box care. Alternatively, it could be complex, and possibly not fixable, like when dealing with a cat that had been declawed. Declawed cats, unfortunately, make up the majority of cats with improper elimination. I will go into the details on the effects of declawing a bit later.

There are two common ways people explain the situation of a cat with improper elimination habits. One way is honesty. The person will say, "My cat is urinating on the carpet and I can't deal with it anymore, I need to get rid of him." I immediately ask if the cat is declawed because in most cases, that is the fact of the matter.

A dishonest manner is the other way a caregiver handles the phone call. The person will say, "I have a neutered, declawed cat and I can't keep him any longer." Typically, a person will use some of the common reasons cats are given away, which are; moving, allergies, don't have time for him, and had a baby. Shelter personnel should inquire if the cat is having any behavior problems, such as eliminating in the wrong places.

Most people will be more honest at this point. The majority of people try to sugarcoat the truth to protect their cat. More than likely, they feel by revealing he has a problem that a good no-kill shelter will not want to take him in and there would be great difficulty in adopting out a cat with a problem like not using the litter box. The truth about improper elimination is that once a cat is in a different environment, he may never repeat the bad behavior.

The way to handle this topic is by asking a few questions. First, find out whether the cat is declawed. This question presents a clearer picture of the situation. Whether a cat has all of its paws intact or only a portion of that anatomy left, one should go over a series of topics with the person.

Litter Box Etiquette

Inadequate cleanliness of the litter box is most often the cause for improper elimination. This is especially the case when the cat actually goes potty outside the box. Keeping the box very clean is critically important. Tell people they must pick out the box daily, at a minimum.

When more than one cat lives in the home, scooping the box more than once daily is necessary. Adding one more litter box in the home may be the solution to the problem. Both of these actions can greatly benefit the caretaker and cats. The cats appreciate having a choice in the matter of box selection. Single cat homes can be rewarded, too, by ensuring there is always a clean option.

All the litter must be thrown away each week, from the box, no matter what type of box filler is used. Particles of litter fall off the scoop, back into the box. The particles contain odors, which we may not smell, but the cat will detect them. The odor will get progressively stronger. Cats are very clean animals. They will not use a dirty, stinky box.

Cleaning the actual litter box thoroughly is imperative. Use a small amount of bleach or some good cleaner, but nothing that leaves a strong scent on the litter box. Not dumping and cleaning the box weekly is the most routine error that people make in litter box etiquette.

Always try to keep a cat's perspective on things. A cat's cool, moist nose contains double the amount of olfactory sensitivity than the human nose. Their smooth scent-detecting anatomy is just inches from the litter, not five or six feet away like our noses. Be courteous to the cat by providing him with a clean potty!

> **Elimination Enactment**
>
> Not dumping all litter box contents weekly and cleaning the box itself, is the most common reason cats will avoid the litter box.

Proper Amount of Litter in the Box

A common mistake people make with setting up a litter box is lack of enough digging material. Some caretakers put only an inch of litter in the box. Whichever type of litter one chooses to use, there should be at least three inches of the substance for the cat to dig. Cats enjoy being able to reach their paw into the spreadable matter and visually detect a hole being created by their labor. This also allows for enough substance to cover the pile of excrement, which is a matter of importance to the cat.

Litter Options

The litter itself can be a factor. Box filler is sold in many varieties today.

- Clay litters come in two varieties, clumping and non-clumping. All are dusty at varying degrees. Clay litters contain silica dust, which is not good to breathe. In fact, it is a known carcinogen. Inhaling silica dust repetitively can cause silicosis, a debilitating and deadly lung disease and other lung conditions. Clay litter dust must not be healthy for a cat to breathe daily, either! Clumping ones are rather fine in texture, similar to sand. The non-clumping ones tend to be a larger piece of litter, like small gravel.

- Pine tree remains, comes in the form of a pellet. This type is not dusty. The cats like it. However, a declawed cat may find the texture rather course on his or her extremely sensitive paws. I like this type very much. It has a mild, natural scent.

- Wheat litter is dusty and adheres like glue onto the litter box, once wet.

- Corn litter is not dusty and works great. Corn litter is my personal favorite. Cats love it and it has a very mild, natural scent.

- Recycled newspaper litter comes in pellet form.

- Litter made of silica crystals claim to last a long time by absorbing the urine. Being rather expensive, the cost is justified by using the litter for a month, according to the manufacturer. Though there is no cloud of dust visible, like with clay litters, upon pouring it into the box, there is a dusty resonance in the air. This type gets odorous quickly. Keeping the litter box in this foul condition is unimaginable to me. Cats are extremely clean animals. I am an advocate for dumping the box weekly for the happiness of the cat and hygienic purposes.

- A litter is available that turns different colors to alert guardians of possible health problems with a cat. When the PH of the cat's urine is not in the proper range, the litter will become a specific color. The guardian can then take the cat to the veterinarian to be examined. If urinary tract crystals are beginning to form or are present, the cat can receive prompt medical attention. Crystals are life-threatening.

- To mask odors, some litters come with a strong artificial fragrance. Most cats hate scented litter. The scent is made for humans' olfactory preferences, not cats. The essence becomes quite pungent to a cat's excellent ability in detecting odors.

Knowledge of what is currently being sold is important, so one can explain to interested individuals some of the options. Changing a cat's type of litter can completely resolve a problem. The best way to switch a litter is to mix the current litter with the new one, so that nothing drastic is happening. Most cats do not like a sudden change of any kind. Cats have preferences just like humans.

Box Options

The size and design of the box can be a factor in the situation of dealing with improper elimination. The largest box size is the best choice. Cats need to be able to comfortably turn around. In most situations, the high-sided boxes are the best. This helps in keeping the area more orderly, with less litter going over the side, onto the floor.

Hooded boxes can be used to combat a spattering of litter across the floor, but just be sure the cat accepts this situation. Some cats are serious diggers. A caretaker will benefit by using a hood, for these situations.

One thing about a kitten whom is a serious digger is that as he gets older, he may stop digging so intently. A guardian does not need to be alarmed with the thought that you will have thrown litter to clean up for the cat's entire life, if your kitten makes a game of trying to dig to China. Butterscotch is a precious kitty that outgrew this behavior of flinging litter. His story will be told, upon completion of the litter box factors.

Short-Sided Box

Some situations require short-sided boxes. For instance, an older cat and a young kitten are best suited with short boxes. An older, senior cat may become arthritic, consequently experiencing difficulty getting into a tall litter box. A very young kitten is not able to climb into a tall box, so a short, yet normal perimeter size box is the best option. A ramp can always be provided on any box, if necessary. A thick, non-slippery book is one way a ramp can be provided. Another option is using a block of wood. I must point out, at this time, a common mistake made is to give a very small (perimeter) box to a kitten.

The problem with the small box is that a kitten needs to use the litter box very frequently. If someone is not home with the kitten constantly to pick out the piles, the box will get full quickly. This could lead to the kitten going potty outside the box, trying not to soil its clean, sensitive paws. A full, dirty litter box is a set-up for improper elimination habits to begin. Always be sure to use a large spacious box.

Location of Litter Box

Location of the box is an important component of proper elimination. A quiet, calm area of the home is ideal. Loud appliances like the dryer can upset some cats, but I have not really found this to be a problem for most cats.

Easy access is critical for cats with mobility problems. An older, arthritic cat is a prime example of a cat that you would not want to force to climb stairs to use her litter box. However, all of these topics should be brought up so the guardian can try all options. After all of these topics have been discussed, there is one more thing to mention. This may be a particularly useful piece of information for someone who has tried the previously described litter box methods, but the cat is still eliminating in the wrong places or spraying.

Mood-stabilizing Medication for Litter Box Avoidance

Mood stabilizing medications can sometimes help correct a cat's behavior when nothing else will work. Cats get anxiety, just like people, which can get triggered in any number of ways. A guardian going on vacation for a week can trigger severe stress in a cat. Territorial changes, like an addition to the household (human or animal) can cause anxiety to increase. Sudden, constant noises, like construction next door can evoke stress in a cat. Problems such as spraying may begin.

When any of these factors or others upset a cat so badly that he can't control his behavior any longer, anti-anxiety medication for the cat should be considered. Cats can develop obsessive-compulsive disorders. Licking themselves bald or sucking wool are examples of behaviors that occur with these types of disorders, where medication may be the only thing that helps.

A veterinarian visit is called for when a new strange behavior begins, to rule out a possible medical cause. After medical causes are ruled out and ample time has passed while trying different non-pharmaceutical treatment methods, the time may come when you are ready to try any other option, such as medication.

Go to the vet again to discuss which medication is best for the cat. I am not one to promote taking medication for humans or animals, but in some cases medication is necessary. When the guardian has tried everything except medication and is ready to relinquish a cat to a shelter, pursuing the medication avenue is certainly warranted.

Jessica Barbazon

Story of Butterscotch

Butterscotch, named due to his captivating hues of butterscotch orange and white, has a remarkable story. This five-month old kitten from southern Florida appeared in my grandparent's retirement community. My grandparents told me about this cat. They asked their neighbor, who has cats, if he belonged to her. She said that he did not. This neighbor brought him to a different neighbor who likes cats. He did not belong to anyone who lived there. This young cat was a stray. I was concerned for him, but I thought I cannot rescue every cat in Florida.

Butterscotch, a DSH, is completely comfortable in his forever home.

My grandparents described his appearance to me. The description revealed that he was very thin and looked about half grown. This white and orange beauty was extremely friendly. It sounded as though he got a home with one neighbor. My thoughts continued to include this cat, though.

A week later, I went down to visit. My cat carrier was toted along for this trip, just in case this cat still needed a home. I asked where the cat was living now. My grandparents had not seen him for several days. They inquired about him to the neighbors, discovering that someone took him to Animal Control.

Glades County recently formed a nuisance animal removal service. The reason most places form an animal control service is out of sheer need. This place would not be one that would be doing much as far as adoptions. When county populations are small and Animal Control's budget is even smaller, animals are not kept around very long. In rural places, adoptions are extremely rare. Most county run facilities, rural or urban, give three days maximum of life allowance.

Fear consumed me because there was a huge probability this cat was dead as it was about five days prior since anyone had seen him at the retirement community. I decided that I must go see, if by some miracle, this cat was still at Animal Control. Upon driving up to the small building, there lying on the porch, was a small white and orange cat. A man came out, picked him up and said, "Are you looking for him?" And I said "Yes, that must be him." I told him where my grandparents live.

The animal control officer said that a man brought the cat in a few days ago saying that he was going to drown him, but instead dropped him off at Animal Control. The officers at the County facility recognized that Butterscotch was a very affectionate and loving cat. They could not believe the level of nastiness of this elderly man. The animal control officers just could not put him in a cage to be euthanized. Those officers have spared several other cats in the past.

This was a miracle! Butterscotch had been spared! The county officials were thrilled to see he was now going to have a wonderful home with me. I went back to my grandparents before heading home to show them that this once homeless kitten was safe. I proceeded to tell them the story of him being brought there. My grandparents were glad he was going to have a great home.

That adorable little cat slept the entire four and one-half hour ride home, with the exception of drinking some water. Butterscotch was exhausted from his tireless week, or maybe longer journey. This adorable young cat was trying desperately to find a home.

Butterscotch was so fatigued for a couple more days. I was concerned about his health. He had a good appetite, however. I de-wormed him then took him to the veterinarian soon afterwards to get tested for FeLV (Feline Leukemia Virus) and FIV (Feline Immunodeficiency Virus), both of which were negative. He was not ill, just completely drained of energy for a short time.

His story of rescue is one I will always cherish. There are so many instances where this adorable kitten could have been killed. Luckily, he was not. I drove a long distance and there he was, almost waiting, for me to arrive to give him his final and forever home.

Eli and Butterscotch, both DSH's, take a nap together.

My precious boy was an insatiable digger in the litter box, as a kitten. Butterscotch would throw litter quite a distance. The energetic boy would go to different boxes and dig. He evidently enjoyed digging a hole. After about three months, he did not dig frantically any longer. This lovable guy is quite neat now. Most cats don't fling litter out when digging. My housecats are all very meticulous, luckily for me. As far as using a hood on the box, it would be more work in my situation, as I would need to remove the lid every time I need to pick out the box. One will need to discover what best fits his situation.

Territory Issues Regarding Litter Box Evasion

A cat who feels threatened, in a physical sense (not that of being beaten up, but rather territorially invaded), in its territory can begin improper elimination behavior. The familiar terrain can become a threatening place when new people or pets are introduced into the household. Sometimes new visitors, more often ones that come frequently, can cause problems to arise. For example, a new boyfriend or girlfriend that is spending lots of time in the house may be receiving time and attention that once belonged to the cat. The cat feels threatened and insecure. These feelings can provoke the cat to begin to "spray" or actually eliminate on places or things belonging to his or her long-time guardian. What the cat is doing is expressing that this is "his or her person."

The presence of a new animal can trigger such events to occur. For example, a friend comes to visit along with her dog. Cats and dogs have scent markers in their paws. The pheromone of the "intruder" will remain in places the dog has touched. The result is that the resident pet may begin to "spray" or eliminate completely in places it should not, to claim the territory. The improper behavior can continue, as long as the new odor endures in the territory. Thoroughly clean areas the visitor has encountered. Once areas have been improperly eliminated on, tenaciously remove that lingering aroma to discourage repeat offenses.

Express to the person calling that the cat is not being mean or spiteful, as sometimes people believe. The cat is re-acting to its instincts. Positive association, like giving treats, and giving lots of attention is crucial when the new person or animal is present. Understanding the instincts of a cat is so important.

Introducing New People

Permanent new residents should be introduced in a regimented manner. The introduction of the scent, from the new addition, is important because cats identify others by scent. When expecting a new baby to be joining the household, before it arrives, put baby items around the house. The smell of the new toys along with items required for babies will already be familiar. Play recordings of a crying baby. The cat's sense of hearing will be introduced to the sounds that the baby will present. An adult joining the family should leave his or her slightly worn shirt, for example, near the cat's food bowl. This familiarizes the cat with that odor.

Introducing Animals Together

New pets should be kept in a separate room from the existing cat, until they gain familiarity with each other's scent. Rub a towel on each animal and put it in the other animal's area so it becomes acquainted with the scent. This method just makes for a smooth transition. It helps to prevent fights between the animals because they will be accustomed to having this scent in their territory.

Persons should keep a few topics in mind when adding a new cat to the family. Giving each cat her own set of food and water bowls, near the original set of dishes is a good way to help the resident cat not feel invaded. Eventually, once the cats are great friends, the removal of one set should be fine. Maintaining two litter boxes for some length of time or forever may be necessary. A litter box can be a very personal possession to a cat. There are cats who absolutely don't want to share this item with another cat, at least until they are friends. I have never had a situation where a cat refused to use his box in this scenario, but there are those who are more finicky.

Use caution in introducing a cat when a resident dog is already present. A lot of time, patience, and supervision will be required if the dog is not familiar with cats, in a kind way. Dogs that like cats should adjust fairly quickly. However, some dogs will never learn to be gentle with cats.

These dogs have an intense hunting and chasing instinct that they just cannot overpower. This type of dog is a serious danger for society. They will chase children, any cat, squirrel, or other animal they can find. This type tends to be very aggressive, also. Fighting with other dogs is common. Additionally, take great care when an additional dog somehow gets with this particular dog because a pack instinct can take over, causing a fairly calm dog to become a vicious killer.

The majority of dogs have no problems in getting along with cats. They can become the best of friends. My Great Dane became best friends with a young, feral kitten that I rescued. This black and white tuxedo marked cat, Ody, became tame through following the lead of the dog. The kitten began copying the actions of the dog. Ody even began to eat peanut butter off the spoon, just like the dog. The dog learned about cat behaviors and mannerisms from Ody, as well. Armani touches noses with cats for a greeting, which is a cat behavior, instead of sniffing the backend as a greeting, which is a dog salutation. The Great Dane grew up with many cats, but these two grew up together. These two have the closest bond I have ever seen between a cat and dog.

Armani, a Great Dane, resting with her best friend Ody, a DSH kitten.

> **Animal Acquainting**
>
> Keeping a new pet in a separate room until all pets have become familiar with the new pet's scent encourages a peaceful introduction and relationship.

Unexpected Way that a New Animal Scent Gets in the Home

A non-suspecting way a different pet's scent could end up in your house is through the purchase of used furniture. One should definitely keep this information in mind before purchases of this nature. All of these improper elimination topics are important to discuss when someone calls with a problem.

Chapter 5

Scratching and Claw Topics

"To be nobody-but-yourself in a world which is doing its best, night and day, to make you everybody else---means to fight the hardest battle which any human being can fight; and never stop fighting. E.E. Cummings

Scratching is an action all cats perform. Scratching is part of a cat's physiological health. It is not a destructive behavior. Many benefits are gained from this behavior. Cats must scratch to strengthen and stretch the tendons and digital extensor muscles. When cats scratch, it helps to shed the claws' outer sheaths, keeping them healthy. Scent marking occurs through scratching, though that is not something we, humans, will ever smell. It is part of being a cat.

Scent glands in the paws release an odor that remains on the object used for scratching. Visual marking is also paramount in the cat world. While performing this instinctive exercise, they are signaling to other cats, "This is my territory and I was here." Other cats visually detect the claw marks on designated scratching objects.

Scratching

Scratching is a natural feline activity. Every cat needs a scratching post. It is shocking to me how many people don't think of the scratching post as a necessity, but rather as an option. Cats come with claws, just like they come with all their other anatomical parts!

This behavior needs to be directed to an appropriate place in our homes. Cats are easily trained to use a scratching post. Show the cat right away upon moving into your home, the proper scratching device. Each cat has his preference for a post. Not one post fits all. The most common mistake guardians make is thinking that the cat will love any post given to her. Another error is that the cat is not properly trained to use it. One buys a post at the store, sets it someplace in the house and gives the issue no further effort.

Scratching Post Options

Lots of options are available when it comes to purchasing a scratching post. Alternate surfaces are available. Different heights, widths, and shapes are other considerations to be given to the post purchase. The option of scratching horizontally or vertically is yet one more alternative to consider. These choices exist because each cat has preferences on the way she likes to exercise her muscles and claws.

The surface of the post is probably the most important option for the cat. The feel of the texture upon the cats' delicate paws is what sways her inclination towards or against a particular substance. Sisal rope, a thick twine, is the most preferred. Carpet is a very close runner up. The tight knit short type most commonly found on commercially made posts is fine. Real wood is another great option. Cardboard, corrugated material, types are an option available.

Height is an important determinant when making a decision for your purchase. Many posts available are totally too short. A very young kitten could use one successfully, but these are absolutely not acceptable for an adolescent or an adult cat. The most critical factor is to be sure the cat will be able to stand upward, completely stretched on his hind legs to comfortably scratch. No limit exists, other than your ceiling, on one being too tall. Cats love to climb, being arboreal creatures by nature.

The width of the post is mostly a matter of preference by the guardian. I have not seen any on the market with a width that was unacceptable. Get one as wide as you prefer. The device must be at least four inches wide, allowing the cat to comfortably grasp it. What is absolutely crucial, however, is the stability of the post.

If the unit purchased is wobbly, it must be secured. A steel platform could be bolted to the post. Another method for stabilization would involve tying, with either a string or an elasticized cord, the post to the wall with an eyehook placed in the wall. Some other option could involve placing a heavy weight onto the post or inside it, for a hollow post.

With the current prevalence of "cat condos" many shapes of scratching apparatus are available. Condos are great purchases for cats. A condo provides a horizontal and vertical scratching surface. It also provides a place for the cat to call his own with the inclusion of a sleeping section, an arboreal view, and most include multiple surfaces, like sisal and carpet.

Round, flat surfaces are what cats prefer for sleeping. Condos can include round tunnels, square and round sleeping areas, and holes to go through which lead to other "areas of interest", for the cat. Soft, squishy beds that are meant for the floor of your home are often appreciated.

Vertical or horizontal posts are other varieties available. Most cats prefer to scratch vertically. The majority of posts one will encounter in the marketplace are for vertical stretching and scratching. Posts to avoid are these wobbly, feeble devices that hang on doorknobs. Should a knob hanging device ever be purchased, secure it onto a wall. A minority of cats will favor scratching horizontally. The most common device being sold specifically for flat scratching is made of corrugated cardboard.

Options abound when it comes to purchasing a post. A lack of interest in the post, by the cat, could indicate the wrong type was purchased for this particular cat. One could design a unique post and build it.

Claw Commandment

Every cat must have a stable, scratching apparatus with the cat's preferred clawing material.

Build Your Own Post

Building a scratching post oneself is certainly an option. Adopters or people that are on the phone need this particular data. By building a post, more control can be maintained over the products used in the cat scratching and / or sleeping apparatus. Natural materials can be selected, like wood and sisal rope. A minimum of a four-inch wide tree limb will work fine for a post, once secured in a steel platform or some other manner.

These products are not only highly preferred by cats, but they are healthy to have in the home, for the people and the cats. Some of the store bought posts and condos are made with structural components which contain toxic ingredients that seep into the air, as well as, the surface of the product. Particle board is a commonly used material which is manufactured with a glue-like substance that comprises formaldehyde. Carpet can include virulent ingredients, too.

The person may want to design a really eccentric style of a cat condo. A very creative person might have an unusual style preference and could build a unique design for his or her cat or cats. Giving people ideas and options is important because one does not know which one will work in their situation. The goal is to have the cat get what he needs.

Kittens on a condo my husband built.

Proper Scratching Location

Location of the post is very vital. A rather prominent position in the house is the best choice for the cat. Since the house is their territory, a place that the cat knows others (cats) would immediately detect the visual and vomeronasal (scent) evidence upon entering this territory, is a top choice location. However, many cats are fine with placing the post in more secluded areas of the house.

Simply find the locale that functions the best in one's own setting. The main point of finding a good location for the post is to place it where the cat likes it the best. If, for instance, the cat scratched the couch, then provide a post in close proximity to the couch. Using a material similar to the couch would be a good choice since the cat obviously likes that material for scratching. Be sure the cat understands that the couch, hypothetically in this case, is not an acceptable place for scratching.

Deterring Methods When Cat Scratches Wrong Object

Harmless deterring methods can be utilized in teaching the cat where not to scratch. All of these methods act as deterrents and use negative association, providing an unpleasant experience for the cat when it does the undesired action. Cats are smart and learn quickly. Never use something that could harm the cat. If one method is not effective, then try something different. A cat that has been allowed to scratch on furniture for a long interval of time and now the guardian decides that this behavior is no longer acceptable, could take several weeks of effort to be re-trained.

Caretakers must give scratching the same consideration as the litter box or food bowl. Upon utilization of any of the following deterring methods, go to the cat calmly, speaking to her in a soft voice. Pick her up and carry her to the correct scratching post immediately. This combination of actions, the deterring method and bringing the cat to the proper place, strongly establishes the message of exactly where the correct location is for scratching.

These methods or objects work great to prevent scratching in unwanted places;

- A loud noise; Clapping of one's hands and vocalizing the word "no" in a firm voice works very well for training purposes. The cat should stop the behavior she was doing.

- Double-stick tape; By placing it on the furniture where kitty should not scratch, upon getting it stuck on his paws or feeling resistance from the tape, he will most likely not return again. A few trials may be necessary to establish a firm message.

- A rough mat, with the raised up plastic bristles, like the kind used to wipe off feet before entering the house, provides an uncomfortable surface to touch. It's great for countertops or furniture.

- A water gun; spray the cat when it scratches where it should not. This method is not one I have utilized, but it may assist some guardians. I would be greatly concerned about spraying the cat in the head, which would be a terrible thing to occur.

Training the Cat to Use the Post

Cats are easily taught to scratch on the correct furniture. Scratching is an instinctive behavior. Training the cat to use the post is simple, yet critical.

For vertical scratching, follow this series of actions;
- Carry the cat to the post.
- Set the cat on the floor.
- Pick upward on the front of his body, placing his paws onto the post.
- Grasp the paws gently, performing the scratching motion with his paws, on the post.
- Repeat this procedure as many times as is necessary, until the cat automatically goes to the post to scratch.
- Sometimes setting the cat's whole body vertically on the post will help. All four paws will be on the post. The vertically-inclined kitty will have to move his paws along the post, to get down to the ground.
- Discourage him from jumping off.
- Encourage him to walk down, by staying very close to the cat, as to be in the direct path if he were to try to jump off. Once or twice is usually all that will be required.

If the cat is avoiding the post and getting him to use it is a bit of a battle, perhaps you will need an alternate scratching post.

For horizontal scratching, follow this procedure;
- Set the cat down, on all four paws with the front ones on the post.
- Perform the scratching motion with the paws, as mentioned above.
- Rubbing catnip on the post can be helpful, if the cat involved responds to catnip.

Trimming Claws

One very important fact, about claws, is how to trim them. Trimming the cat's claws on the front paws are usually all that is needed. Some people may want to trim all of the claws and that is fine. Pet nail clippers are sold in the stores. Trimming the nails is painless to the cat, providing you don't trim too short, cutting the quick of the nail. Trim the hooked ends off the nail. The cat can still scratch normally. By clipping the claws they won't catch on furniture and blankets, or be sharp when holding your cat.

Other crucial benefits to the cat include not damaging any skin. This could be his own or another feline friend. In particular, the cat may have an itch and subsequently scratch himself. Another situation could involve rough play with some feline friends, resulting in a bad skin slash from a claw.

A sleeping cat presents a good opportunity to trim the claws, especially when first learning about this procedure. The cat will wake up. Providing that you are calm, the cat shouldn't do much other than stretch and roll over. A cat usually becomes accustomed to claw trimming with time. The cat realizes it does not hurt and is not a big deal. Just use positive association, like giving treats, to help the cat realize trimming his nails is a harmless experience.

> **Nail Nip**
>
> **Push on the nails very gently to extend them a bit. This tactic helps provide a good view of what is being clipped.**

Claw Sheath Option to Protect Furniture

An aid is available in the marketplace that prevents the claws from ever touching the furniture. The use of this gear involves placing plastic sheaths directly onto each claw. The manufacturer claims they stay on for up to six weeks. They are inexpensive, so one can buy more as needed. These glue-on caps come in many colors, allowing kitty to be stylish. This product offers a kind alternative for declawing. Next, the physical and mental destruction caused by the procedure of declawing will be discussed.

Declawing Reality

Declawing, the intentional removal of a cat's claws is a horrendous human invention. We really need to stop it from happening. Society must look at the actual effects of declawing. It's not some simple little operation that the cat will forget ever happened in a few weeks. The effects are so detrimental to cats in every way, emotional and physical. Don't for a minute think the cat is not aware of exactly what has happened. Cats feel completely defenseless, losing their claws.

Physically this is just torture to a cat. His balance is forever challenged. He must learn how to walk again, like when he was a kitten. The cat wants to keep his muscles tone, attempting to scratch. The mutilated, live being discovers he can no longer grasp anything at all. As a result, his muscles deteriorate. The cat continues desperately, trying to grip something and gets frustrated, eventually becoming depressed when he continually fails.

Now he gets sharp nerve pains in his toes at any given time. The paws are constantly aching from bone fragments and torn tendons that often occur from this torturous procedure. He feels like a freak, missing parts of his limbs. He just does not know why he must live this way. This is not the way he was born.

I urge everyone to try to view situations from a cat's perspective. To be a good caretaker for cats, one must embrace their perspective. Let's call this practice what it really is, one can call it: phalange removal, finger-tip extraction, or cutting off the keratin containing portion of the toes, but it all boils down to legalized mutilation.

Declawing is not an expression of love towards your cat. I absolutely don't understand when I am speaking with someone, who had her cat declawed and claims to love the cat. I am befuddled by the proclamation of love after choosing to remove a portion of the cat's anatomy! What this person truly loves is her furniture.

The person assumes the cat is determined to destroy the furniture. I completely understand one does not want furniture destroyed, but we can't mutilate a living creature. A cat needs the proper scratching post along with a lesson or two on its use. That's it! It is really that simple. If declawing was not legal, this torturous and ridiculous idea of tearing out a cat's claws would not even be an option to consider. Such attitudes anger me greatly, I must admit. However, my educating effort is of the utmost importance in this situation. People need to be informed about the physiological necessities of scratching and how to direct it in a house, so that hopefully she will never have a cat declawed again.

Conversing with a potential adopter is where one can become an advocate for the cats. This person has not yet legally mutilated a cat, so a life can truly be saved in this situation. I would never turn someone away from visiting the cats by mentioning that so foul word, "declaw" because obtaining a cat is easy, as there are so many of them homeless.

The person seeking a cat simply would go someplace else to get a cat then have it declawed. I want this person to come to my shelter because I thoroughly understand this issue. Passion pours from within when I speak on this topic, as it should from any cat advocate. Conversing with a person creates the opportunity to save a cat's life. Perhaps many lives can be saved, as this person may adopt other cats throughout his or her life. Once told the facts, most people will not declaw the cat.

Claws are as much a part of critical anatomy as any other body part. A cat controls its claws in the following manner. When a cat is resting, ligaments on top of the paw are relaxed, and a sheath of flesh, cover the claws. The way a cat exposes its claws is by contracting the digital flexor muscles in its legs, and then pulling the flexor tendons under the paw tight. Cats have a rich supply of nerves in the paws.

Some proponents of the declawing procedure argue that it allows more cats to get adopted. But, the fact is that many of these cats end up being euthanized because of behavior problems that result from the surgery. Declawing causes more cats to get killed! We are not doing a cat any favor by allowing him to get mutilated in order to get a home. In most cases, the improper behavior issues from declawing can't be corrected. These issues are the result of permanent emotional and physical problems brought on by declawing the cat.

Physical problems are what most guardians are cognizant of, which are caused from declawing. Improper elimination is the most common result of this barbaric practice. One always needs to discuss all of the options about litter box etiquette that was previously mentioned when someone calls with an improper elimination situation.

In many cases, when dealing with a declawed cat, it is the type of litter that is the most significant factor that can be changed which may help alleviate the problem. Since the cat's paws are so tender, the cat needs the most soft and fine litter available. When a cat experiences pain, it will associate what is most prevalent in that situation, or area, with the pain. For instance, the litter box is perceived as the source of pain because as the cat steps in it and digs, its paws begin to feel intense discomfort. Therefore, the cat will avoid the source of such agony, the litter box.

The most common complaint from guardians is that the cat is relieving itself on the upholstered couch or on the bed. These surfaces are soft and squishy. Eliminating on these surfaces indicates the paws are very much in need of this type of surface to avoid irritation. Suggest to a guardian to actually create his or her own litter, if commercially available ones are not a solution. Since the cat likes these fabrics, tear a shirt or sheet into pieces and place them in the litter box. Position the litter box, at least temporarily, in close proximity to the location in which the cat has been improperly eliminating. Cover the area with plastic, so the cat can't use that spot anymore. The cat should be diverted to the litter box, which provides the same soft feeling on the paws that the "wrong" place furnished.

Declawing being named as the source of the problem is not very common. This needs to change. My belief is that it is a matter of not wanting to denounce a practice that most veterinarians will perform. After operating a no-kill cat shelter for several years and personally handling every phone call and every cat, I absolutely am aware of the direct correlation of declawing and behavior issues. Veterinarians certainly have to be aware of the correlation and causation.

The Veterinary Medical Association wants to keep declawing legal. Many veterinarians promote declawing to clients. Vet clinics often present declawing as part of the spay or neuter package. Cat guardians are not as inclined to question something, even when it seems wrong, when their cat's doctor acts as though it is fine. These attitudes need to change. Making more money, at the detriment of the cat, is absolutely wrong!

The sad fact is that there is not a cure-all solution for cats destroyed by declawing. Many cats acting out physically will continue to eliminate in places they should not. The problem lies much deeper. The mental and emotional aspects of declawing are very serious. After the cat is mutilated, symptoms may be revealed immediately after coming home with phalanges, metacarpals, carpals, and forelegs wrapped in bandages or it may take years to witness the effects.

Cats may become aggressive, especially with biting. A cat is safe in our home, but he is still an animal with instincts, fully aware of the fact that he is prey, at times to other animals. Now one of his best defense mechanisms, his claws are gone. All that is left are the teeth for defensive purposes. The cat is very conscious of this fact.

Methods in Use for Declawing a Cat

Different methods are used for declawing. One procedure, called an onychectomy, is performed by chopping off the phalanges, at the outermost joint. To better understand, imagine cutting off your finger at the knuckle below your fingernail because that is exactly what is entailed for this technique.

The cat's bone is hacked apart, causing the part that the nail grows from to completely detach. Tendons leading to each claw are also severed. With the cat's anatomy dismantled, he has dangling open-ended tendons and bones left under his skin. The pain is excruciating!

Another mode is a tendonectomy, in which the tendon leading to each claw is severed while the nail is left on the cat. This prevents the cat from extending or controlling the claws. The nails will continue to grow. However, now the cat is not capable of caring for and maintaining his claws. Many cats that got mutilated with this process end up with their claws growing into their paw pad. This situation allows an infection to occur. The guardian needs to keep the nails trimmed. There is yet another way to remove a cat's body parts.

Laser surgery can be used for declawing. A laser beam is an intense form of heat and light, which cuts through tissue. The searing beam burns through the sensitive flesh by heating and vaporizing it. There is much less bleeding that occurs with this method. The cat will still suffer long-term effects of declawing, though. The result for the cat is essentially the same because he is still without some of his natural physiology.

Story from a Declawed Cat

Tremendous trauma has transpired and the cat knows it! His world is total chaos. What is normal now? The cat thinks, "Should I go potty in that plastic box with hard gravel in it? It hurts my paws. Am I even a cat anymore? If I wanted to climb a tree, I could not. I can't grab a mouse if one were to run across my food bowl. I'm staggering often, since these bandages were removed, and I can barely do the things I once could.

My family who feeds me took me to the vet and picked me up after my toes were removed. Did they do this on purpose? I thought they loved me. Surely, I was wrong. Certainly my health is more important than my family's love of inanimate objects, like furniture. Someone who loves someone does not have his body parts removed. Why would someone get a cat only to cut off some of his natural parts?"

Geographical Attitudes Vary about Declawing

This atrocity of declawing is predominantly performed in the United States and Canada. However, I can applaud two communities in America, for their banning of declawing. These areas in the United States are the city of West Hollywood, California and Norfolk, Virginia. In West Hollywood, California on April 7, 2003, this law was signed into effect, declaring declawing illegal. However, there was opposition from who most people would consider an unlikely organization. This group was the California Veterinary Medical Association.

The CVMA sued the city of West Hollywood and the judge. They appealed the wonderful humane law to ban declawing of innocent cats. The argument they brought forward was to say a vet and the client should decide whether they want to declaw a cat. The truth is that the bottom line of their reasoning was that they did not want any vets losing money, though supposedly there were none in this two-mile vicinity. Their main concern was that other communities would follow West Hollywood's example. In February 2006, a California court struck down the ban on declawing.

The good news is that this is not the end of the Hollywood court case. In June of 2007, a California appeals court overturned the 2006 ruling. Justice finally prevailed! Cats are protected by law to be free of the legalized mutilation of declawing in this locale in America.

There is even more good news. Just as the California Veterinary Medical Association feared, another locale did follow West Hollywood's precedent. In April 2007, the same type of law was passed in Norfolk, Virginia. This is just wonderful for the plight of cats in America.

One other very positive thing California has done for felines must be mentioned. This law applies to wild and exotic felines. Many wild felines are kept in captivity. Some individuals or organizations cruelly declaw these magnificent cats. Since some people attempt to raise these wild beauties for pets and the fact that circuses are, unfortunately, allowed to keep these creatures in cages, they will sometimes declaw the big cats to prevent a human from getting scratched. By the way, circus acts that cage confine beautiful animals that belong in the wild, and make them do stupid tricks is appalling! A glorious day it will be when these heinous acts are outlawed. A law was enacted that applies to the entire state which bans declawing on large wild and exotic felines.

In January 2005, The California Anti-Declaw Act was signed into law. The act was introduced by assembly member Paul Koretz. It was called the Paw Project, AB 1857, when introduced. I commend Mr. Koretz and Governor Arnold Schwarzenegger, as well as, all others who participated, in making this historical legislation happen. I greatly hope other states and communities will follow California's example, of protecting all felines from mutilation.

There are other countries in the world that recognize this human-invented mutilation, for its true nature. Numerous countries have either completely outlawed the practice or it may only be used in some very extenuating circumstance. These countries are as follows: England, Scotland, Wales, Italy, France, Germany, Brazil, Australia, New Zealand, Yugoslavia, Japan, Austria, Switzerland, Norway, Sweden, Netherlands, Northern Ireland, Ireland, Denmark, Finland, Slovenia, Portugal, and Belgium. As you can see, many countries from all corners of planet Earth recognize declawing as mutilation and extreme cruelty! They all are so correct.

The behavior problems associated with declawing are absolutely preventable. Just don't declaw a cat. It's that simple. It is completely unnecessary and needs to be against the law everywhere. Mutilating a majestic cat should not be a choice. Like I said, cats come with claws. Claws are not detachable, like a Velcro strap! They are part of the animal's body. I am all for having freedoms, but destroying a beautiful pet is just plain wrong in every possible facet of the matter. There is no positive side to mutilating a cat. All every cat needs is to be loved and appreciated.

Paw Law

A cat comes with retractable claws. If this is a problem, then don't get a cat!

Chapter 6

Helping Stray Cats

"Not everything that is faced can be changed, but nothing can be changed until it is faced." James A. Baldwin

Strays are cats that are currently homeless. They were once someone's pet, having been abandoned, either this generation or some previous generation. This generation is usually quite friendly. The generations born in the future most often will be feral because they will not be reared around humans. The subsequent generations are taught by their mother to regard humans just as they would any other predator.

These cats are true victims of our society. We, humans, domesticated the cat and cats deserve to be properly cared for, not abandoned. Each and every one of us must band together for this common cause of helping these victims of our society. Anytime a stray cat appears in your yard, take the initiative and do something to help it!

Strays

Stray cats number in the millions across the United States of America. These cats live a very meager lifestyle, scrounging through trash or hoping a rodent crosses their path, to get a meal. A lucky cat will cross paths with a nice person, who will give them a descent meal. Most cats must work very hard to keep eating.

Most strays are not spayed or neutered. Consequently, they produce kittens that are born into this deprived environment. More mouths need nourishment resulting in even less resources per cat. At least fifty percent of kittens born do not survive to adulthood.

Many dangers confront strays, whether they live in an urban or a rural environment. For instance, there is lack of food and water, and predators such as: dogs, coyotes, owls, and snakes, which all present the danger of death. Other hazards include: cars, mean people, getting stuck in precarious places, like a storm drain or wall, and parasites, which literally suck the life right out of the kittens, especially.

I must emphasize that evil people are a very common threat facing any cat or kitten, particularly those outside. Many felines fall victim to people who find joy in torturing and killing an innocent animal. It is beyond sickening to even think of intentional torment being inflicted by a human to a pet. However, this is reality. It is so important to get cats off the street and into a safe environment.

I have taken in cats that were abused. One cat was hung from a tree, by teenagers, with a noose around his neck. I describe other stories later in the book. I found a mutilated, dead kitten in the road one time. It was a truly horrifying, traumatic event for me to find this murdered kitten!

The television station, Animal Planet, features shows, like Animal Precinct, which details stories of abused animals. Some examples include; a man beating a kitten, the kitten survived, but was blind; two teenagers opening a window of an apartment, removing the cat and beating it to death, all caught on film from the building's camera; a puppy being stabbed to death, and two nursing kittens placed in a box in an apartment to see how long it would take them to starve to death (authorities were called and one kitten did survive). Animal abuse is a serious problem in our society.

We took cats into our lives, in different capacities, but nevertheless, under our protection and guardianship. Some cats worked in our barns to rid the area of pesky rodents, saving farmers loads of money by reducing loss of grain and increasing production of the farm (no matter what the farm was producing; forage or livestock). In later days, when machinery and electricity were invented, cats contribute to saving all these wires from being destroyed by the nuisance rodents who love to chew any wires they can find. Other cats came into homes to provide affection to the family. They protect it from damage caused by vermin, too.

Think back, for a moment, to eras when people lived in caves or feeble homes of sticks and mud while they slept on beds of straw. Imagine the family's cat attacking and killing a rat that was gnawing the newborn infant's toe off while everyone was sleeping. This cat is a hero! Now, generations later, this is how we repay the cat by abandonment only to be caught and killed by an Animal Control agency. What if that baby was your ancestor, remember any infected wound usually resulted in death back then, you wouldn't be here today! Thank a cat the next time you see one.

The number of cats escalates by starting in one home, then a community, then the state, and to a national level, which is where the millions come from each year. When hearing these statistics of "several million," animals euthanized each year, it's hard to grasp such a large number. Just think of a stray you saw wandering in search of food, or that neighbor who has a sign up trying to find homes for kittens because she never spayed her cat. Each cat placed into a home from an advertisement, takes a home away from a cat currently in a shelter on death row. So, don't think by allowing a cat to breed and by finding homes for those kittens that this is acceptable behavior. These innocent felines, in every neighborhood, are part of the "several million" we all hear about in the statistics. Everyone has definitely seen one or more of these cats and maybe knew some very well.

It is critically important to personalize these statistics in order to make people understand that by helping out even one cat, one person can make a huge difference to end the suffering endured by these innocent cats. The "kill numbers" are not from some far away land. When operating a shelter, one will certainly be made aware of the enormity of the stray cat situation.

The majority of phone calls received will involve a stray cat. Those who bother to call a no-kill shelter are often concerned that the cat gets a descent place to go and will not be euthanized. The fact is that no-kill shelters can't always take in every cat that needs placement, as there are so many. I always put the cats with no other options, like in the following situation, as a priority to accept.

One portion of callers must get the cat placed somewhere. Most often this consists of people living in apartments where pets are not permitted. They can't take the cat in, but know that by leaving it where they found it the cat will surely meet death. The cat could starve to death. A mean person may cross the cat's path, in which case it will be harmed and/or killed. The apartment building's manager may call Animal Control, to catch the cat, in which case it would most likely be euthanized.

The other type of callers could keep the cat, but would rather get the cat a safe place to seek an adoptive home. Make these callers aware of the benefits of keeping the cat. Explain about the massive numbers of homeless cats in the community. By the person deciding to keep this cat, it would be a great service to all cats. Include the fact that cats are territorial, defending their territory from others. By sterilizing and providing for this cat, this will prevent other non-sterilized cats from residing in the yard.

Financial expense is often what people are most concerned about when deciding to take in a cat. Many communities have some very low-cost sterilization options that are available. Have phone numbers ready to give out. Tell the person by utilizing low-cost vaccination clinics, at large animal feed and supply stores for instance, he can save money. Calling local veterinarians to get prices on vaccines and other treatments is an excellent way to comparison shop for the best price. De-worming is very inexpensive. Yet, it is critical for the cat's health. Proper de-worming agents can be bought over the counter.

Be Prepared to Help a Cat;

- Carry cat food in your vehicle to feed a stray cat anyplace you see one. Cats can be found at gas stations, restaurants, and hotels. A hungry kitty will appreciate a meal. It may be the meal that saves his or her life.
- Haul a pet carrier in your vehicle, using a collapsible one if space is a constraint.

Story of Jasmine

I encountered a situation where a litter of kittens were found in a wall. They were in an office building, where my husband is employed. Someone heard them crying. My husband got them out of the wall, by cutting a section of the wall out. They were about three weeks old, cold and starving. One of the three kittens was dead. The other two were barely alive.

I got them immediately, putting them on my lap as I drove home to get them some food and turned the heater on full blast. I kept rubbing them and telling them not to die. When I arrived home, one kitten died. The seal-point Siamese kitten was still hanging in there. She ate some kitten formula. I put Jasmine on a heating pad and fed her every couple of hours. She began to gain strength and eventually blossomed into a beautiful, affectionate cat. Her will to survive was immense.

Jasmine, a Siamese kitten, nurtures Jack, a DSH kitten, found on the floor of a straw barn at three weeks of age.

Jessica Barbazon

Orangey, is a DSH cat that I rescued from a life as a stray cat. His gratitude is immense.

Rescuing a Needy Cat

Allowing a once homeless cat to reside in one's yard or home is a great thing. In some cases, the yard is the only option, as people may already have all the indoor cats their home can accommodate. The cat now has a loving guardian who will provide the necessities.

Cats are territorial, often keeping other cats out of their territory. Unclaimed territory, in the cat world, is simply territory that is available for claim. Therefore, if one does not keep his newly neutered cat in the yard, the chances of another cat, probably not spayed or neutered, moving in are very high. It is just a matter of when the new stray cat will arrive. Un-sterilized cats moving in to the territory presents problems.

Detrimental consequences materialize from the act of these cats breeding. The process begins when a queen, an un-spayed female, moves to your yard. She will attract tom cats, un-neutered males, and certainly not just one. As a result, fights for the "mating rights" will occur. Loud yowling and screeching sounds will transpire. The fights get very brutal. Cats bite and scratch each other in, literally, rolling battles. One of the worst tragedies happens next. Once mating takes place, kittens will be born about sixty-three days later. By everyone simply sterilizing their cats, all of this legalized killing in shelters would not happen to innocent kittens. What a tragedy!

Sterilizing and providing for that one cat just makes sense. Many people can see the worth of allowing a stray cat to remain on his or her property once given the facts about cats. I always explain the benefits from the human point of view, which in turn will reward the cat. Now that the stray cat has arrived, you are not sure of the best method to catch the cat. A very domesticated cat, at first, might act almost as though it is feral, by keeping a good distance from you. But, pulling the trap out may not be necessary.

When a cat is abandoned, it goes through a series of actions, in most situations. A very friendly cat that was recently abandoned will be scared. You will know the cat is not feral if it responds verbally to you when you speak to the cat. A domesticated cat likes people and communicates by meowing to the person. The discarded feline is so terrified after being tossed into a foreign environment it probably will not allow anyone very close at first. After a few feedings, petting the cat should be possible. Be patient, the cat just needs to know you are well-intended. The cat will now have something constant in its environment, you! An abandoned cat that is not fortunate enough to find a nice human to befriend it may end up turning rather feral permanently. Of course, a cat's history and age can cause differences to occur with either remaining or deserting domestication.

Spraying Urine

Males and females are capable of spraying urine. Cats do it to attract a mate and claim territory. When the sex hormones become active, instinctively the cat is inclined to do what it takes to get a mate. Spraying urine involves the motions of backing up to an object and spraying urine upright onto it, while wriggling its tail, in a small range of motion, from side to side. The resulting urine signals to other cats that come into this territory that this land is already claimed. The urine reveals information about this particular cat to the other cats that sniff it. Pheromones are present in the urine.

Pheromones are a chemical substance produced by an animal. They serve as a stimulus to other individuals of the same species for one or more behavioral responses. These innate chemicals signal to other cats whether a specific cat is ready to breed.

Cats spayed or neutered before puberty will almost never spray urine. Spraying urine is a nasty and smelly behavior, as far as humans are concerned. It is not acceptable when it happens in the house. This is another point exemplifying the importance of getting a cat sterilized. I don't want to imply that every un-sterilized cat will spray, however. By getting the cat "fixed" though one should never have to deal with this issue. The only other reason a cat will spray is because of territorial-related issues.

When other animals, especially cats, and usually many others need to come into this cat's territory, the cat may feel threatened (not necessarily physically, but territorially). The cat gets a feeling of not having enough space of his own. He feels resources are too limited to allow this many other animals in the territory. After getting an adult, sexually mature cat altered, the likelihood of it continuing to spray is either completely eliminated, in most cases, or greatly reduced.

Spruce, a Polydactyl Maine Coon cross, has never sprayed urine because he was neutered at an early age.

Females "In Heat" Behavior

When the queen is ready to breed, she is in estrus, also called "in heat." Heat cycles are brought on by increased hours of daylight, in the spring. This helps ensure the kittens are born at times when food will be most available and the weather is not so cold.

Females have their own methods of expressing their hormone tendencies. They can "spray" just like male cats. The urine is laced with hormones that will attract male cats. Other symptoms of "heat" include: yowling loudly, rolling around, being very affectionate and becoming very energetic. Once sterilization is performed, the cat will not have to go through hormone-induced behaviors.

Fighting

Fighting is another behavior problem, especially with un-neutered males. When males are not neutered, their hormones drive them to fight other males that come into their territory. Each cat wants to have "breeding rights" with any females in the area.

Tom cats have loud, screeching battles, leading to severe lacerations that can become infected. Bite wounds and scratches will often form an abscess. A cat that has gone exploring territories and with no one to care for him, these abscesses can become fatal, without medical treatment. Another behavior difficulty is that of a male cat wandering around, searching for a queen to breed and territory to claim.

Wandering puts the cat in danger. This behavior puts the cat at risk of coming into contact with vehicles and predators. Infection, vehicles, dogs, and predators can all cause death for the cat.

Story of Mr. T

Once I encountered a situation that involved a chronic "yowler." A friend of mine has a horse farm. One day a stray cat appeared. This friendly, young cat has black and white tuxedo markings. After visiting the cat, I determined he was about one year old, just going through puberty.

The farm owner said he would be willing to keep the cat, except that he is constantly hollering near the house and everywhere, therefore, becoming understandably annoying. I said, "Once the cat gets neutered, he won't yowl any longer." By me offering to take the cat to be neutered, the farm owner agreed to keep the cat as long as neutering proves to keep him quieter.

The cat stayed with me for a couple of weeks while he healed up after surgery. Then he was returned to the farm. The farm owner was amazed how the neutering quieted this once very vocal cat. This gorgeous tuxedo now proved to be the perfect barn cat. Through joint effort of the people involved, he found a permanent residence. Getting a cat neutered can make a huge difference in the quality and length of his life.

Trapping

Acquiring the skill of trapping is necessary knowledge for a rescue entity. Humane traps do not harm the cat. Purchasing the correct size of trap is critical to have success. Traps that catch raccoons, opossums, and skunks are the ones that trap cats. The inclusion of this point is pertinent because when advertising, the trap manufacturers name these particular common nuisance animals. Now you need to select a trap.

A trap that opens only on one end is the best, as chances of escape are greatly reduced. Follow the instructions that go with your specific trap to learn how to properly set the mechanism that will trigger the door. Once you understand how to operate the unit, it must be baited.

Odorous, aromatic bait works well. Sardines or tuna fish are wonderful attractants for cats. I have used tuna quite often, having much success with it. Canned cat foods are another good option for use in luring a cat. After obtaining the enticing food, proper placement of the bait is the factor that can truly cause this attempt to be a success or a failure.

Most traps will call for the bait to be placed on or behind the trigger plate, the flat metal structure that causes the door to shut when the cat steps upon it. Proper placement alone is sometimes not enough to lure cats that fall on opposite ends of the intellectual spectrum. A cat whom is very trap-savvy or one that is perhaps a bit lacking in intelligence often need extra incentive to get into the trap.

Some cats are very leery of traps. Those who have been caught in the past may not go into a trap again. Feral cats may be completely afraid of going into the device that reeks of human scent and appears so foreign to the environment (this reason is why I recommend a food containing a strong smell with a very tantalizing, irresistible flavor). Use gloves when handling the trap to reduce your scent from remaining on the trap. A method used when trapping coyotes is to spray apple cider on and around the trap to remove human scent. Perhaps this natural spray would work for a human-scent aversive cat.

Other cats just need some help to be able to find the entrance of the trap. I learned from watching cats that I was attempting to trap, how some of them just absolutely could not determine the method in which to retrieve this food. The cats would go to the back of the trap, close to where the delectable sustenance lies.

Sticking their claws through the wire trap is a common maneuver. Next, the cat will walk adjacent to the side of the cage, reaching and pawing towards the food. Finally, the little fellow will jump onto the top of the wire enclosure to sniff and stare downward at the prize with the desire of retrieval, but without the trail to success. This is when I knew what must be done. It works like a charm.

A trail of food, leading towards the trigger plate, should be properly positioned. The first morsel goes immediately in front of the entrance to the trap. Placing the food a few inches away from the temporary prison is fine. In fact, another sample should be placed even farther back on the journey into the trap.

The cat will be able to see and smell the enticing bait. Place a smaller portion of pleasing chow just within the trap on the wire bottom. Now, go a few inches further inside to situate more vittles there. One more allotment can be dropped through the wire, from the top, far into the device, yet not quite onto the trigger plate. The creation of this trail of aromatic food ensures success nearly every time. There is one more trick that sometimes needs to be utilized to catch some cats.

Covering the trap with a towel can encourage some scared cats to go inside. Use of this method provides darkness. Most feral cats feel more secure in the dark. Cats do not suffer vision impairment in the dark, as humans do, provided there is some light in the environment. A cage is more camouflaged to cat eyes, for some cats, by having that solid appearance versus a wire metal containing a square pattern. Of course, do not cover the entry port with any fabric.

This practice of using a tarp on the trap was not one that I executed for the most part. My intent is to include all the tricks available for use in trapping for any situations that may arise in your endeavors. Sometimes one little tidbit of information makes all the difference for successfully trapping a cat. Avoid having the cat escape because it will become more frightened with each failed attempt.

> **Trapping Tip**
> Place a trail of food, starting just outside the trap entrance all the way past the trigger plate, inside the trap.

Behavior Quirk from Some Feral Raised Cats

I have observed an unusual behavior with some feral raised cats, the type that ends up rather friendly. Some feral cats swat, with their paw, at the caretaker and other cats regularly. It mostly tends to occur at feeding time. Usually, it is not a very aggressive swat. I think it is due to lack of socialization with humans at a young age and some other element involving the method of rearing. Some of these cats were raised with siblings, others were not. What each of these cats has in common is a feral kitten-hood.

Handling Ferals

Safety precautions must be observed when handling feral cats. Equipment you should have includes:

- Thick leather gloves

- A long sleeved shirt, preferably a leather jacket
- Long pants, like denim jeans
- Closed toed shoes, such as sneakers
- Protective eyewear (safety glasses)
- A fishing net (For Your Information: there are nets sold specifically for cat capture), a long and short handled net for whichever situation it will work best. The net, with a handle, is the best item I ever discovered for working with feral cats.

The net allows capture of a wild cat without being bitten or scratched. The cat can be caught and put into a carrier by using the net. One's body parts will never be very near to the cat. This procedure can be used out on a site where you need to catch a cat that you can get a few feet away from or inside your cat pen.

Catch the Cat in the Open Outdoors

When attempting to catch a wild cat in the open outdoors, the net makes all the difference between catching the cat or not. Let's say there's a feral cat that won't go into a trap. One can get three feet from the cat, but no closer. This is a perfect situation to use a net and a pet carrier to catch this cat. A critical factor to perform before beginning the trapping process is that the carrier is bumped up against a stable object. The carrier must not be able to slide backwards or the cat will escape.

Once the carrier is firmly in place, follow this series of steps to net the cat;

- Situate the carrier within the three-foot radius that the trapper will be working.
- Once the carrier is secure with the door wide open, move onto the next step.
- Feed the cat in the usual place at the same repetitive time of day.
- Have safety gear on and be ready with the net.
- When the cat comes and begins to eat, put the net over her, taking care to be sure the rim of the net is firmly on the ground. Otherwise, the cat will find a small escape avenue and use it.
- Drag the net, as it is, over to the pet carrier.
- Once the net is as close to the carrier as it can get, lift the end up that is towards the opening of the carrier.
- The cat will find the escape route.

- She will run into the carrier.

- Once she gets to the back of it, she will probably turn around and be facing the front, so the door must be shut before the cat turns around.

- As soon as she gets mostly out of the net, slam the door shut. Be sure the net is not in the way (the netter should pull it back towards him or herself), of obstructing the door from closing.

- Once the door is shut apply pressure on it, to prevent it from opening.

- Work the latch of the carrier so that the door will be permanently shut.

The feral cat is now caught! She can be brought to the cat pen at this point. After the cat is released in the large cat pen, the day will soon come when she needs to be put into the carrier again to go to her veterinary appointment to be spayed and vaccinated. The procedure to capture is almost the same as when you caught her outdoors.

Catch the Cat from Within the Pen

Bring the net in the pen. Calmly set it down. Then bring the carrier in the pen. Decide on the location that will provide the easiest angle of entry. Push the pet carrier against the wall so it won't move, with the door wide open. Have a clear path to the carrier opening, with no obstructions in the way.

The cat is probably acting frantically at this point. She knows this equipment and that something strange is taking place. She may be literally flying off the walls. This reason exemplifies the validity of the safety equipment. Basically, hold the net to block off her leap in mid-air or try to capture her on the floor. As she "flies" around the pen a couple of times, one will become familiar with the pattern of travel she is using, more intricately.

It can take a couple of minutes to catch a cat in the pen. The good news is that if she escapes the net a time or two, you will have other chances to catch her within the walls of the pen. With a mid-air capture, the cat can get out of the net before you can place it firmly on the ground or get it to the carrier. Move as quickly as possible towards the carrier or the floor, whichever is closer.

Once on the ground, whether capture takes place there or you have managed to keep her in the net long enough to get to the floor, from a mid-air catch, hold all edges of the net's rim firmly on the ground. Drag the net to the carrier door opening. Lift the edge of the net up that is facing the doorway. The cat will run into the carrier. Shut the door swiftly and latch it. The feral cat is ready for transport.

Using the net is a safe method for capture. There is no need to grab the cat to place her in the carrier. Handling the cat puts you at a great risk for being bitten or scratched. Wearing the thick, long clothing is somewhat protective in itself, but if you do not have a material like thick leather, the teeth and nails can penetrate it. Regular leather gloves can even allow teeth to possibly get through and the pressure of the jaws squeezing down whiling biting will cause great pain with possible damage to your body. Trust my assurance that the jaw pressure is tremendous.

The cat "flying" around the pen could happen regardless of whether the net is used because if you go in and grab the cat with your hands, she will be scared. One escape from your hands and the cat will be off on her "flight." The best way to promote calmness in the cat is to have the carrier in the pen a few days in advance of when you're going to attempt to catch the cat.

By placing the carrier in there, it will not be something new in the pen. Calmly walk in with your net, placing it over the cat before she knows what happened. Don't leave the net in the pen unattended as the cat could become entangled in it, getting seriously hurt.

Housing Un-socialized Cats

Feral cats should not be kept in a pen where visitors go to view cats. Cats that are essentially wild can hurt someone unintentionally, due to fear. Most feral cats are not mean, just scared. There is a difference.

Once your ferals become calm enough to feel comfortable around people, you could place them up for adoption. Becoming barn cats may be the best scenario for them, since they may not ever be tame enough to feel happy living inside a house for the rest of their lives. They have been free to do as they please outside for their entire life. However, some feral cats will become very tame at a rapid pace, and becoming indoor cats is very suitable for this type.

Domestic tame cats sometimes have a mean disposition. Don't put mean cats with visitors either. Mean cats are extremely rare, but odds are that you will get one or more at some point in time. When cats come from a household where they were not treated well, their attitude can be, understandably, bad. A mean cat will usually have a day where its attitude changes in a positive manner. The cat will decide that it wants an adoptive home and the attitude could change literally overnight, when the decision is made.

Chapter 7

Caring For the Cats

"Thousands of years ago, cats were worshipped as gods. Cats have never forgotten this." Anonymous

Once tiny orphans or adult cats arrive at the shelter, they must be handled properly. Determining the requirements of each feline is necessary. A visual inspection of the cat is mandatory. The purpose of the exam is to identify any major physical problems.

Once the cat is physically comfortable, other needs and comforts must be met. Getting a nutritious and tasty meal to the kitty is necessary. Whether that is a delightful, warm milk formula or dry kibble, all the information to mix and select the proper meal will be discussed in this chapter. The time may come to bathe the cat. A bath is fairly simple to administer, in most cases. Do not fear, proper bathing techniques are described here.

Raising Young Orphans

This segment of the feline population is very labor-intensive. Newborn kittens are completely helpless, not being able to see or hear. The adorable newborn felines use scent to identify their mother. The queen purrs to them. They feel the vibration of her purr. She licks them to stimulate their bodily functions. When a litter of kittens no longer have a mother, they need someone else to provide for them.

Maintaining Body Temperature

The most important aspect of rearing young kittens is to keep them warm. They are not able to regulate their body temperature. Keeping a litter together or adding other kittens similar in age together can be helpful. By having several kittens together, the proper body temperature will be established and maintained. This would be one less element for the human parent, to be concerned about providing.

Without other potential littermates to pair together, the caretaker will be responsible for regulating the kitten's body temperature. Room temperature is way too cold for tiny kittens, so an additional heat source is required. A heating pad left on low heat, with a towel or thin blanket in between the kitten, is a very good source of steady heat. An empty coke bottle or milk jug can be filled with warm water. Have a cloth of some type, placed between the bottle and kitten.

Always keep the kitten in a box or carrier large enough so that if the kitten does get too hot, it can crawl away from the heat source. The youngest newborn can't really move far at all, so always check him regularly. Once the kitten's body heat is accounted for, he must be fed properly to survive.

Formula Selection and Feeding

Regular feeding sessions are important to support the kitten's survival and growth. Newborn kittens should be fed about every two hours. With about each week of growth, the time intervals can be spaced out farther, throughout the day. Always feed the kitten as much food as he wants to eat. He will stop eating when he is full. There should be an increase in the amount of formula consumed about every couple of days. Kitten formula is obviously a critical component in the survival of an orphan.

There are several formulas available for purchase to raise young kittens. I have used three of the main ones anyone would find in the store. KMR powdered kitten milk replacement happens to be my preferential choice of formulas. The kittens love it the best. This awesome life-saving powder transforms into a consistency of thick milk when mixed with the proper amount of water and the nutritional elements listed seem to be optimal. Whichever brand is used, I definitely recommend using the powder formula, as opposed to the liquid, which is all ready to use.

The liquid has some drawbacks, including;

- The need to store it in the refrigerator once opened, which means it must be heated up before each use.
- It does not mix up very well even when shaken vigorously, so clumps (of nutrients) are left at the bottom of the can.
- It is quite sticky and adheres almost like glue to the kitten's fur, even after wiping him down properly after his feeding.

When using the powdered formula, mix the amount needed for each feeding. The amount needed will become evident as the feeding sessions continue. Any leftover can be stored in the refrigerator until the next feeding. Simply mix the cold formula in with the new, warm formula to easily achieve the desired temperature for feeding. Do not keep remixed formula for more than about two feedings. This rule serves as a precaution for not harboring really old milk, which can become contaminated rapidly. Bacteria are a young kitten's worst enemy.

Cleanliness of the feeding utensils is a crucial factor in preserving a kitten's health. Use a bottle or a bowl to mix the formula up, but be sure that regular disinfecting of the feeding apparatus is performed. The nipple or syringe that the kitten eats from needs to be kept clean. Without proper cleaning of the feeding utensil, harmful bacteria will grow.

A kitten will subsequently ingest these microscopic organisms. Consequently, the kitten will become ill with death being the possible result. Once daily all of the utensils should be allowed to soak in a disinfectant, preferably chlorine bleach. Then scrub and rinse them thoroughly. The best method in which to administer the feed to the kitten will be discussed next.

The feeding bottles that are most commonly found, for orphan kittens, do not work very well. The nipples are stiff. Trying to poke a workable hole in the end for the kitten to use is very difficult. These nipples create such a challenge for the kitten to squeeze milk from them. Air passage into the bottle to allow ease of flow of the milk is yet another obstacle with the bottle. I discovered a couple other options to dispense the milk formula more easily.

One option is to use an eye-dropper or an ear-dropper (the ear-dropper is a bit superior because the nipple-type part is more elongated allowing the kitten a longer gripping area from which to suck). These can be purchased in the pharmacy section of a store and are very inexpensive. Constructed of glass, they can be easily disinfected (just pull the rubber, suction part off) on the pro side. Another advantage is that these instruments are so cost-effective that simply replacing a dirty one with new ones, to avoid washing these tiny gadgets is practical. The con side is that possibly the kitten could break the glass in her mouth. Glass breakage has never occurred while I was feeding, however.

Since not a lot of milk can be put into the dropper at once, this would be best suited in a situation where only one orphan is being fed. Having several kittens to feed would be very time-consuming using this dispensing device. A litter of seven that I was feeding with the ear-dropper was too grand for this method of feeding. It took forever, it seemed. More orphans needed my care. I just had to find something that worked faster.

A syringe became my best discovery for feeding kittens. Notice that the tips of syringes are very different from one another. There are ones that have only a nipple-like protrusion on the end. Other syringes have the nipple, in which to attach a needle to, but it also has an outer sheathing around it.

The type of syringe that works best for feeding kittens, are the ones that have a longer tip with no outer plastic sheathing. The kitten can get a secure grip on it. A caregiver can very gently push on the dispensing portion of the syringe as the kitten is sucking. Often one won't even need to place any pressure on the dispenser because the kitten exerts enough pressure on it to move itself. Some kittens, however, may need a little help. Never force milk into the kitten's mouth! This would cause his lungs to get milk in them. Obviously, this situation could result in death. Always feed an orphan at her own pace.

The syringe will need to be replaced after a few days, depending how often daily and how many kittens are being fed, because with more use, it becomes harder to push. It will even become jerky in its motion, which is very bad. The syringe seems to lose lubrication and ease of smooth motion with increased use.

Advantages of using a syringe for feeding are numerous. They are cheap. Syringes are fairly easy to clean and certainly cheap enough to be replaced anytime. Another good feature is that different sizes can be bought for whatever size works best for the number of kittens being fed. The larger ones have small or larger nipple areas so the appropriate one can be selected.

There is a method that works best for feeding several kittens;

- Give one kitten a serving of milk
- Then go to another kitten, giving each one a turn and then back to the first baby again.
- Keep rotating along until everyone is full. This gives each kitten time to fully swallow, resting a few moments before eating more. Each kitten is very hungry.

- Utilizing this rotation system ensures that no one is forced to wait longer to eat while he smells the milk, knowing someone else is eating.
- Once all the kittens are fed, it is time to stimulate each kitten to excrete any urine or feces that needs to leave the body.

> **Orphan Ordinance**
>
> **Bacteria growth from improperly disinfected feeding apparatus or old formula can be a kitten's worst enemy.**

Wiping the Kitten for its Health

A paper towel or cloth, moistened with warm water, is the next supply one will need, to continue with the care of the orphans. This accessory serves two important functions. One is for wiping any milk from the kitten's face. If milk remains dried onto the kitten's fur and skin, eventually the hair will fall off.

The other, and most important purpose served, is to gently wipe the kitten's genital area to stimulate it to go potty. A mother cat licks her kittens' genital area to cause them to defecate and urinate. Young kittens are not able to do this critical bodily function all by themselves.

A kitten will not relieve herself every time after she eats, but the caretaker should always gently wipe, in case the orphan needs to go. An orphan will urinate nearly always after a meal, but may defecate only once per day, possibly every other day. Once the kitten is about three or four weeks old, it probably will not be necessary to wipe his bottom any longer. Make sure that the treasured kittens and their living quarters are always kept meticulously clean. Eventually, the baby will be able to eat other foods.

Teach the Kitten to Eat Canned and Dry Food

As the kitten approaches four weeks of age, soft food can be offered to him. When first learning to eat, a kitten essentially sucks the food into his mouth, just how he has been used to eating milk. Canned food is the best option to get a kitten started eating. The scent is more tantalizing than a plain, dry food. If one has no other option, the dry food can be moistened with warm milk or water and offered to the kitten. However, with canned food, the consistency is perfect.

Do not get a food, such as the kind "in gravy" unless you want to remove every little chunk. The inconsistent texture of smooth gravy and chewy chunks could cause a learning kitten to choke. A consistently textured food from a can will be the optimal choice in the beginning of this process. Mix a small portion of the kitten's milk formula with the canned food to get started. The ease of slurping it up will be enhanced. The milk already has a familiar scent and flavor.

This new formulation must be presented to the growing little cat. At feeding time, some could be placed on the caregiver's finger, so the kitten can get familiar with slurping it up. Another means for successfully administering soft food to the kitten is by cutting one end of a straw half-way off, to create a platform to place food on, that can easily go in a kitten's mouth just enough so she can eat the food. It's kind of like making a spoon for a kitten.

The food can be left with the kitten on a rather flat saucer. Something with the edges slightly raised-upward to discourage runoff of the soupy mixture, and to attempt to keep the kitten from walking through it too much, is ideal. A teacup saucer would be fine. A metal lid from a glass spaghetti jar is another example of a useful item. A bowl, with high sides is an example of the wrong type of bowl. Never use anything with sharp edges that could cut the soft, little fur-ball.

Take care not to leave a particular specimen of canned food out at room temperature for an extended duration of time. Microbiology experts say bacteria may grow in one or two hours at room temperature. Pathogens are very bad for a kitten.

The kitten's eating skills will improve with each day. At four weeks of age, dry kitten food can be placed in the living environment. Dry food may be left for a long time, days, without ever spoiling, but I recommend swapping out the uneaten portion after two days, to keep it optimally fresh. The food will become somewhat stale after sitting in the bowl for days with oxygen and light constantly making contact with it. The kitten may not eat the food for a few days, but by it being accessible, when that precious moment of maturity comes, the kitten will be able to make that big step. Now is time for that really grand step towards adulthood, which is using the litter box.

Litter Box Training

Kittens are capable of using the litter box in their fourth week of age. Each kitten develops at his own pace. Do not be discouraged if one kitten takes more time to achieve this task. Some may be five or six weeks old before proper potty use is accomplished. The fourth week is when most are ready to have a litter box placed in their living quarters.

A valuable morsel of information regarding litter box training is that some kittens eat the litter. Always have dry kitten food in the pen with the kitten, before adding the litter box. This can help to stop a kitten from eating litter. The kitten can smell the food as being just that, food. This way if the kitten wants to chew on something, such as for teething reasons, hopefully the genuine chow will be the option it chooses.

The reason why kittens eat litter is not in my parameter of knowledge, but this can be very dangerous, especially if any clay litter is being used. Clay expands once wet. This absorbent substance can become like a hard rock inside the kitten's body and kill him. Clay litter was the type I always had, usually the non-clumping large granule type.

Kittens that are first learning about the box would sometimes begin to eat it. This stage does not seem to last for a very long duration of time, though it can be deadly with a small amount eaten. Perhaps a different type of litter would not encourage the kitten to eat it. I never recommend clay litter anyhow because I have lung damage from inhaling such massive amounts of the dust, which contains silica dust, a known carcinogen!

Once the short-sided litter box is ready to be introduced to the kitten, there is a more advantageous time to introduce the box to the kitten. After the kitten has just eaten a meal is the best time to place him in the litter box. Gently place the kitten in the box. Grasp one of his front paws in your fingers. Perform the digging motion with his paw.

Some kittens will begin to dig, will go potty, and never need to be shown anything further. Others will need this step repeated a few times. Place the kitten in the box anytime and, do the pawing motion, until he has learned this innate skill.

Additionally, always do the potty lesson after his meal. This is when he most likely will need to urinate or defecate. The reason cats dig a hole to relieve themselves and then follow-up with burying the waste is because through evolution they learned to try to keep their whereabouts unknown to predators. Burying the waste kept the scent and visual appearance of excrement to a minimum, thus not alerting the predator that a cat was just here.

Young kittens require lots of attention.

Medical Exam

When a cat is taken in, it should be carefully examined to notice any major health concerns or injuries. A very experienced person that is very familiar with cat anatomy and ailments could perform this function. During a professional exam, the vet looks over all of the same body parts looking for possible health concerns. After taking numerous cats to the vets for exams a person does acquire some basic knowledge as to what to look for on a cat. This exam should not be a replacement for a professional exam because a vet palpates the abdomen to assess if abnormalities are present in the organs, in addition to viewing the external parts, but this in-house routine allows a shelter to catch any obvious problems needing immediate attention. By doing the exam right away, a cat will not need to wait to have serious conditions addressed immediately.

Extensive medical care, such as, blood work and checking the urine, are not included in just a basic exam. Some cats may require this type of in-depth investigation. Senior cats would be good examples of cats to take in automatically to the vet to get an extensive exam.

Begin the exam by starting at the head, continuing towards the back of the cat. First, examine the eyes to be sure they are clear of any discharge. When a discharge is present, it will be either bacterial or viral. A bacterial infection is thick in texture and yellow in color. Neosporin, the clear Original formula, can be placed directly into eyes to assist in killing bacteria that are causing a thick, crusty discharge from the eyes. This is essentially Neo-Poly-Bac, an eye ointment prescribed for bacterial eye infections. A viral issue will be a watery and clear discharge. The viruses have to run their course. When discharge is in the eyes, it is likely to be in the nose.

A couple other important parts on the head need careful observation. Observe the nose of the cat. Is there any discharge? Is there any dry drainage encrusted on the nose? Upper Respiratory Infection (URI) is common. This nuisance predicament affects the eyes, nose, and sinuses. Look in the ears. Is there a thick, dark wax present? This likely means ear mites are living in the ears. Ear mites have many different cures available.

The mouth is an important place to examine. A lot of cats have dental problems that require professional attention. Look for red or inflamed gums. These are symptoms of gingivitis. The back of the mouth could be red, inflamed, and even bloody when a serious case of stomatitis is active. Cats can have broken or decaying teeth. Some require extraction by your veterinarian. Sores or ulcers could be present in the mouth. These irritations can result from rodent ulcers, allergies, or autoimmune disorders, like pemphigus. They are often on the inner upper lip.

Lots of thick tartar on the teeth, indicate that a cleaning is needed. Veterinarians perform dental cleanings for cats. The cat is placed under anesthesia for a dental cleaning. Cleanings should be performed when plaque forms on the teeth and along the gum-line.

When tartar is ignored, it becomes thickened plaque on the teeth. Plaque can cause serious health problems for the cat. Portions of plaque can break off, becoming ingested. Loads of bacteria in it can harm the liver and other organs. Organ damage due to bacteria that live in plaque is a preventable condition, by maintaining good dental hygiene.

Brushing a cat's teeth oneself is possible. Soft brushes and rubber finger sheaths for the person to slip onto his finger are products that are sold to assist with this process. Pet toothpastes are available. Self-cleaning a cat's teeth on a regular basis can help reduce tartar buildup. My preference is to take the cat to the vet for a professional cleaning when needed. The cat's teeth should still be examined by a vet and be kept clean, one way or another. Find a plan that best suits the cat's needs.

A cat that is not eating properly may have dental problems as the source. Many people forget to look in the mouth when an eating issue arises. Do not make this mistake. If a cat is not eating as she should be, look in her mouth. Do this before assuming the cat is internally sick, elsewhere in the body.

Run your hands along the cat's body continuing down his legs, assessing the inner parts and the outer parts. Do any bones feel out of place? Are there any fleshy lumps? Notice whether the skin feels smooth. A cat may have a flea allergy when numerous tiny bumps are on the skin. Look at the paw pads for any tears or splinters. Notice the nails themselves to look for any swelling, redness or ingrown nails.

Continue to examine the remaining portions of the cat's anatomy. Feel the abdomen, just by petting the cat, for any odd lumps. Touch the cat's back carefully to see if there is tenderness when touched. Pet the tail to feel that all of the vertebrae are in the correct place. Look at the genitals to see that everything looks normal. Notice whether any tapeworms appear to be present. When tapeworms are living in the cat, seeing some dried ones around the anus is common. Once the cat is thoroughly examined, now a bath can be given, if desired.

Most cats never receive a bath in their lifetime. There is a misconception that all cats hate water and baths. This certainly is not the truth. One who understands some of the different breeds of cats knows that specific breeds tend to enjoy water. I have given many baths to cats that have never been bathed, most tolerate it very well. A few absolutely hate a bath, but these types are more the exception than the rule. Most cats are initially a little scared when the water begins to touch their body, but they soon realize nothing is hurting them and begin to relax. Using a non-intimidating procedure of giving a bath makes all the difference.

Justice For Cats

Ebony, a DSH, has stomatitis which flares up at times.

> **Medical Mandate**
> Lack of dental care can increase the chances of organ damage, due to ingested bacteria harbored in the plaque.

Giving a Bath

Find the basin for use during the bath. A laundry sink is an ideal size, but a bathtub or large sink can be used for an adult cat. A kitchen sink is a fine size for a kitten. Get all the supplies required at arm's reach.

The necessities are;

- Cat shampoo; have the bottle opened

- A large plastic cup (to put water in and pour on the cat)

- Two towels; one for drying, the other is optional: for placement under the cat's feet for slip prevention and comfort

- Safety glasses should be worn because a cat may thrash around some. Eye protection is important.

Get further prepared before acquiring the cat. Get the water to a comfortable temperature. Run the hot water before you begin. Preparing in advance prevents wasting time for an event (the bath) that should be short in duration. Once the hot water is coming out of the faucet, turn it off. Now get the cat. When using a room with a door, like the laundry room, close the door. This action will prevent the cat from escaping. He will not be able to go far. Catching him and beginning again will be possible.

When bathing a cat for the first time, the cat's reaction to a bath is not known. Set the cat in the washing basin. The following tip is very important. Do not allow the cat to face the door. The cat will struggle to escape when his eyes catch a view of the way out. Always keep a firm grip on the scruff (skin on the back of the neck) of the neck to avoid being bitten or the cat escaping, until knowing the cat will remain calm. If two people are giving the bath, things will be easier. I never had help, with the exception of a couple times, so this is certainly possible alone, however. Turn the water on to a warm, comfortable temperature. Hold the cat in the path of the water flow. Do not wet the cat's head. Never plug the drain.

Let the cat become accustomed to how the water feels. Talk calmly to the cat. Work your hand through the fur persuading the water to reach the skin. Keep in mind the entire bath will be a relatively quick process. Most cats are not going to want to spend a long period of time for this procedure. Use the plastic cup to help wet the cat, especially when a spray nozzle is not available. A spray nozzle, with a hose pullout, is perfect for bathing. It will penetrate the fur and skin quickly with acute thoroughness.

Squeeze some shampoo onto the cat. Use one's hand to gently scrub the cat, working your hand around the back, tail, and underside. Begin to rinse the cat. The cat is still essentially being washed. Be sure to get all the bubbles and soap residue off the cat. Run one's hand over the cat's body, removing excess water off the fur.

Grab the towel, wrapping it around the cat. Massage the towel over the body absorbing excess water. Depending on where the cat is going and what the temperature of the environment is, one can decide whether it is necessary, to blow dry the cat. Cats enjoy licking their fur after the bath. They feel happy and clean. If a cat is restless during the bath, one thing for sure is that after the bath, he will feel great.

When blow-drying, start the drier on low pressure to acclimate the cat to the noise and air pressure. Most cats do not like being blow-dried. A small room is ideal for this situation. The cat could be placed in a carrier. Give the cat a break from it though, no matter how it is done, but especially if he's in a cage.

Have some fabric or something on the floor of the cage. The plastic or metal gets hot quickly. The cat's tender feet need to be protected from burning!

Cats will usually swat and hiss at the blow-drier. Some will even pounce at it or one's fingers when attempting to touch them to tousle the hair to speed the drying process. Approach the cat with caution. With kitty clean and dry, a good meal should be served for his pleasure and nourishment.

Cat Food

Cat food comes in several varieties. There are dry foods, moist foods, and "wet" or canned foods. Dry foods are the most beneficial foods and convenient to feed. They promote dental health by assisting in the removal of tartar on teeth. Dry foods supply a full range of nutrients for a cat's health. Cats should always have dry food available to eat.

Moist foods are moistened dry food ready to feed, usually in sealed individual packets. Most of them are very inferior nutritionally. The cats don't seem, even mildly, thrilled with the flavor.

Canned foods are great to have around. They are beneficial to teach kittens to eat on their own. The cans of delectable nourishment are handy to have when required to trap a cat. Most cats enjoy canned food thoroughly. However, with the link to toxic substances from the non-stick type of lining present in all cans, human foods included, one should use cans sparingly. The options are numerous when it comes to selecting food.

My top choice of canned food is Fancy Feast Fish & Shrimp food. I do not consider the other flavors of Fancy Feast to be superior to any other canned foods, but this particular flavor is outstanding. It is actually real flakes of fish and has real whole shrimp, though only one or two, in it. It looks good enough for people to eat. I've had sick cats that would not eat anything at all, actually eat this food. However, one should feed it sparingly because of its fish content.

The foods range from average cheap brands to the premium foods. The ingredients are of a higher quality in the premium foods, but the cats like some of the average brands just as much as any high quality and high priced brand. It is very important to feed the main part of a cat's diet, which in most cases will be dry food, an immensely high-quality food.

Never buy the cheapest dry food because one does get what one pays for when it comes to dry cat food. However, there are some companies that grossly overprice their food. The best way to know what you are getting is to read the ingredients.

Ingredients are listed in order on packages. The first ingredient is what consists of the highest content in the food. The last ingredient is the item with the smallest amount. The first few ingredients listed are the most important because they make up the majority of the content. The type of meat in the food should be examined. Ones that list an ingredient with by-products are not very good quality, like chicken by-products. A better option would be chicken or chicken meal. Look for a very high percentage of protein in the food. Cats are carnivores, though they love some blades of grass for a snack. Many foods are deficient in healthful levels of protein for cats. I mean they are acceptable I guess, to be allowed to be sold, but a higher level is better. This is why I love the Innova brand's Evo formulation of cat food. They don't skimp on what a cat needs! The foods that are the cheapest do not contain very quality constituents.

Foods that contain red dye, which make many cats very sick, are never good to purchase. I wish these dyes were banned from foods. The cheapest dry foods often have red dye. The cats do not like the flavor of the majority of these cheap, red foods. Some cats get diarrhea from red dye. Many cats are allergic to it. A simple way to tell whether a food contains red dye is to notice if the food is red.

All high quality, or premium, foods have distinctive characteristics from low-quality foods. All foods with the possibility of being high-quality, foremost must be some shade of brown. The food should contain nutritious, highly digestible ingredients. A filler ingredient, like corn should not be listed in the first five ingredients. Stools will be smaller and denser when feeding a high quality food.

Commercially produced foods have standards that they are required to meet to be able to be sold. Granted, the standards need uplifting. At least an essential nutrient, like Taurine, is required to be in the food. Cats will become blind without Taurine. The retina of the eye will slowly degenerate without this nutrient. Besides blindness, the lack of this nutrient also causes feline dilated cardiomyopathy, a heart condition.

Someone that thinks just feeding cooked fish to a cat would be sufficient, know that this would not be a balanced diet. In fact, too much fish can be unhealthy. It is believed to cause urinary problems for cats. Too much Magnesium can be detrimental for urinary health. Magnesium crystals can form in the bladder, giving high-alkaline urine, which can become life-threatening for the cat.

Fish presents other health problems for cats when fed often. Fish is low in calcium. It is high in phosphorus, which is bad for the kidneys. The cat will accumulate high levels of Mercury in its body. There is also a possible connection to hyperthyroidism. Something in the fish can cause a mimicking of the thyroid hormones. A vitamin E deficiency can occur.

This vitamin deficiency can lead to Yellow Fat disease or steatitis. An abundance of unsaturated fat and the antioxidant, vitamin E, deficiency begin the onset of this ailment. The cat becomes hypersensitive to touch. The cat will experience great pain when touched. A cat will lose its appetite. Other symptoms include: greasy, dull coat, flaky skin, anorexia, fever, and not wanting to move.

Feeding raw fish has a unique problem that it causes for cats, in addition to the previously described symptoms. Thiamin, vitamin B-1, is destroyed. Raw fish contains an enzyme, thiaminase that destroys thiamin. A thiamin-deficiency sets the cat up for neurological problems and seizures to take place.

There are ingredients that are in some cat food that must be avoided. Refrain from buying any food with artificial preservatives. BHT, BHA, and ethoxyquin are ingredients that should be averted. They are known to promote kidney failure in the cat over time. Luckily however, there are some good additions to certain foods.

Probiotics are the best supplement to cat food I have found. These are the natural, good bacteria that aid digestion in the intestines. One place these probiotics are found is in yogurt. They drive pathogens out of the gut. Lactobacillus acidophilus, Lactobacillus casei, Bifidobacterium thermophilum, and Enterococcus faecium are these good bacteria. A food containing probiotics is essential and the more types it contains is optimal.

Any cat that has problems with digestion such as: chronic diarrhea, colitis, or irritable bowel syndrome could greatly benefit from eating a food containing these probiotics. Probiotics also help to reduce gas and upset stomachs. It could truly be life changing! I went through this exact situation with my precious cat, Elijah.

The cats are enjoying some food.

> **Cuisine Canon**
> Only high-quality food should be fed to cats.

Story of Elijah

Elijah was brought to me in a box, along with five other siblings. These six colorful kittens were two weeks of age. A man found them in his yard. He did not see a mother cat.

The kittens were all beautiful. There were two calicos, one with long hair the other had short hair. There was one orange tabby. There were two orange and white tuxedo tabbies. Then there was Elijah, white with burnt-orange spots on his upper body.

I fell in love with this bundle of pure joy immediately. He was like a combination of two of the most special cats I had ever met. They were no longer in my life.

The desire to have an extraordinary bond again with a very special cat was devouring me. Since suffering the loss of my two special cats, I tried to find a bond with a few different kittens that now live with me, but that extra special connection was not there. Before I got too attached to Elijah, I wanted to attempt to verify that we would bond intensely, after suffering such heart-wrenching losses with my other two cats, Nolan and Salmon.

At night, I took some of Eli's siblings to bed with me, one at a time. One wiggled constantly. He kept moving and pawing at me. Another pulled fiercely at my hair. Eli was a perfect match for me! Elijah slept with such contentment. This little pleasure ball slept quietly and remained still through the night. I knew for sure he was the perfect cat. We would bond, just as my other cats and I had a very unique connection.

His spots were the color of Salmon, like an orange with a suntan. Eli's marking patterns were just like Nolan. My golden child made the same facial expressions that Nolan made. This warm ball of fluff slept almost exactly like Salmon, though Eli and I sleep cheek to cheek. He curls up beside my head and places his cheek against mine, while gently purring. We experienced more of a bonding journey than my heart could have ever imagined.

Eli, a DSH, is relaxing comfortably.

My new fur ball of joy became ill while very young. Many other orphans were in my care at the time Eli's litter arrived. Many of them were sick with URI and a horrible affliction of the eye. This very special little kitten got the URI terribly. His nasal passages were severely clogged. He did not have the desire to eat very much food. This sick little boy was sneezing while retaining a fever. Then something really terrible happened! He nearly lost one eye, but fortunately did not. This occurred when he was about six weeks old. The cause of this predicament was Chlamydia, I learned after going to the vets. Some kittens lost an eye because of this horrendous affliction.

Once he became four months old, something unexpected happened with Eli's health. This silky soft kitten developed an irritable bowel type syndrome, constantly getting severe diarrhea. Food appeared to be the trigger of the severe diarrhea. He would immediately have to go potty after eating. But it got even worse.

My adorable boy was placed on anti-diarrhea medications upon being taken to the vets. He was also treated for other possible ailments. The anti-diarrhea medicine barely improved his condition. Any results were short-lived.

This beautiful burnt-orange spotted kitten was getting worse overall. Eli would wake up constantly in the night screaming because he could feel the diarrhea coming. I carried him to the other room where his litter box was, sitting there with him as he strained to get the diarrhea out. This went on constantly through the night, for nearly three months.

A litter box was set up next to my bed. Setting him in the box again, continually every night became a ritual. His anus was of course very sore. Different foods were being fed to Eli, hoping that one would work out for him.

All the prescription diet formulations were tried that were geared toward sensitive systems and intestinal health. The hypoallergenic foods were also tried with him. None helped him. I tried a rabbit and green pea formulation, among many others that were made for cats with specific food allergies. Still, none improved his condition.

Eventually, a couple of foods helped a little. My vet mentioned some cats improved from eating Tender Vittles. After reading the ingredients, there was no desire to try it, but there was desperation to get this little kitten comfortable. It was tried on him. It helped him some, but he got tired of eating it very quickly.

Then Eli was switched to a very similar food, but one that is more specifically formulated for cats with problems like Eli. This food is Purina E/M. There was some improvement, but he quickly lost interest in its taste. I can't say the ingredients were impressive, either.

Through a different veterinary practice, he was prescribed another food. This was a canned food. Science Diet was the manufacturer of this d/d formula. It is made especially for cats that have digestion issues. This food drastically improved Eli's condition, giving him much firmer stools, though perfection was still not attained.

The problem was the taste. It became detestable to him after a few days. With all of these diets, he was only supposed to eat that one particular food. The search was still ongoing for the food that completely made him well, that was healthy and tasty.

One day, more than two months later, I discovered the ultimate healing food. Upon shopping for cat food, my eyes zoomed in on a bag that read, "New, with yogurt," and since Lactobacillus Acidophilus was the next ingredient to be tried with Eli, this food would be a perfect means of administering this live culture in his diet. How convenient to finally find a food with probiotics.

Others did exist, I now know, but they are not too common in regular stores that sell pet food or in vet offices. A couple of these foods are present in pet-specialty stores, I have since discovered, but they certainly do not claim this glorious ingredient visually on the package. Animal feed stores that carry farm supplies happen to be the ones, at least in my area, that sells the very high quality foods, beyond many premium brands.

Purina One with yogurt was the food I discovered. This food was absolutely life changing. Elijah had a perfectly normal stool for the first time in months within only a day or two of eating this food! I was thrilled!

My bowel-distressed boy was a normal cat once again. He had no pain in his intestines or any of the resulting irritations that go along with having constant diarrhea. Elijah would get blood in his stool at times. Finally, sleeping through the night once again became possible. How precious it is to sleep all night without any disturbance.

At the time of discovering this food, Eli was still a kitten. The only formulation of this food with yogurt was a kitten-formulated food. Once Eli was over a year old, finding a food that was specifically geared toward adult cats was a goal of mine. No drastic actions would be taken with regards to changing his food after all I went through to find a food that made him healthy again. I wrote Purina a letter about Eli's success story with this food and encouraged them to produce other formulations. There are many other cats that need Lactobacillus Acidophilus to be healthy. Purina did not respond. Elijah remained on the kitten food.

About two years later, an adult food was on the store shelves. I was ecstatic! Now Eli could eat a food made specifically for his age group. The ingredients would remain essentially the same, so as not to disturb his internal organs because it was a Purina One food. The golden child remained on this food until he was nearly four years old. He would still get blood in his feces on occasion, though. A friend told me about Innova brand cat food and the high-quality ingredients it contains.

I went to the only store that sells it, in my area, to read the ingredients. This food contains many probiotic live cultures. The Evo formulation, as it's called, is the one my friend told me about. This high-quality food was most impressive, of all the formulas to me. There are no grains at all in it. It does contain a small amount of carbohydrates. The ingredients are varied and healthful. The protein level is very high, being fifty percent. This makes a lot of sense, as cats are carnivores. Innova Evo turned out to be a remarkable food. Eli has completely normal stools and there is no blood in them any longer. My other housecats eat it and love it.

Eli grooming little Oleander.

Eli is my best friend. We have a special bond. This coddled beauty overcame the odds, as an orphan newborn, kitten born to an apparent stray queen in someone's yard by actually getting a wonderful, life-long home. If I did not take in this litter of kittens, they would have been taken to animal control and euthanized. Had I not recognized how special this kitten was and kept him myself, it is quite likely someone else would not have been as determined as I was, to find a cure for all the ailments this kitten presented. I started Feline Estate, Inc. to rescue cats and this little cat (not so little now at 19 pounds 3 ounces) was just what I needed. It is fair to say that we needed each other. I am grateful for each day that we have together. Elation overwhelms me to have this treasured cat in my life.

Jessica and Elijah.

> **It amazes me how much joy can come in such a small package, as a cat!**

Better Cat Food Standards

The good news is that natural, healthier foods are becoming more of a standard in pet food. The horrible incident with the tainted pet food from China has definitely prompted consumers and consequently manufacturers to be more cautious and health-oriented in pet food production. The trend in human food, which offers consumers many organic and other natural food options, has inspired some pet food manufacturers to have higher standards. When consumers have higher standards for their own food, they expect their pets to have higher quality food choices.

Chapter 8
Feline Medical Concerns

"Ever occur to you why some of us can be this much concerned with animal suffering? Because government is not. Why not? Because animals don't vote."
Paul Harvey

There are many organisms in the environment just waiting to occupy a host, like a cat, to continue its life cycle. As cat guardians, we must take a pro-active approach to protect felines. There are anthelmintics, which kill worms, and vaccines, which help prevent diseases that are used to maintain a cat's health.

Sterilization is obviously an important procedure for cats. It is the key to stopping pet over-population. Many benefits are gained for the cat from being spayed or neutered.

Intestinal Parasites and Protozoans

The topic of intestinal parasites is important to discuss. Many cats have been brought to the shelter with serious infestations of worms. Lots of people are not aware of the facts on worms. Most cats are not de-wormed enough. Worms can kill.

Hookworms and Roundworms

Hookworms are a horrible parasite. They are extremely miniscule in size, but catastrophic in the amount of damage inflicted on a cat. Attaching to the small intestine lining, blood is withdrawn directly from the flesh. Holes are drilled in the intestine causing the cat to become anemic.

Various symptoms manifest in a cat from Hookworms. Visually the mucous membranes of the cat, like the gums, become very pale. The cat acts extremely weak and lethargic, eventually loosing the will to even eat. The worms continue to multiply. The cat becomes thin. Blood may be seen in the stool. The stool may even appear black and tar-like, which is blood the cat is losing from damage caused by these worms.

These nasty little worms migrate out of the intestine, as part of their life cycle. They head towards the lungs. The cat will begin to cough. Once the worm is coughed up into the throat, it will then get swallowed. Being swallowed eventually gets the worm back to the intestine.

Roundworms are very damaging intestinal parasites. These worms can migrate through the intestinal walls. They can get into the eye or the liver, for instance. You can actually see it swimming in your cat's eye. Roundworms look similar to spaghetti, being round and white in appearance.

Adult worms are three to five inches long. A cat infested with this parasite will develop a round, bloated abdominal appearance. The ribs and hip bones will be protruding since the cat is extremely malnourished. The cat will always be hungry. Diarrhea and vomiting are common symptoms, as it is the body's way of trying to eliminate (no pun intended) these annoying trespassers.

The cat will choke and gag when infected with Roundworms. Coughing up some worms is not uncommon. Life-threatening blockages can result inside the cat when too many of these worms are present in the intestine. Try and imagine a cat having thirty five- inch long worms compacted in his intestine. That visual alone should compel people to realize how important it is to de-worm their cat.

Cats become infected via three main methods and one less common method;

- By ingesting worm larvae from the mother cat's milk
- By eating a rodent that is a carrier of the worm larvae
- By ingesting eggs that are passed in the stool of an infected cat
- Another way the Hookworm can enter the feline's body is by going through its skin. A cat can lie on the ground where a larvae, is waiting for a host. It will enter the cat's body. Kittens are in the most danger

when getting these worms, since their immune systems are not fully formed and their tissues are thinner.

Hookworms and Roundworms are nematodes, which have un-segmented bodies that are narrowed at each end. Their shapes are cylindrical. These worms are killed by the some of the same medication. De-worming medications are sold in stores right over the counter. Pyrantel Pamoate kills both types of worms. It is currently available in Animal Feed stores, not in pet supply stores or supermarkets, in my area anyhow. Generally, I have not found it to be labeled specifically for cats, though this anthelmintic is safe for cats, one cc per five pounds.

Veterinarians use this exact same liquid to de-worm a cat at exam time. However, anytime a medicine is not labeled for cats to use, do not use it until being verified as safe for cats. There are flea products only for dogs that will kill a cat. Ask a veterinarian for information.

Pyrantel Pamoate is a liquid, which is easily given on food or orally with a syringe. This product is easily accessible and inexpensive. Some cats even enjoy its taste. It is convenient because it kills these two worms. Other de-wormers only kill Roundworms.

The treatment needs to be given in sequential doses about two weeks apart. The follow-up dose is very important. Only worms that are in the intestinal tract will be affected by the de-wormer. All the worms that have migrated into other parts of the body need to find their way back to the intestinal tract, where they can be killed by subsequent doses. Only two doses are required in some cases. More will be required in other situations. Always thoroughly read the dosing instructions on any medication.

Some anthelmintics only kill one of these worms. Hookworms are killed by Mebendazole and Fenbendazole, which is commonly called Panacur. Carefully read all instructions. Roundworms are killed by even more de-wormers than hookworms. Febantel, Piperazine, Selamectin, and Emodepside are some additional pharmaceuticals that can be used to kill roundworms.

Tapeworms

Tapeworms are an intestinal parasite that requires a unique killing agent. Tablets are sold at pet stores and other places. The worm is very long, living throughout the intestine. However, the way it multiplies is by portions of it breaking off. These pieces, which look like a grain of rice, will be seen on the cat's rectum and /or in the stool. The cat's sleeping quarters is another place one could view dried worm segments. The good news is that this worm is totally eliminated with one treatment of de-wormer.

Cats become infected with a tapeworm by a few methods;

- A flea is the most common method of infection. Fleas carry the larvae on them, so when the cat ingests a flea, the tapeworm begins its growth cycle.
- Rodents present a method of infection, being carriers of the larvae.
- Another, but extremely rare, method of infection is by way of a cat stepping on feces from another animal that has live eggs in it then proceeds to lick its paws. The cycle could consequently get started within its body. This mode is uncommon because cats are very clean, being careful not to step in fresh dung. For places with multiple cats, since cats bury their feces, transmission from cat to cat, is unheard of essentially.

Various Parasite Killers Available at Vets and Internet

Veterinarian offices have many new products available for sale that kill worms. Most of the products kill several parasites, including fleas, hook, and round worms and heartworms, which are transmitted by mosquitoes. These products tend to cost more than over-the-counter types because of the convenience of killing multiple parasites with one product, the middleman (the vet office), and the "newness" of the product.

The Internet is a great place to purchase these products much more cheaply. Giving all the options to a caller, is critical so whatever his or her economic earnings are, a cat can receive all the necessary medical care. Currently, all heartworm medication will require a prescription from a vet, to purchase it online. Every cat deserves to be healthy, no matter whether his guardian is rich or poor.

Coccidiosis

Coccidiosis is another organism that is harmful to cats. Commonly found in bird feces, this protozoan ends up on the ground. Coccidia enters the cat's intestines, after he has come into contact with it from the ground or via eating prey harboring it. Kittens are most likely to die from this organism, if they are not treated, for the reasons mentioned above, regarding their immune systems. Adult cats have often had the time to develop somewhat of a resistance to this deadly culprit.

An orally given sulfonamide antibiotic is the medication needed to kill coccidian, commonly called Albon. The symptoms are severe diarrhea, which is yellow in color and watery, blood in the stool, flatulence, weight loss, intestinal bloating, and straining to defecate. Lethargy and extreme gauntness are visual symptoms one will notice with an infected cat. Do not delay in getting treatment, as the kitten will fade quickly.

Story of Arian

A beautiful white kitten who desperately wanted to get out of the cage, I adopted from Animal Control, had this terrible affliction. I picked her up several days later once she was spayed. She was ill, though not from surgery complications. Yellow diarrhea was plaguing her.

I took her back to Animal Control to be examined. The vet there gave me Albon to give her because she had coccidian. She nearly died. It was really rough for her. I gave her tons of intensive care. She finally pulled through. I am glad I adopted this very intuitive feline. Recognizing a problem, when it is present is a key factor for saving an ill cat, so treatment is sought after promptly. Now that one has information on common parasites, that are not very expensive to get rid of, when detected early on, I'll get onto ways to protect cats from contagious diseases.

Arian was a sensitive and intuitive DSH who always knew when I needed comforting.

Preventing Contagious Ailments

Upon arrival, a new cat should ideally be isolated for about two weeks. The reason for isolating a cat is that it could be harboring an upper respiratory disease. The quarantine time limit given allows the illness time to reveal itself, so as not to expose the other cats to it. Soon they would begin to show signs of the illness.

Let me expand on the topic of isolation. I do not agree with making a cat live in complete isolation for any period of time. One other cat, as a minimum could be housed with a new arrival. This way, if by chance the cat is harboring something, at least the entire population of cats will not have been exposed to it. The other alternative could be allowing the new cat to be able to see the other cats and vice versa. They can all become familiar with each other in this manner before physically meeting. This would be an additional benefit of the situation.

When a young kitten gets brought in, such as six weeks of age, it should never be left completely alone, in my opinion. Young kittens depend on the other kittens for body heat and proper emotional development. One or two other kittens could be housed with him. If no other kittens are currently available, then pair up a suitable adult cat for the baby's companion, while in his state of transition into the organization. The goal of semi-isolation is simply not to expose all of the cats to some contagious ailment.

Mixing litters of kittens is not a good idea, until it is known they are very healthy. Kittens are very susceptible to medical ailments. When kittens are infected with an illness, but are not showing signs yet, they can infect all the other kittens they are contacting. A situation of all the kittens becoming ill is clearly a bad predicament.

Sanitation Policy

Health of the cats is an aspect of operating a cat shelter that cannot be stressed enough. When one cat is sick, others that come in contact with that cat have the potential to become ill. This could become a detrimental mess. Treating one sick cat is much easier and cost-effective as opposed to treating ten sick cats, for instance.

A sanitation program for anyone handling the cats is very important to have in place. Germs are easily spread between cats when someone touches a sick cat then a healthy one because we act as fomites. Our clothing and hands will get microorganisms on them, from wherever the sick cat comes into contact with us. Subsequently, this is often how the transfer of pathogens occurs. Hands should be washed very frequently in a cat shelter. Numerous hand-washing stations will play an important part in maintaining a healthy cat population. Putting out waterless anti-bacterial solution is another way to prevent germs from spreading. A cat that is clearly ill should be somewhat isolated from the rest of the clowder, so as not to infect all the cats.

Objects and living quarters must be disinfected properly. Certain materials are able to be sterilized more effectively than others. The best type of litter boxes and food bowls for shelters to use are stainless steel ones. They can be completely decontaminated. Plastic can't be sanitized very well and this is especially true when it has been damaged, as with a scratch in the surface. Plastic food bowls are not good to use in any setting. These bowls harbor odors and germs. Cats, who are forced to eat from plastic bowls, sometimes develop acne on their chins. Cats do not like drinking water from plastic bowls at all. Since the bowl can never truly be purified, odors and germs can thrive in it. I like ceramic bowls, though they are more porous than stainless steel. They are perfect for home settings.

I am a very chemically sensitive person, just like cats are, but to kill certain pathogens a chemical cleaner is necessary. Sodium hypochlorite, or bleach, is truly the best disinfectant and it is definitely not as toxic to be around as some others. Always use in a well-ventilated area. Do not have the cats near the substance or the fumes. Bleach is just about the only product that kills the Feline Panleukopenia Virus. One-half a cup of bleach mixed with one gallon of water is the correct concentration to annihilate FPV, or Distemper, and many other nasty microorganisms. It must be left on the surface for ten minutes, when the goal is to obliterate this particular viral disease. Always rinse off all surfaces very thoroughly after cleaning.

A precious kitten, like Oleander will appreciate a sanitation policy in place so he will not become ill.

Chlamydia

Chlamydia is a bacterial infection mainly affecting the eyes. It causes Conjunctivitis which is inflammation of the inner surface of the eyelid and the white part of the eye. Watery discharge is the earliest possible symptom one will notice. The eye begins to swell immensely and the discharge will convert to typical bacterial discharge, being thick and yellow. Some other URI symptoms may also be present. The worst case scenario involves the kitten's eyeball swelling and bursting. This can happen quickly! The kitten must now go through life with only one eye or with no eyes, if he loses them both. Death can follow, if the kitten is not treated, as the bacteria will continue destroying the body.

There are treatments that effectively kill Feline Chlamydophila. Antibiotics, such as Tetracycline, given as an eye ointment or orally can defeat this atrocious bacterium. Oral treatments should be included, as part of the treatment plan because the bacterium can exist in other parts of the body, in addition to the eyes.

Upper Respiratory Infection

Upper-respiratory infection is the most common infliction of shelter animals. Stuffy nasal cavities, watery eyes, and sneezing accompanied with fever and lethargy are symptoms of this affliction. Generally, it goes away after a few weeks, but depending on the previous exposure each cat has had to the infirmity, it can be severely debilitating to some.

Kittens can easily die from URI. They can barely breathe and certainly can't smell. An infected cat or kitten will often hold his mouth partly open. His nasal passages are so clogged this is the only method that the cat can inhale air. Felines can't smell their food. Lack of olfactory abilities inhibits their desire to eat and drink. Dehydration is sure to follow. If not addressed immediately, death is the consequence. Kittens have weaker immune systems than adults making fighting the ailment nearly impossible.

When plagued with this common ailment, the cat may have afflictions of the mouth. Oral ulcers are common. These ulcers can form on the tongue, gum, lips, or anyplace in the mouth. URI can come from different sources.

URI can be caused from bacteria or viruses. A thick yellow-green type discharge indicates the cause is bacterial. Clear, watery discharge points to a virus being the cause. Antibiotics may or may not help, depending on the causative agent.

Subcutaneous fluids are usually what will save an affected kitten or cat that is severely dehydrated. Fluids need to be combined with a high calorie supplement, like Nutri-Cal. Nutri-Cal can be offered to the cat by putting it on one's finger or a dish to allow the cat to lick it up. Some cats have no desire to eat. In this case, one needs to apply it to the inside of the cat's mouth frequently to provide critical nutrients. Eventually, it will stimulate the cat's desire to eat. This miracle gel has helped me save many lives.

Jessica Barbazon

Lilac, a Polydactyl, nearly died from URI when she was a kitten.

> **Ailment Alert**
> Bacterial causes produce a thick, yellow discharge. Viral causes create a clear, watery discharge.

Distemper (Panleukopenia)

Distemper, or Panleukopenia (without white blood cells, from its Latin origin), is a highly contagious disease. It is spread by many different means. Fomites are a common transmission method, meaning any inanimate object, substance, or person can spread the disease to uninfected felines. An insect can become a fomite by walking through an infected surface. It then carries the ailment on itself to other areas. An infected cat's entire body is an infective agent. Anything it touches with its body and any bodily fluid will become infected. This hardy virus can live for beyond one year at room temperature!

Young kittens are the most susceptible to this ailment. This "cat plague," as it is often referred to, is the most common cause of sudden death in shelter cats. The cat may seem fine then the next day it is dead. However, symptoms can become apparent quite quickly. The blood and lymphatic systems, the gastrointestinal (GI) tract, and the nervous system are all affected.

When a pregnant female becomes infected with distemper, there are consequences for the kittens. Their brains will not form properly. The cerebellum of the brain becomes damaged from this disease. A high-fever will occur, such as one of 103* F. Brain damage and neurological problems usually result from distemper. The kittens' growth will be affected. Kittens that do survive usually will have neurological problems for their entire lives. They wobble while walking and lack coordination.

Other symptoms show up when a cat or kitten becomes affected. Vomiting and mucus-yellow diarrhea are other common symptoms. This results in dehydration. The intestines are affected. They become bloated and may not work properly. When a blood test is performed, the white blood cell (WBC) will be low on cats with this disease. Although, low white-blood cell counts does not necessarily mean this disease is the cause because other ailments have this same evidence.

Survival rates can vary. Many kittens will die soon after acquiring the disease. Some will survive. Keeping a kitten hydrated is a critical factor for survival. Hydration can be obtained by giving subcutaneous fluids and electrolytes. Syringe feeding water into the kitten is another method to incorporate in your hydration program. Nutritional supplements can help the cat. Antibiotics can be useful to help eliminate any secondary infection the kitten may have caught due to the low white blood cell count.

Vaccinations against this disease should be given. The name of the vaccine is the Feline Viral Rhinotracheitis Calicivirus Panleukopenia (FVRCP). This vaccine comes in a few varieties: a 3-way, 4-way, or a 5-way vaccine. Any of these vaccines will promote herd health for all the cats. The shot does not prevent a cat from getting one of these URI afflictions, but it will reduce the intensity of the illness.

The name implies the number of ailments it protects against.

- The 3-way is for Rhinotracheitis, Calicivirus, and Feline Distemper.
- The 4-way includes all of the ailments in the 3-way and adds Chlamydophila.
- The 5-way includes all of the previous illnesses while including the Feline Leukemia vaccine.

Kittens can receive a distemper combo shot at about six weeks of age. All felines, six weeks of age or older, entering a shelter should receive a vaccine upon arrival. She will need three or four subsequent doses, depending how young the kitten is when she receives the first one. Vaccines are given about three weeks apart. A kitten that is twelve weeks old before receiving a vaccine will only require one more dose. An adult cat that was never vaccinated for this before would need one follow-up booster shot. After the booster series, whether one shot or several, an annual vaccine is the general protocol for immunity protection. Other ailments exist that are contagious.

Feline Infectious Peritonitis (FIP)

Feline Infectious Peritonitis is a very peculiar disease. There is currently no accurate test for the ailment. There is no cure. It is difficult to diagnose. One can never know for sure whether a cat will come down with the illness at some point.

This disease is a part of the coronavirus family of ailments. Most cats are exposed to the coronavirus at some point early in their lives. Many cats will get diarrhea, and then just get over it without any further complications. However, in some cases the disease will mutate. This mutation becomes the deadly strain called FIP. There is no predictor of which cat will recover completely and which cat will get the deadly form.

Titer tests are available to test the blood for antigens of coronavirus. The problem is that currently there is no distinction between the mild, non-lethal coronavirus or fatal FIP. The titer number, in a blood test, is not an accurate indicator of whether a cat will come down with lethal FIP.

The disease is spread through alternate methods. The most prominently known method of spreading the disease is when kittens share a litter box with adult cats, resulting in the kitten coming down with the disease in roughly one year. Other cats that are prone to getting this affliction are those with compromised immune systems. For instance, cats that already have FeLV (Leukemia) are more likely to come down with FIP. Perhaps the coronavirus is able to mutate easily in a cat with an inadequate immune system. Kittens can be born with FIP if their mother had it. Fading Kitten Syndrome is the most common death of newborn kittens. Death will come a few days after birth for no evident reason. This is a result of FIP.

FIP can take on one of two different forms: a "wet" form or a "dry" form. With the wet form, fluid accumulates within different organs and in the body cavities, like the abdomen and/or the chest. The body detects the foreign disease within itself. While attempting to fight the disease, it creates some of the excess fluids. Other fluid originates because the disease causes the leaking of blood fluids and serum out of the blood vessels.

This disease presents some symptoms in a cat. The most prominent will be the fluid accumulation in the abdomen, should the wet form come about. The wet form is the most common. Other symptoms a cat exhibits are; unexplained fevers, lethargy, weight loss, or eye disease. Secondary symptoms are liver or kidney disease. The dry form of the disease manifests in a different manner. No fluids accumulate in the body cavities. However, fluids accumulate in the organs themselves and will eventually cause organ failure, just like the wet form.

Feline Leukemia Virus (FeLV) & Feline Immunodeficiency Virus (FIV)

Every cat that comes into the shelter should be tested for Feline Leukemia Virus (FeLV) and Feline Immunodeficiency Virus (FIV). Both of these afflictions compromise the immune system. A certain area or specific pens should be designated for cats that test positive for the illnesses. Cats that have either of these diseases can live very long lives before the disease ever bothers them.

No one can know for sure when the cat will begin to succumb to the ailment. It could be at the age of one year or it could be at age nine, for instance. Attempt to not allow exposure to other illnesses because the cat's immune system is not able to fight germs off the same way that an uninfected cat can. It is best not to allow uninfected cats to mingle with infected cats.

Cats can become contaminated by way of saliva or other bodily fluids. These cats can be adopted out only into a home with no other cats and that will be an inside only lifestyle. There are vaccinations available for these diseases, but the FIV one in particular has some drawbacks. One being the cat will test positive for the disease, though he may only have non-infective antibodies. Discuss all the details with a veterinarian.

Rabies

Rabies vaccinations are a requirement by the law in most places. This is definitely an advantageous vaccine to give to every cat. Wild animals will be carrying Rabies at some place sometime, so one never knows when a rabid animal may make contact with a cat. Since there is no cure, there is no way to save the cat once infected with the disease.

Rabies is a neurological disease that affects the brain. This fatal disease manifests in one of two different ways in an infected mammal. One form is an aggressive form which causes the animal to attack another animal or person. The other form is called "dumb rabies" where an animal acts unusual, but calm. For instance, if a wild raccoon starts following you while on a walk and seems disoriented, it very likely has rabies. Wild animals should fear people, to a certain degree.

Jessica Barbazon

Sherbert, a DSH, feels safe knowing he has a current Rabies vaccine.

Sterilization

Sterilization is the act of making the cat sterile, preventing the ability to produce offspring. This operation can be safely performed on both sexes at six weeks of age. The reason for doing it so young, is mostly for shelter settings, to ensure a kitten is spayed or neutered before leaving. Four months old is a perfect age. Cats need to be sterilized before going to a new home. There are many benefits obtained by having this procedure performed on a cat. The most beneficial aspect is to prevent the cat from contributing to the massive overpopulation problem, which results in about four million pets being killed each year in our country. Other rewards of sterilization contribute to good behavior for the cat, which essentially boils down to not being relinquished by his guardian for preventable, undesirable behavior. Some health rewards exist for the cat from this medical process.

> **Sterilization Statute**
> Sterilizing a cat before puberty will prevent undesirable behaviors, which are often triggered by hormones. When performed after puberty sterilization usually stops unwelcome actions.

Health Benefits of Sterilization

Health benefits exist for cats that are sterilized. For females, it will eliminate the risk of cancer to the reproductive organs. Breast cancer risk will be reduced. For males, testicular cancer risks will essentially be eliminated.

An indirect health reward of being sterilized is the reduction of fighting and wandering which reduces the risk of deadly dangers. Sterilization is a commonly performed procedure by veterinarians, which involves a specific sequence for each sex. Both sexes are fully anaesthetized for sterilization. Before making an appointment to sterilize the new stray cat, you must first determine the sex of the cat.

How to Determine the Gender of the Cat

When a kitten is young, it is more difficult to determine the gender of the cat. However, with a description of the appearance of each sex's characteristics, this should simplify the process for accurate detection of the gender of the cat. The description of this process can be used for kittens and adults.

For a female cat;

- Look at the genital area, under the tail.
- The anus will be visible.
- Extremely close to the anus will be an oval-shaped opening called the vulva.
- The most noteworthy thing to mention that helps one in determining that the cat is a female is that the opening will be very close to the anus.

For a male cat;

- Look at the genital area and locate the anus.
- In a young kitten, there will be about one –quarter of an inch of a space between the anus and the penis opening, which is a tiny round opening.

- A young kitten will have this space clearly visible. The testicles will eventually begin to become visible at four months of age, as they descend into the scrotum.
- The testicles size will slowly increase with age.
- At age ten months to one-year, the testicles will be quite large and pretty much full-grown. The space between the anus and the penis opening will appear larger than a very young kitten.

How to Establish Whether a Cat is Already Sterilized

When a cat arrives, determining whether the cat has already been spayed or neutered is necessary. For females, it is more difficult to ascertain by simply looking at the genital area. One way to obtain an answer would be to bring the cat to a vet facility to have the cat's abdomen shaved, or do it oneself, and look for a scar from a spay surgery. There are other more subtle, yet less definite ways, to make a determination.

First, notice if the female's belly is really rounded, indicating she may be far-along into a pregnancy. Take note that a rounded belly on a cat could indicate a severe infestation of roundworms or the wet form of Feline Infectious Peritonitis (FIP), a rare deadly disease. The nipples are the key to assessing a possible pregnancy. A pregnant cat will have nipples that are elongated with the width being swollen.

The nipples are important indicators in determining whether a cat is pregnant. The nipples elongate and swell long before the cat shows any other visible signs of being pregnant. If the nipples are rather large, like one-quarter of an inch long or more, then this cat may currently be pregnant or just recently finished nursing a litter of kittens, who may or may not be weaned. This certainly means this cat is not already spayed.

Run your hand along the female feline's abdominal underside to feel the nipples. A cat that has never had kittens will have extremely tiny nipples, like not even one-eighth of an inch long, and are so tiny that clearly nothing has ever nursed on them. One that had given birth to kittens who have survived and nursed previously will have teats that are slightly larger than that, but not as tiny as ones that never had kittens.

When an adult female cat shows up that has never had kittens, this is a good indication that she may already be spayed. Not much time will pass before a tom cat finds and breeds an un-spayed female. The possibility exists that this cat could have just escaped from her indoor only home and is not spayed, nor is pregnant yet. Most stray cats are not sterilized, but looking for signs of past or current pregnancies is about the best way to determine the cat's status on sterilization, without clipping the fur off the belly.

It is always best to get the cat to a spay clinic, when there is any doubt at all. Once the cat has her abdomen shaved, the spay staff will soon know the status of the cat. It is better to be safe than sorry on this issue. There are way too many un-sterilized cats running around and breeding.

A male cat is easier to determine as to whether he has been neutered or not. An adult male will have visibly large testicles, like three-quarters of an inch protruding from his scrotum that are visible. A cat that is six-months old, for instance, will have smaller testicles, but they will still protrude.

One can feel the scrotum to assess if the testicles are in there. They will feel round while sticking outward. A neutered cat has a flat surface within and upon the scrotum. The space will still be present between the anus and the penis. It will just be an area of flat surface. An adult male whom is not neutered has a large, round head from the testosterone in his body. When a cat gets neutered before adulthood, he will not get that massive head.

A Spay for Females

When a female cat or queen is sterilized, it is called a spay. This process involves a series of procedures. A spay is an ovariohysterectomy, which removes the ovaries and Y-shaped uterus, down to the cervix. Cats have two ovaries and two uterine horns. An incision is made in the cat's abdomen, on her underside, in most surgeries, to access these organs for removal. Sutures are used to close the cervix and to close the abdomen, though glue is often used. The cat will be fully healed in about ten days. One must visually inspect the surgery site daily to monitor for any discharge, swelling, redness or heat at the incision.

Most surgeries have no problems associated with them. However, anytime surgery is performed, there is always some risk of complications. Grimalkins, older female cats, usually have no problems from this procedure, though they should be monitored like any cat that gets a procedure performed. Go to a veterinarian immediately, if discharge is present. The cat will be examined to see exactly what is medically occurring. Discharge can indicate an infection is at hand. Antibiotics will be prescribed.

When swelling occurs, there are a couple of reasons this can happen. One reason is the internal stitches or glue used to seal the internal flesh can cause an allergic reaction, which goes away in a few days. Another reason for swelling may be an infection or an indication that something was not properly sealed off inside the cat.

As far as redness of the skin, a little bit at the incision site is normal after surgery. However, if the red area expands along the skin, then it is possible an infection is present. A hot incision-site, much warmer than other nearby areas of the body, can also indicate an infection. With any of these symptoms, seek medical attention for the cat.

Bridgette is a calico DSH cat. Nearly every calico is female.

A Neuter for Males

The procedure of sterilizing a male cat is called an orchidectomy, or commonly, a neuter. A neutered cat is called a gib. A neuter begins with making a slit in the scrotum. The spermatic cords and associated blood vessels are cut to remove the testicles. These cords and vessels are then tied. The scrotum slit is left open, though it appears closed. It simply heals within about a week.

A great benefit for sexually mature male cats is that his very pungent urine will go away about two weeks after neutering. Male cats are less likely to have problems after surgery than females, but they too should be monitored daily. Upon the arrival of any of the previously mentioned symptoms, medical attention should be sought out for the cat.

Noah, a classic orange tabby is a DSH. Almost every cat that is all orange is male.

Sterilization through a Vaccine

Research is being conducted to produce a more efficient and practical means of sterilization. The whole method would simply involve giving the cat a shot, as opposed to any surgical procedure. This technology is already being applied on male dogs. This would be so practical for feral cats. Just imagine the efficiency for sterilizing feral colonies. Cats would need to be trapped, given the shot, earmarked (to be identified as already sterilized), and released. With sterilization being performed at the location, it would greatly reduce stress on the cats. Labor and financial costs for the humans would be greatly minimized.

The University of Florida is exploring this method, along with financial support of the Morris Animal Foundation, in creating a sterilization vaccine for cats. Currently, the vaccine is not lasting for the lifetime of the cat. It is sterilizing a female for about two years for the majority of the cats being injected. Research is continuing for the perfection of this vaccine. This vaccine could truly change lifestyles for feral cats, particularly by reducing their numbers very quickly. Scant resources, in a feral cat lifestyle, would last longer with fewer cats utilizing them.

Description of a Cryptorchid

A cryptorchid is a very rare occurrence, but this is a good place to mention them. This means the testicles have never fallen into the scrotum, which normally occurs at four months of age. At a glance, these cats absolutely appear to be neutered. However, within the prepuce (the skin covering the penis) the penis will have the normal spiny barbs just like any unneutered sexually mature male tom cat. These penile barbs form due to male hormones. They serve the purpose of stimulating the female to ovulate, as cats are induced ovulators, upon completion of mating. The truth of the situation becomes clear by the smell of the urine, as I will describe in my experience with Owen. The urine continues to smell like a non-neutered male, the very pungent odor that develops from the male hormones.

Story of Owen

Only one cryptorchid had crossed my path through many years of rescuing cats. This male cat, Owen, lived in the barn area near my residence. At times, he was friendly. One day I caught this elusive, light orange tabby upon going to the vets with another cat. My goal was to get him tested for Leukemia (FeLV) and FIV. The results came back that he was negative for these diseases.

This tough, older tabby had another issue, I wanted to be examined. He had dried blood coming from the inside of one of his ears. Upon his examination, it was determined that he had a tumor in his ear canal that needed to be removed. Needless to say it turned out to be a much more expensive day at the vet office than I planned. He appeared to be neutered, which was a very pleasant surprise for an abandoned barn cat.

However, as he was kept in the pen for treatment after surgery, I noticed how his urine reeked, like a non-neutered male. This was puzzling to me. I never had a neutered cat continue to have smelly urine. That odor always goes completely away within two weeks following a neuter. I brought him back to the vet clinic when he completed his post-surgery treatment, mentioning this situation to the vet. She examined him, discovering that he was a cryptorchid. By visually noting that his penis was still barbed, it was determined that he really was not neutered. The fact is his testicles never descended. The male's barbs normally go away after a neuter.

Chapter 9

Reasons by Which Cats Come up Missing

"The reasonable man adapts himself to the world; the unreasonable one persists in trying to adapt the world to himself. Therefore all progress depends on the unreasonable man." George Bernard Shaw

    Losing a cat is a horrible situation to experience as a cat guardian. One day the beloved cat just disappears and feelings of helplessness and bewilderment are plaguing. Where could the cat have gone? Did he wander away, following the scent of another animal? Did someone steal her? Did a predator eat him? Did a car hit her? I completely understand the anguish one experiences in this situation, having gone through it myself. I want to offer someone, every possible option to help him or her explore where the cat may have gone, when he or she is forced into this devastating situation.

Predators

    The majority of lost cats fall victim to predators. These creatures come from many different Classes. There are Amphibia, Reptilia, Mammalia, and Aves (birds). Coyotes are by far the ones that kill the most cats. Coyotes live nearly everywhere across the United States. They are immensely skilled hunters.

A well-known fact among those who study coyotes is that they prefer to eat cats rather than other types of prey.

Coyotes: The Most Prominent and Prolific Predators

Coyotes are responsible for causing many cats to vanish. Operating a cat shelter, many calls will come in about lost cats. The coyotes are eating the majority of lost cats. The cat simply vanishes. No trace of the cat is usually ever seen. A collar may be found at some distance from the house or a mass of cat fur, but that's all that will be found. People must be made aware of the coyote's abundance and the danger they pose.

The keen coyote is very astute at not getting hit by a car. Very rarely will you see one that has been killed by a vehicle. This is one reason individuals are not aware of their presence. For instance, since we (in Florida) see countless dead opossums on the road daily, we all know they live everywhere, even if you have not seen one walk across your yard.

People falsely believe when they live in any area that is not completely rural, that they do not have to be concerned about coyotes. This is very far from the truth. These shrewd creatures hunt predominantly at night, in the majority of places, so humans rarely see them in most areas of the country. These quadrupeds only need the cover of a few trees to build a den. The requirement of some expansive forest to find a home is not necessary. The distances they will travel are immense. These scavengers hunt ten-mile areas of land. The pack may not live in your back yard, but be assured they are visiting it.

Coyotes are bold and intelligent. While living in the city limits, I had a serious problem with the coyotes. They quietly come in the night, stalking my yard. My dogs would wake me with their loud bark. The bold carnivore would be standing at my wire fence with the desire to get in the yard. Eating a cat was its goal. The cunning coyote knew the dogs could not get through the fence. It was just hoping a cat would cross the fence, so it could grab him. I am not alone with this situation.

Jake, a Black Lab, was part of my coyote repellant team.

Katie, an Aussie, is a great cat protector.

Armani, a Great Dane, is the youngest member of the coyote brigade.

Armani portrait.

Coyotes not only pose a danger to pets. They are known to attack humans. Since the 1970's there have been more than 100 attacks on humans in California alone. From about the year 2007 through only the beginning of 2008, there have been seven ambushes on children in the Chino Hills area of California.

The common occurrence is the coyote grabbing a child and attempting to run away with it.

Most instances of sieges on humans occur during the day. These bold predators have mauled joggers, bicyclists, and have snatched people's lunch bags from them. They have even grabbed dogs being walked on leashes by their guardian! Across the country, one state has had a couple of human raids by coyotes. In New Jersey, a child was attacked by a coyote on May 23, 2007. A three-year-old child was attacked on his swing-set in 1998. I have mentioned to people, don't leave young children outside at dusk, for this very reason. Most likely, they did not take me seriously. Hopefully, they now know I was not delusional with my words. Coyotes' capabilities do not fool me. They will do whatever it takes to get a meal.

This canine has virtually no enemies, other than man. Wolves are their only enemies, but implanting wolves into places is certainly not going to help cats or livestock. No solution there. These sneaky animals are not easy to kill. Trapping can be tricky and shooting provides difficulties. These speedy creatures can run forty miles per hour.

Coyotes continue to breed. They run rampant throughout Florida. The sly canines are in most communities across the country. Recently, some communities have actually turned packs of them loose, like in North Carolina and Maryland, in hopes of them killing deer. These survival oriented critters sure will kill deer along with everything else they can catch, too. Cats, small dogs and livestock are all perfect meals for coyotes. All of us in Florida and other parts are already well aware of this fact. The intentional release of this stealthy predator is disturbing to me because coyotes proliferate so quickly and are unchallenged. I fear that many people, who have never dealt with these creatures in their areas, will most certainly lose many innocent pets, livestock, and children to coyotes.

My best friends (felines) had been killed, before I was aware of the prevalence of these carnivores. My sheep and goats had been killed, as well. I know other people that had foals and calves decimated by coyotes. I can't even begin to add the numbers of precious cats taken by them, from farms and yards. The only difference I've encountered living in a rural setting as opposed to a suburban setting is that one can hear extremely numerous packs howling in the far and near, great beyond, in the rural area.

Packs of coyotes come howling near and through my land. Fences often don't stop them. Their strong, sharp claws dig under them. My dogs do their best to keep them out of my yard, once again. Coyotes are a constant battle, being way too numerous to even dent the populations by any means of an individual citizen or rancher. Where is Parvovirus, when one needs it? Coyotes could sure use it!

Humans are partially responsible for the detriment caused by coyotes. I think every animal has been affected by our extreme population growth in the world. We have cleared a lot of habitat that animals use for their homes and food sources. We are encroaching into what, was always "their" territories. However, with coyotes, we have also transported and released them in places where they are not native. These creatures originally lived in the western part of our nation. They currently live in forty-nine states.

These hardy animals learned to flourish in whatever environments they were inserted. They have become the dominant predator, though certainly are not given enough credit for the devastation they have caused to pet and livestock guardians. Coyotes will eat nearly anything. They love to eat cats, which is even listed on websites about coyotes. If you have ever had your cat come up missing, never to return again, it very well could have fallen victim to a coyote.

Coyotes are capable of breeding with domestic dogs. In some situations, when a dog has been abandoned, it will join a pack of coyotes. The product of these two species interbreeding is called a coy-dog. They are wild predators, just like the rest of their group. Everyone needs to have this knowledge about coyotes, so cats can be protected. They probably live close to each of us. Enough precautions cannot be taken to protect cats.

Whether one lives in a rural setting or a suburban setting, coyotes visit or reside in many neighborhoods. With any areas of moist sand, a footprint is evidence of their presence. A coyote footprint is distinguishable from a dog. The two hind pads, of the four pads, on an individual paw are visibly larger and wider than the front pads. This applies to all four paws.

Coyote Footprint.

> **Coyote Fact**
> **Coyotes are known to attack pets and humans!**

Other Predators

Other predators can take cats away. Depending on what area of the country one lives in, there will be different predators, in addition to the coyote. Large owls are known to swoop down, taking a cat away in its talons. Any other bird of prey that is large enough to carry a kitten or cat off should be regarded as dangerous. Owls hunt predominantly from dusk until dawn. Hawks often hunt in the daytime. Snakes are a danger to felines. Those huge pythons that idiots have released all over South Florida are definitely pet killers. Any poisonous snake can bite and kill a cat. Foxes don't usually bother a cat, but a young kitten could be in danger. Alligators will gladly eat a cat. A snapping turtle is another creature that could grab a cat, especially if the cat is lurking near the edge of a pond.

When a predator does catch a cat, the cat will simply vanish. Usually there is no evidence at all left behind. However, if a cat is wearing a collar, the collar may be found not too far away, within one-half a mile. Other than the possibility of finding a collar or matted hair, there would not be anything else to find. There is another animal to fear, which I would not consider a predator because they kill for sport, not for food.

Dogs can be dangerous, especially when in a group. Dogs assume pack behavior when more than one is present, in most situations. A dog that may be a relatively nice, harmless dog can completely change its attitude when another free-roaming dog joins it for company. The dogs can have killing another animal on their minds, once in a pair or a pack. One main difference in this situation, as opposed to a true predator which kills for food, is that the dogs will maliciously tear the cat apart, as they have their fun. The other difference is that finding the missing cat not too far away from where it was killed is common.

Dogs can be vicious because they consider this torture to be an extracurricular activity, or a sporting event. Free-roaming dogs are common in country settings, as people think its fine to let them wander. When that dog comes up missing, his guardian should be aware that a farmer probably caught him in the act of killing his livestock or pets and that dog's life has now been ended by means of a rifle. There are ways that cats come up missing that does not involve any other animals, rather people.

Research Labs

"I abhor vivisection. It should at least be curbed. Better, it should be abolished. I know of no achievement through vivisection, no scientific discovery, that could not have been obtained without such barbarism and cruelty. The whole thing is evil." Charles Mayo, M.D.

> **Please make a law preventing the use of cats and dogs in research laboratories!**

In areas where animal research labs exist, which usually are metropolitan urban regions, pets face the threat of being stolen to be sold to one of these legalized torture chambers. There is nothing worse than going to a research lab, if you are the subject that is going to be brutalized. And what a betrayal! A precious kitten that grew up in a loving home with people playing with him and petting him is stolen by some loser, trying to make a quick dollar, that says, "Here kitty, kitty" and snatches the unknowing kitten. The pathetic scumbag throws him into a burlap sack, hauling him to the research facility to sell.

Research labs do horrendous procedures to innocent animals. Scientists remove portions of their skull and attach electrodes onto their brains. They can administer shocks to the cat in this manner. Cats are intentionally starved to look at some cause and effect situation, for instance. Their spinal cords are severed and the cats are forced to live this way for months. Then they are killed. Cats are a preferred species for neurological experiments. Many neurological experiments involving the spinal cord are carried out this way.

Cats are tortured by numerous methods. Eyeballs are removed from their head. Eyeballs are switched into the opposite sockets, as well. Their skin is burned. Cats are sleep-deprived by being forced to walk on a moving treadmill for twenty hours or more at a time. Cats are shocked when they fall off the treadmill. Sleep deprivation experiments are conducted in yet another heinous manner. A cat is forced to balance on a small plank in a huge barrel of water. If the cat goes to sleep, subsequently falling off the plank, he will drown.

Metal rods are drilled through their heads to force the cat into immobility, as they are further held in place with metal vices. These few examples that I have described of what really happens in research labs should get the point across of how awful this life is for a cat! Can you imagine your best friend that you raised from infancy, being treated this way? The little baby that has never been hurt by a human, fully trusted humans all his life, is now being brutally tortured day in and day out by humans. That's why I say the betrayal is just so wrong.

Wonder has always brewed in me as to why our government allows torturous research to be performed on our companion animals. I don't like any animal research, but how can the government possibly permit our best friends to be treated this way? Cats and dogs are our best friends. Billions of dollars are spent on pets each year in this country. Someone that needs proof of the love for the animals that live in our homes, it's there. We even pick up their feces. Performing this task for anyone is a display of true love because it is not a pleasant task.

There are different types of dealers that supply research labs with animals.

- Class A Dealers; specifically breed animals to sell to labs. They are not likely to steal someone's pet because they often breed animals with certain characteristics to sell to labs.

- Class B Dealers; gather animals from "random sources" then sell them to research labs. They may steal a pet from any place to sell it to a lab.

Well, a cat is a cat! Just because you torture one that was bred with the purpose of torturing it, does not make it any less of a cat than one who was stolen from someone's yard or taken from an animal pound and sold to a lab. A cat, no matter where it came from, is still an individual and still feels pain! Every cat should certainly have the right to live or die free from torture.

Dogs should also be banned from research labs. Cats and dogs are the animals we, humans, domesticated thousands of years ago. Cats and dogs have been our loyal companions. They assisted our survival and this is the thanks we give them. Hey, government officials, I know many of you share your homes with a special pet right now, so don't pretend the cat or dog being legally maimed in a lab right now is any different from your pet.

Please make a law preventing the use of cats and dogs in any research laboratories! There are large animal rights groups that exist who have been trying to eliminate animal research for many years. It is very challenging to change such a common method of practice that has gone on for decades in this country, but could we at least ban the use of cats and dogs in these facilities? What takes place in these labs is beyond immoral, to mutilate companion animals that we have made into our friends and helpers.

Pound seizures allow research labs to take animals from animal shelters, specifically the county operated animal control facilities. Many states have banned this practice. Other states still allow them. This means when someone is forced to give up a beloved pet for some reason and the only service available in a particular area is the county run facility, the cat is taken there with the hope that he will get an opportunity to be adopted. Instead some research lab needs more cats this week, so they come and get this friendly cat, among others.

Labs specifically request nice, friendly pets because the researchers are not as likely to get bitten or scratched when they attempt to torture the cat. Researchers do not want any feral cats. They are too difficult to handle and force to remain in a small cage or a head-locking immobility device. Most people do not know the fact that their precious pet could end up in a research lab, but now everyone does.

School Dissection Labs

"We need a boundless ethic which will include the animals also."
Albert Schweitzer

Cats can be stolen for the horrible reason of dissecting their bodies in schools. Cats are mutilated across the nation in schools, though at least they are dead first, as opposed to the previous example, in research labs, involving vivisection. Science labs, which start in middle school and go all the way through college, commonly use cats for dissection.

These unfortunate cats are often obtained from random sources. Each pet is at risk to be taken for this reason. All ages of cats, including pregnant ones are killed with their bodies preserved with formaldehyde. The cats are killed in a gruesome manner.

The fact that cats are used in such a barbaric manner is just absolutely appalling. These dissection labs teach children that it is fine to chop up a beloved pet. Many children are completely horrified from being forced to do this procedure. They have a beautiful beloved cat at home, then must come to class and slice open a cat's body and rip the organs out!

I was very fortunate to somehow have avoided this confrontation, of dissecting a cat, through primary school and college. I would have taken a failing grade because I could not chop up a cat that was killed just to be hacked to pieces for something, so stupid and wasteful, as looking at the dead body, then putting the cat in the trash. This is not education. This is cruelty. Cats are my friends and this is not the way one treats a friend.

Fortunately, there is some recognition nowadays to the emotional trauma this curricula inflicts on many students. There are some states which allow the student to make a choice without penalty. Students, in one of these states, can opt out of the actual animal dissection. The same knowledge, of viewing anatomy, can be obtained by using one of several completely accurate computer models or by using an actual plastic model. Take action to protect a cat from theft.

Hit by Car

After reading what some humans intentionally do to animals, being hit by a car doesn't sound so bad. But, yes of course that is a horrible thing to have happen. A lost cat may have accidentally been run over. Sometimes the body can be found along the roadside.

The cat will often be found close to home. Always drive along all roads near the cat's residence. Look in the ditches, as well. Walking the roads and ditches is necessary to see more closely. Perhaps friends and neighbors could walk the roads to give more chances of spotting the cat. When a cat is missing, one can't do too much in trying to find her.

Stolen by Human

Another horrendous possibility to consider is if a mean person intentionally stole the cat to kill it. It is difficult to think of this as a possibility, but this does happen. Summertime is the worst time for this type of situation because kids are out of school. Some children look for mischievous things to fill their time. For example, a thirteen-year-old boy may have just received a BB gun for a present. Now, he wants to shoot a live animal. Cats are easy to locate, becoming easy targets.

There was a story on the Orlando news recently about a five-month-old kitten that had about fourteen BB pellets in her. A couple of teenagers actually left her at a veterinary clinic. Perhaps they saw what their friends did or just had a change of heart. This kind of illegal torture happens more often than we would want to think. For every mistreated pet that is found, know that there are many more that no one ever discovers.

Another news story told of a man living in an apartment complex that shot two cats. This derelict used a BB gun, continually shooting the cats in the head. One cat died. The other cat was left in critical condition. These are examples of what can happen to a cat, by an evil person.

People that recently lost a cat often want to believe that another person stole the cat because they liked her. This does happen, but is not as common as we want to believe. Everyone wants to get their cat back, but when time goes on and the cat has not returned, we hope for the best. Like for instance, instead of believing a coyote ate the cat, we are very hopeful that a nice person that saw the cat came to steal her. At least with this scenario, she would be alive and well.

Leaving With a Visitor via the Vehicle

When someone comes to one's house, a cat can get into or onto that person's vehicle. Cats are quiet, slipping into vehicles unnoticed. The visitor could be a repair person or a friend. The bed of trucks should be checked. The interior of cars and trucks needs to be visually scanned in case the cat slipped inside while the door was open.

There is another important place to look in a vehicle for a cat. This location would be under the hood of the car or truck. Cats often seek out a place they can hide. Once running underneath a parked vehicle, the cat may look up, seeing all those nooks and crannies he can hide in.

After the cat gets situated someplace under the hood, starting the vehicle can be deadly for the cat. One should always tap on your hood before starting your vehicle. This action gives the cat an opportunity to get out. One could hear the kitty beginning to move around, giving awareness the cat is in there and assistance can be provided to him for getting free. Cats are especially prone to crawling within the engine components after it has just rained or a storm came in suddenly. A cat that recently escaped from inside the house is also prone to finding her way within the hood contents. Attempting to flee from a predator is another cause forcing a feline to obtain the shelter of a car hood.

Story of Garlin

I encountered a situation of my kitten getting on a repairman's truck. The man came to service my well. A couple of hours later I realized Garlin, my beautiful five-month old kitten was missing. After searching everywhere, it occurred to me that she got on that truck.

Garlin was a beautiful DSH kitten.

Calling the repairman was the first step in finding my missing girl. He said he did not see or hear the cat. He stated he will look thoroughly in the vehicle. I asked him where he stopped and where his work for the day took him.

That day I drove the entire route the repairman traveled. The restaurant where the man ate lunch was one of my stops. His route took him quite far. I traveled nearly two hours, several counties away. Going to the repairman's county of final destination, animal control facility could be beneficial. If Garlin got off the truck in someone's yard, then they could have taken her there.

My sweet tuxedo tortoiseshell was not in Lake County Animal Control. Information about her was left there, in case she was brought in. A few days later, an employee from animal control called me, stating a cat came in that looked like Garlin.

Lake County Animal Control was my destination that day. It was not Garlin. She was never seen again and was greatly missed. Two of her brothers, Twinky and Bronson, still live with me, nine years later. They were all rescued after I trapped their feral mother. These tiny kittens were two days old. All the kittens were so nice, lovable and uniquely marked.

Twinky, a DSH, is very affectionate.

Bronson, a DLH, loves to give hugs.

Getting Trapped in an Inanimate Object

Cats are curious creatures by nature. They explore new items brought into the house. They can get into the oddest places. When your cat vanishes, one must think carefully what was going on that day. Was someone packing a suitcase? Are you moving, packing boxes? Is there a large moving storage container in the yard that boxes or rolled rugs are going into? Was furniture removed from the home? Think very carefully.

Cats are small and quiet. They can easily crawl into tiny spaces. Try to think like a cat. Where would a good exploration destination be in the house on the day the cat became missing?

This scenario happens more frequently than we can all imagine. People don't consider this possibility when a cat disappears nearly enough. This possibility needs to be brought to a guardian's attention.

Story of Koshi

My beautiful Devon Rex, Koshi, crawled in the hole in the net-like fabric on the bottom of the couch. I realized my cat with light-green eyes was missing a couple of hours later. I looked everywhere for him. This curly-hair soft cat was an indoor cat. He was hiding in that couch, which was now in the garage.

The outcome could have been awful if we hauled the couch to the dump or sold it. I may have never seen my affectionate tan and white bicolor cat again.

Koshi is a Devon Rex and quietly found his way into the bottom of the couch.

Indoor Cat Escapes and is Terrified

A cat that is not familiar with the outdoor world will be terrified upon escaping from the home. A cat can run out a door or fall out of a poorly secured screen in a window. Loud noises or unusual activities in the home may provoke a feline into a scared state of mind, therefore seeking an escape route. In many cases, the cat will look for an isolated hiding place. The feline could be very close to home. Searching in the trees and under sheds are great places to begin searching. Dusk and dawn are optimal times to retrieve the cat. In other situations, the cat runs a great distance trying to escape whatever caused him to take off in the first place. When one finds him or herself in the unfortunate situation of the cat being gone, what can one do to find her?

Chapter 10

Ways to Find a Missing Cat

"We can judge the heart of a man by his treatment of animals." Immanual Kant

Time is of the essence when a cat disappears suddenly. There are many alternatives one can explore to get the cat back. Investigating all options is important because any may result in bringing the cat home. This is a very emotionally challenging time. Fear, anguish, and sadness set in with not knowing whether the cat is safe. I hope these tips will assist in bringing many lost cats home safely.

Locate a Missing Cat

There are many things we can do to find a lost cat.

- Go to the county sponsored animal control facility. Animals are allowed three days of life in most county animal control facilities before being killed.
- The cat may have been caught in a trap set by an animal control officer someplace. Someone could have found the cat, bringing him to the county facility as a stray. Get there first to look in the cages.
- Begin looking close to home. The cat is usually closer to home than farther away.

- Talk to the neighbors. Let them know the cat is missing. Find out if they heard or saw anything unusual.

- Tell them a reward will be given to anyone that finds the cat or gives information that leads to the cat's return.

- Put up a large, visible sign in the front yard so that people will know exactly where the cat lives. Regular 8"x11" paper is not sufficient. A very large sign that people can read while driving by is necessary.

- Have flyers made up, include a picture because many cats have similar descriptions, but a picture can truly make all the difference. Hang the flyers all around the neighborhood and at stores.

- Get an advertisement placed in the newspaper. Be sure to include the reward amount. Make it as large of a dollar amount as possible. Rewards can make the difference between getting a pet back or not. Some people, that would not be inclined to look, will do so, when money is offered.

- Utilize a local Internet classified ad section.

- Call all regional animal rescue agencies because someone might bring the cat in as a stray. Leave a description of the cat along with the contact information with them.

- Stroll through the neighborhood and any wooded areas nearby. Holler the cat's name. The cat may have been chased by something, climbed up a tree, and is still very scared.

- Promenade along ditches because a car may have hit the cat.

- Communicate with any teenagers seen in the area. They often hang-out outside. The youngsters may have seen something or know other information.

- Drive along local roads. Should a car have struck the cat, the body may still be there.

- Local veterinarians are a possible resource in case someone brought the cat there after being hit. Someone may have found him wandering as a stray, subsequently bringing him to the vets to be scanned for a microchip.

All of these methods should be explained to callers that have lost a cat. As a cat-lover, I want anyone in this tumultuous time to have all the information possible that can be of assistance during this critical situation. As a rescue organization, with the mission being to rescue homeless animals, we must do everything possible to keep a cat that has a loving family with her family and help make a reunion possible.

Actions to Take Which Help Prevent Losing a Cat

There are many things we can do to reduce the chances of our cat ever being lost. One way is to keep a cat indoors at all times or especially at night, when most disappearances take place. For a cat that goes outside, a collar should be worn with an identification tag. A safety collar is the kind that should be worn, so a cat will not strangle if he ever gets caught on an object.

Microchips are one of the best ways to help in getting your cat back home. These devices can't fall off the cat. They get implanted under the skin with a needle, usually between the shoulder blades. I can't emphasize the value in these tiny chips enough.

Collars

Collars can pose a huge danger. A kitten, whether indoors or outdoors, faces this danger. When a kitten or a cat is first learning to wear a collar, it must be constantly supervised. They usually try to bite at the collar. Kittens also attempt to get it off their neck, since they don't know what this thing is circling around their neck. When placing a collar on the kitten it is important to tighten it to a proper fit. This will involve sliding a size adjuster or placing a buckle in the correct hole. If it is too loose, the kitten will get his bottom jaw caught in it. One should be able to get two fingers under the collar, to know it is not too tight.

Only a collar with a safety, breakaway device should be worn, in case the cat gets caught. The proper tightness is important. Always constantly supervise any cat first learning to wear a collar. Inside cats should not wear a collar, unless in your situation there is a great likelihood the cat may escape.

In outside situations, wearing a collar will just depend on the likelihood of the cat wandering or the guardian's preference. As long as a safety collar is utilized, it is a good idea to have one on for identification purposes. Too many cats that are lost don't get reunited with their guardian because they have no identification. However, collars can fall off. Collars can be lost, so a permanent solution for identification would be a microchip.

> **Collar Code**
> Safety collars are the only type that should be worn. Always supervise any cat first learning to wear a collar.

Justice For Cats

Story of Oleander

A situation with my cat, Oleander became terrifying, involving a leather non-safety collar, with a buckle. At the time, he was six-months old. Oleander is as white as cotton, with three small splashes of black hairs, which appear gray, on his head. In fact, Orchid, the black cat whose story will be told later, is his mother. Oleander was the only white kitten born in a litter of all black kittens. A black queen giving birth to one white kitten, while all the others are black, is extremely rare. These raindrops of black hair on his head have faded with age. At one year old, only a few black hairs remain. This velvety soft cat never goes outside.

Oleander with his four siblings.

He needs to be comfortable with wearing a collar. When I travel with him, he will need to keep a collar on at all times. It was put on him at the correct tightness. He had the collar on for about thirty minutes.

My curious little boy was intrigued by the tag, with his address and phone number, on it. Otherwise, he seemed to be adjusting well with it on his neck. I went in the other room. Being there for only thirty seconds I then heard a strange noise. I immediately ran towards the noise, worrying that it was he, in distress. It was!

Oleander had the collar caught on his bottom jaw. He could not breathe. Oleander's collar was so tight, it would not move. His tongue was blue! The terrified young cat was pawing frantically at the collar. I tried to move the leather strap back through the holders, but it would not move.

The understandably panicked kitten was clawing my hands because he was trying to get the collar off his mouth. The collar was so tight it would not slip off his head, either. Grabbing my leather gloves just a few feet away, I managed to get one on before I got back to him. Now, I could maintain my grip on the leather. Finally, I was able to push the strap back through the two holders. Then the buckle could be released to free him. I was exuberant to have saved his life! Knowing how close that adorable kitten came to death is still terrifying. What if I had stepped outside, just for a moment, when I came back in he would have been dead. This is exactly the reason that a cat or kitten just learning to wear a collar should always have supervision.

Oleander likes to carry this big toy cat around and play fetch with it.

Microchips

Microchips are essential for every cat. They can't fall off the cat, as collars often will. The microchip is tiny, like the size of a grain of rice. It gets implanted using a needle beneath the skin, between the shoulder blades. Each microchip has a number. This number, when pulled up on a computer database will have the guardian's contact information. This allows the pet to be reunited to his home. A scanner can detect whether a microchip is present in an animal.

Nearly every animal shelter and veterinary clinic has a scanner to check for a microchip. Many animal control facilities allow longer time, like ten days versus three days, for an animal to live, if it contains a microchip. Sometimes people forget to update their address when they move, so no one can contact them when the pet is found. But, by the animal having the microchip, animal control knows someone will be looking for the pet. A microchip can make all difference as to whether the cat will get home.

Microchip Mandate

A microchip is the best way to get a lost cat back home. Get one for your cat!

Story of Zipper

A cat was returned to me by someone who found him because he had a microchip. The woman that found Zipper took him to a veterinary clinic, having him scanned to determine whether he had a microchip. This story has some surprising twists in it. The cat's name is Zipper, a short hair black and white tuxedo. He was a stray that showed up where I live. I began feeding him. Zipper would not let me get close to him for quite some time. The bad thing was half of his tail was gone with bare flesh exposed.

My assumption is that a horse stepped on it, cutting it off. Zipper was a smart tom cat. This elusive, handsome cat finally became friendly towards me. I got him neutered, vaccinated, and got his tail fixed. The bare fleshy part with no skin was further amputated and the skin was sewn together. This shiny tuxedo cat, healed up in no time. He felt better having his tail healed up as good as new, just shorter.

Zipper got adopted as a barn cat on a big horse farm. In fact, the people adopted a couple of cats. Zipper got a great new home.

About six weeks later, a phone call came in from a lady that found a cat. This cat showed up at her home. She could not keep him, as pets weren't allowed where she lived. No space was available to take another cat right now, I explained to her. She said she would take him to the veterinary clinic that was practically across the road from her, to have him scanned for a microchip. Information about trying on her own how to find a home for him, should he not have a guardian, was explicated to her.

The next day a phone call came in from a lady that said she had my cat. It was the same lady. I said, "You called me yesterday, I have the cat rescue." It turned out she had Zipper. I was amazed. I further explained to her that he was adopted about six weeks ago, living way across town. I was baffled as to how this cat landed so far from his home. Anyhow, I told her I would come to pick him up.

The person that adopted Zipper was then called. I asked her how things were going. She said Zipper had been missing for three weeks. She said her family missed him and wanted him back.

We were trying to figure out how he got so far away. He could have walked. The journey would have included cleared pasture and a few wooded areas with roads to cross. Possibly he got on a feed truck while it was making a delivery, riding to another stop, near where he was found. No one will ever know for sure, but one thing that is for sure is that the microchip got him back home!

Zipper, a DSH, was found because of his microchip.

Other Return Stories Because of Microchips

Other cats have made it back to me because of the microchip. Two other cats that were adopted into homes ended up at Animal Control. Animal Control was called by the mother of the person that adopted the cat. A few months prior, the woman that adopted the cat had a hardship, leaving the cat with her mother, for too long in her mother's opinion. The cat had been at Animal Control for about a week before I was called.

Before he was killed I went to bail him out, by paying a large fee. The fee included the animal control pickup fee and the daily board since he arrived there. I spoke to the lady that adopted him, whom was still out of state. She said she would reimburse me for getting him out and saving his life, but she never did. Eventually, he was adopted into a new loving home.

Animal control called me one other time about a cat named Exxon. He was just brought in by someone that found him wandering near her home in the Northeast section of town. He was adopted out, about six months prior, to a woman in the very Southwest portion of the county. Her phone number was disconnected. Locating her to find out what happened was not possible. Perhaps she moved to the Northeast part of the county and he somehow escaped.

We will never know for sure. Microchips perform a very important function by bringing lost pets home again. None of these three cats would have ever seen me again and probably would have met death without the microchip.

The lady that found Zipper most likely would have called Animal Control to come get him because she already had pressure on her by the homeowner association. The cat picked up by animal control was most likely going to be euthanized because so many are, that come in there. Exxon was definitely going to be killed because he was in extremely poor condition when he was brought there.

Chapter 11

Establish Methods for Operating a Shelter

"The very essence of leadership is that you have to have vision. You can't blow an uncertain trumpet." Theodore M. Hesburgh

Decisions need to be made before beginning to operate a shelter. Before taking in any cats, establish how many cats can be financially and physically handled at one time. Figuring out the amount of labor and supplies needed for each cat will help in assessing the situation.

Records need to be kept on every cat. There are other aspects to explore. Where and how the cats will be housed needs consideration. Will the shelter location be publicly known or private? These are decisions that need to be carefully thought through.

Boundaries

When word gets around that the rescue exists, the phone will not stop ringing. For this reason, one must have some boundaries pertaining to operating the shelter. First, decide what hours communicating with the public will occur. Determine when answering the phone in the morning will begin and at which hour, in the afternoon, that the answering machine will take over. The most important aspect that must be determined is the number of cats which can be properly cared for at a given time. One thing that should absolutely be avoided is acquiring more animals than one can physically and financially support.

The cats require certain standards. They need plenty of food to eat. Living quarters need to be kept immensely clean. Parasite control is necessary, including internal control for worms and external control for fleas. All of these needs must be met.

Donation with Taking in a Cat

It is necessary to ask for a donation with each cat being brought to the shelter. Most people are willing and able to donate something with the cat or kitten. Many folks are happy to have a no-kill shelter that can take the cat. But, without asking there are those that certainly will not give anything.

A donation should be discussed on the phone with the person whom needs to place the cat. This is the best way to generate enough money to keep the shelter operating. Donations from the public are often the only source of revenue a shelter has to rely on to generate funds. People with a cat who needs help are the ones with the most interest in keeping the shelter operational.

People will often ask what amount of money would be a standard donation to make. The request should be for an amount that will cover something that the cat needs, like vaccines or sterilization. Often I would just say whatever you can give is fine. The fact is without any intake donations the number of cats able to be saved will be reduced. Most donations are minimal, but between them all, enough funds can be obtained to continue operating the cat haven.

Some people are not able to give any donation with the cat. Cats with impoverished guardians are often the cats that need help the most, so I would not turn them away. In some cases, a person finds a stray cat or litter of kittens, but just has no money to give to place them in a safe facility. Other times, a very financially-challenged person has to give up her cat. The cat has likely not been given any medical care ever and needs help desperately before the worms he's had since kitten-hood kill him. How could I refuse such a cat? I would just be glad that this cat is now going to get what he needs.

Always remember that the purpose of the organization is to help cats in need of a safe residence and medical care. Reality is that it takes finances to purchase supplies and medical care. Asking for a donation with each cat is necessary so that people whom are able to donate something will donate, but it does not mean refusing a cat that does not come with a donation. Perhaps the next cat that comes in will help cover his costs or maybe the previous cat already did. A donation can be $5 or it could be $500 (this is extremely rare), but whatever the amount, it will buy something so operations can continue.

Get the Best Prices for Supplies and Services

Creating a financial plan is required before taking in any cats. Figure out how much it will cost to take in each cat. Learn what resources are available in the community for low-cost sterilization. Go talk to several different vets to discover the most economical way to get what each cat needs. Maybe you can work out "a package deal" price for each cat.

This package could include a spay or neuter, vaccines, a FeLV and FIV test, and de-worming. Take this warning that many vets are not willing to help at all. A vet that personally loves cats will be the best candidate. I assure you, not all vets love cats. They have preferences just like anyone else in society.

Many individuals will constantly presume that a rescue organization gets all medical services and products for free or next to nothing. This assumption is very irritating. People conclude that because a shelter is doing "a good thing" that many others are not willing to do, vets love animals too and just want to do everything for free to help a non-profit save lives. This is so far from the truth. People would sometimes call me stating they can't afford to get veterinary care for their cat. They inquired if they could go through my organization, assuming that the shelter must get exams at virtually no charge.

The fact that a rescue provides tons of business to a clinic can result in some discounts here and there. However, I have to pay for an exam and any other treatment the cat needs. Unfortunately, there is no Medicaid for cats! Just because one maintains non-profit status, this does not mean that vets want to make less money for the same service they provide to someone else.

My explanation of reality to callers was informative. I would tell them to call around for the best price. Inform the guardian that an examination at the veterinarian office won't necessarily take their entire paycheck. This is an important fact to convey. Getting the cat the help it needs is what is important. For instance, I offer some assistance by listening to the caretaker describe what symptoms the cat is having. I could then tell them what is probably going on with this cat. My conclusion as to what the diagnosis will likely be and what type of veterinary costs may be included during the exam, are helpful morsels of information to the guardian.

There are huge differences in the cost of exams and other services, such as X-rays. When one knows of a vet that is less expensive than others, in the specific area of care the caller's cat needs, advise them to call that particular vet. Calling different veterinary offices is the best way to know what specific services will cost.

Perhaps, the explanation on the reality for an organization regarding veterinary care will enlighten people. Rescue groups have to pay for services, just like anyone else. Anyhow, back to getting rescued cats the care they need. Detection of the absolute most economical way to treat each cat will allow your resources to go further. Don't purchase sub-standard services, just barter the best one can to get optimal prices.

Don't assume money will flow in from the community. Taking on operating a no-kill rescue organization is one of the most important jobs anyone can do, in my opinion. Rescuing innocent companion animals that deserve to live a long, healthy life with a family is a noble occupation. This does not mean that every citizen is going to financially support the effort, though.

Getting the best price on everything the shelter needs is critical, in order to save scant resources. The ability for the organization to save more lives will be possible by being as frugal as possible. Provide the cats with absolutely everything they need to be healthy and happy. The point of emphasis here is that money must not be wasted. Get the best possible price for quality supplies and services.

Here is a pertinent point for cat guardians. Should your cat ever get sick, requiring a very expensive surgery, calling different veterinarian offices can be very important. This is especially significant for persons who live in a large metropolitan area. Veterinary costs can be exorbitantly high in large cities. If it is a struggle to come up with the amount of money your usual vet quoted for the procedure, do not give up on getting what the cat needs.

Call some vets at a place that is about an hour or more away from your metro area. Perhaps a friend or relative lives in a less expensive, smaller location that could get a quote from his or her local vet. One could truly save thousands of dollars. A cat deserves the medical care necessary to save his life, so be resourceful in your planning if that's what is required to get the surgery performed.

Determine the Cat Care Budget

All the necessary requirements added together will determine how much each cat will cost to rescue. Medical services are the main expense category that allows one to know how much simply taking in the cat will cost. Vaccines, tests, and sterilization costs are basic needs. Flea control is another cost to consider. If it costs $10 to de-flea every cat, then add that to the total cost. Every cat needs food, too. Food is one necessity one should not purchase the cheapest food available. One gets what one pays for regarding food.

Calculate how much food each cat eats daily. This will help determine how many cats one can afford to feed each week or month. Determine how many servings are in a bag. This will assist the calculation of how many cats can be fed on one bag. Figure out how many cats should be kept at one time. This number is dependent on financial costs and physical labor available.

The Labor Force

Labor is a very important element to a shelter.

Daily duties that must be performed include:
- Feeding
- Medication disbursement
- Litter box cleaning
- Caring for orphans
- Giving individual attention to each cat.

Other routine duties include:
- Keeping accurate records on each cat
- Transporting the cats to get medical care
- Washing bowls, litter boxes, and cat carriers
- Dispensing parasite control
- Grooming the cats

With a small budget, don't count on having paid staff. Volunteers are a possible source of labor, but often can be unreliable. Only when individuals prove to be dependable, should they be counted on for labor. Foster parents can provide a means to rescue more cats by having a place to house them. When things change at any point, be ready to re-analyze the situation. Determine what modifications need to be implemented. Know that nothing stays the same indefinitely.

Foster Parents

Create specific policies in the organization to handle potential fosters. The person fostering cats or kittens, until they are old enough or are ready for adoption, are the ones doing all the labor involved in their care. Reliability is a very important factor to determine before enrolling specific "parents." Carefully screen potential foster parents.

A visit to potential foster parent's home is essential because it allows a visual inspection of the way the family or individual lives. A filthy home indicates that a person has no standards of cleanliness. This person will not have any standards for the cat, either. Absolutely avoid this type of person. The reference is not about someone that may have dust on the bookshelf, but a truly grubby, grimy house. This person likely will have poor hygiene himself. A non-hygienic person will not properly care for a cat.

Inquiring about other people that live in the home is another important piece of information. Use the answers to the questions to determine whether this family will be an ideal foster home.

Here are some questions to ask:

- Are young children present?
- Does the man or woman of the house like cats?
- Are teenagers a part of the family?
- Do they truly like cats or would they hurt a cat?
- Does the family have pets?
- Are they sterilized?
- Do the pets visit a veterinarian regularly? Check with the vet for a reference.
- Is the person dependable?
- Do they have enough money to buy what the kittens or cat will need? The shelter may want to provide these things to a foster home, but that is totally something it must decide.

Volunteers

Volunteers are another segment of people who need to be dependable. Surely there are some that are reliable, but many will prove not to be responsible. After a few times with people proving not to be bankable, I could not waste precious time "trying out" humans. Rescuing cats is time-consuming. There was no time to spare to teach people how to change a litter box and stand there, attending them, to get the jobs accomplished. I did not want to get in a situation where I was forced to depend on anyone. I found it, in a way, easier to just do the work myself.

Perhaps a person in your group can be designated to screen and train volunteers. That really is a job all its own. With the right volunteers, the organization could go even further with its mission. Until the volunteer is known well, do not absolutely count on him or her to be there. Aside from trying to coordinate human labor, the stars of it all are the cats. Once cats are ready to be received in the shelter, a method must be in place to keep accurate records on each cat.

Records for Each Cat

Records are kept on paper and computer. A paper notebook is handy to quickly look over who is due for a de-worming, for instance. For any records, no matter where they are, some particular divisions should be included.

There are pertinent categories for inclusion:

- The cat's name
- The former and the adoptive guardian's name, address, and phone number
- Dates of intake and adoption
- A description of the cat

    This is useful in helping to remember each particular cat when necessary. Other cats with the same name will surely come into the shelter. It is helpful in distinguishing exactly who was who by memory when you see, DSH tortoiseshell, you can then remember "Oh, this was Misty the tortoiseshell as opposed to the smoke gray tabby named Misty." A photo would be great with the records.

One may want to include medical histories on the cat files. Intake forms will include any previous medical history that the relinquishing caretaker is writing down. It is best to keep all the intake forms for the permanent records. A filing cabinet works well for keeping all the medical records and other paperwork orderly. Include on the form, a statement for the person to sign acknowledging they are signing custody of the cat over to the organization.

This form is titled the "Feline Surrender Form." Some of the questions should be as follows on your form:

- What is your name?
- What is your address?
- What is the phone number?
- What is the date the cat is being relinquished to the shelter?
- How old is the cat or kitten?
- Does the cat have a name?
- Why is the feline being given to the shelter?

- Was the cat found as a stray?
- Is the cat sterilized?
- Has the cat been tested for Leukemia or Feline Immunodeficiency virus?
- Does it have its vaccines?
- Are there any records from a veterinarian's office? Having the papers brought in, if the cat is current on vaccines can save your organization lots of money.

A cat needs to have certain things soon after arriving, if he does not already. Vaccines, especially for Rabies, are needed before he can get adopted into a new home. Proof must accompany the cat or vaccines will need to be given again. Giving redundant vaccines to a cat is not healthy, nor is it good for the budget. Each cat must be properly identified within the organization. With so many cats coming into the shelter, many of them are strays that were found and will not have a name. Everyone needs a name. Name books, which can be purchased at any bookstore, are a great resource to have in the organization's possession. The Internet is also a vast source to find many new names.

All cats should have a nice name, as opposed to just giving them a number. Cats are all individuals. Internally, within the organization, a case number may be assigned to each cat, but the cat still must have a proper name. When cats come in with a duplicate name, in other words someone already used that name, putting a number 2, then 3, then 4, behind the name so as to keep them as individuals, is helpful. For example, there may be Max, Max2, Max3, and so on.

Keeping all the cats' records in alphabetical order, in the computer files, will promote ease for finding information on a specific cat. When receiving a litter of kittens, giving them names that all begin with the same letter invokes ease. This procedure would make inputting the names into the files faster and easier. It also allows simplicity, knowing which kittens are from the same litter.

Hoarding

Do not ever get into a situation that becomes hoarding. Hoarding involves some of the worst cases of animal neglect and abuse. Mostly it is individuals in the community that end up collecting animals past the point where any of the pets are getting any descent care at all. Animal rescue refuges can easily become overwhelmed with animals if they do not set boundaries. Knowing the limits on what they can properly care for is critical. Hoarding does not do the pets any favors.

The animals are kept in deplorable conditions, not spayed or neutered, and barely fed. Keeping a cat in filth and without resources is abuse. Litter boxes are barely ever cleaned, if they are even present in the home. All of these cases tend to involve the cats going potty everywhere in the house, since there is no clean, designated place for elimination. Trash tends to get piled up all over the home. The odor of feces, urine, and trash is literally sickening. The ammonia from the urine burns cat and human eyes, just being present in the environment.

Cats will breed prolifically because they are not sterilized. More cats get born into this neglectful situation causing resources to become even more scant. Many of these kittens will die due to illness, since germs thrive in filthy environments. The mother cat and kittens won't have adequate nutrition to grow properly or to establish a healthy immune system, in which to fight off diseases. The kittens usually remain feral, since they are not given proper interaction with humans. Another factor that contributes to becoming feral is that there are so many cats in a small area that stress levels are greatly increased. Proper development just can't happen in this type of environment. Most cat hoarders do not know the number of cats that live with them.

Animals forced to live in this type of household are always malnourished, sometimes almost to the point of death. Often when the authorities, such as Animal Control personnel, are alerted to investigate one of these environments, many animals are dead and rotting among the living animals. Lack of enough food and fresh water is a common fact of a hoarding situation. Parasites, like intestinal worms, make survival even more difficult. De-worming or de-fleaing is nearly unheard of for these animals.

Veterinary care is null. When imminent illness sets in, it will spread to the other animals. Survival becomes even more of a challenge for these suffering animals. Extreme neglect runs rampant. A hoarding household is a horror for a precious pet.

A particular hoarding situation comes to mind that was featured on the Orlando news. The reason this person was caught for this despicable crime was because the neighbors called Code Enforcement due to the putrid odor permeating all around the house. The smell was from the cat and dog urine and feces piling up inside.

There were forty cats and twelve dogs living inside the house. The cats were kept in small pet carriers with four or five animals in each carrier. The helpless cats were forced to live literally on top of each other, due to lack of space. They had to urinate and defecate on top of each other!

When the officers arrived, they were not able to distinguish whether the animals were cats or small dogs because their fur was so encrusted with feces. Can you imagine living this way? Should anyone ever question whether hoarding is abusive, just remember this particular tragic account. There are many more like it, unfortunately.

Most of the pets were euthanized. This is truly a tragedy because with proper nutrition and some time, these animals could have recovered. They could have a chance to get a wonderful home to see what life should be like. To be forced to live in squalid conditions and subsequently killed after being "rescued" from that living hell is just really tragic. Not having an opportunity to live a nice life at all is just not right.

Unfortunately, this is common. As I've said throughout the book, there are not enough cat rescues. Animal Control facilities do not usually spend resources on animals that will require some time before being ready to find a new home. More no-kill shelters are needed to help rescue all of the animals in need of good homes. When you are ready to take on starting a shelter, a decision must be made where the cats will be housed.

Where the Cats Will Reside in the Shelter

When I first began taking in cats, some were brought into my house, along with my own cats. This was not a good situation. Mostly, the population was tiny orphans that were in a cage, as they would only wake to eat, but it got stressful for my cats. It was not a healthy situation, either. There are a myriad of ailments kittens can be harboring, which could be given to other cats. Tiny kittens can't be tested for diseases with accuracy. A need to devise a different housing arrangement was apparent. This is when the idea of adding some outdoor enclosed buildings became relevant.

The housing units are outdoor buildings, similar to sheds. They are completely roofed with sides partly closed-in with siding and partly open sides with steel mesh, very impenetrable. This allows plenty of airflow and sunshine yet has portions that are protected from wind and stays shaded. Use of heating pads in winter and sometimes fans in the summer helps in maintaining the comfort of the cats. The cats can move freely anywhere they choose in the building. Only in a rare or particular circumstance will a cat be confined in a cage.

Utilization of the fenced yard allows cats that become familiar with the environment to have more personal space. Expansive territory reduces stress when many other cats are present in a smaller environment, like a building. Some cats have remained with me for a year before finding an adoptive home. Cats like to run around at times. Remaining confined permanently in a small building for a year, no matter how nice, is not always pleasant for a cat. The cats' comfort, health, and happiness, is my ultimate goal while they reside with me, until the perfectly matched family comes along. So, for someone with property and a desire to house many cats, outdoor housing units may be an optimal arrangement. An addition to the home is another possibility.

An organization with a network of people may house a few cats in their homes. This method has benefits of having fewer cats together, which reduces chances of an illness erupting. There is additionally, less stress for the cat, by not having to get to know so many new cats. Keeping the cats in this home environment provides another benefit which is that it makes for a graceful transition to a new adoptive home, when that time arrives.

A challenge with this situation could be with performing adoptions. By not having a central location for all the cats to be met, this could prove to be detrimental. If a central adoptive location is not possible, then housing the cats, at each home, into certain populations may fare the best. For example, indoor only type cats could be in one location, so a potential adopter could go to that particular place to see those cats. Since many pet supply stores allow organizations to bring in pets for adoption, if the organization has developed this type of relationship with a store, then not having a central location within the affiliation for adoptions may not be a deficit. Some stores do offer incentives to cat rescues in the form of cash and/or food. The following scenario details why having as many of the cats available for people to meet at one time and place is beneficial.

Many people will call stating that they want to adopt a kitten. Often, a kitten will not be the best suited age group, for their specific household. After discussing this information, while giving the adopter the opportunity to meet kittens and adult cats, the person usually will realize the adult is a wonderful pet. Adopters would frequently meet an adult cat they absolutely love and just have to adopt him or her.

There are alternate methods for housing cats. One other option is to keep the cats in one or two rooms of one's home. Perhaps an unused barn or shed on your property could easily be converted to house cats. Another alternative is to rent or purchase a building exclusively to receive, house and adopt cats out. This plan clearly involves more start-up capital than the other plans. Every person yearning to rescue cats will need to decide what route will best suit his or her circumstances.

With any cat rescue, once people know it exists, and if the location is publicly known, drop offs will occur without your permission or knowledge (that is until you find them the next day). A decision needs to be made as to how to accept the cats from the public. Will the location be public information or not?

This will depend on some of the other arrangements, mainly where the cats will be adopted out from. Will there be a central place that the public can come in and meet the cats? If the answer is yes, then allowing those people who want to surrender cats, to bring them in would be ideal.

John building cat housing facilities.

Secret Location or Publicly Known Location

A public location would be one with a large visible sign and disclosing of the address and phone number in the phone book and other public places. Regular operating hours will be posted for persons to come by, either bringing in a cat or to adopt one. Persons dropping off felines anytime, including late at night, without verifying whether space is available, are more likely to occur with a public set-up.

During kitten birthing season, particularly the predominant one of the year (spring), many people from the community potentially could drop off lots of litters of kittens. Irresponsible citizens are always looking for an "easy out," when it comes to this type of situation. The no-kill shelter especially becomes an easy dumping ground. People know the cats won't be killed and by abandoning cats there, they don't even have to give a donation to help support the cat's needs. It is just too easy for them. Repeat offenders could become a typical occurrence. For instance, an irresponsible guardian who did not spay his cat could leave March's litter on your doorstep, then November's litter, once again, on your doorstep.

Benefits exist from remaining in a secret location. The main one is the number of kittens and cats cared for, at a given time, will be maintained. At this point, the proper number will had been decided upon. Also, know that in this vocation, there are people that try to take advantage of someone that clearly cares about the well-being of cats. Some people can see the federation as a dumping ground for cats they no longer want or attempt to drastically downsize their population.

By choosing to keep a hidden location, alternate arrangements need to be made to receive cats. One option is to pick up the cat. This option is more resource consumptive. A person from the organization will spend time to go and get the cat. Fuel expenditure along with depreciation on the vehicle will be at the organization's (or the volunteer) cost. Some risk could be involved in going to crime-infested areas of town or just some very weird person's home. Another option altogether is to have cats brought to a veterinary office or to a pet adoption center that the affiliation deals with, to relinquish the cat.

I don't know of any organization, kill or no-kill, secret or public that has not had drop-offs. Drop-offs just go along with the territory of being in the rescue vocation. Even those who go to a pet specialty store to generate adoptions have cats get dropped off outside and inside the store. Whether your organization discloses its location or not, know that at some point, an unexpected cat will "arrive." It is fair to say that with a private location, the drop-off numbers will certainly be less overall. There are pros and cons to both scenarios. The results will become clear as choices are made about each aspect of how to operate the shelter.

More resources from the organization will be consumed by doing adoptions elsewhere.

Labor
- Loading cats up in carriers
- Bring them into the store or other facility
- Get the viewing cages ready
- Unload the cats
- Remain present for the hours specified
- Load the cats into carriers (either that day or another depending on the arrangements)
- Clean out the viewing cages
- Carry them back into the vehicle
- Drive home
- Unload the cats
- Wash the carriers

Tangibles
- Gasoline
- Vehicle depreciation

Chapter 12

Advertising Cats for Adoption

"Whatever you believe is real for you." Jessica Barbazon

Advertising is the key to success with placing cats into homes. The way a cat is described can make all the difference in getting the cat placed quickly. The ad must be carefully planned before sending it into print.

There are different sources to use for spreading awareness. Some will prove better than others, but if the lesser source gets just a few connections made then it is well worth using. The more the name of the organization is verbalized in the media, the more people will think of coming to that particular pet refuge to adopt a cat. This works both ways. People wanting to surrender cats will remember hearing the organization's name.

Cat Breed Book

Operating a cat shelter requires knowledge of cat breeds, to be a good rescue. Justice will not be served when trying to find them new homes without knowledge about cats. Buy a book or encyclopedia on cat breeds.

Many different breeds of cats will enter a shelter. In many cases, the person bringing the cat to the cat rescue facility is not aware of predominant characteristics of a certain breed the cat resembles. This information becomes valuable especially when trying to get the cat a new home.

When a cat contains features of a rare breed, or a popular breed, of cat, the cat can find a new home very quickly. Just because a cat does not have registered pure breed papers does not mean that there is not a lot of a particular breed within the cat's genetic makeup. Cats living on the streets came from someone's home. Yes, purebreds get abandoned, too. Purebreds breed with domestic short-hairs or other breeds of cats. Some kittens in each litter will resemble the pure breed cat when this type of mating takes place.

It is fine to call the cat, the breed it most resembles, in an advertisement. This lets potential adopters know what the cat looks like. The cat can have interest generated in it when people enter a search on the Internet for a certain breed. The more people that see the cat, it will stand a better chance of finding a new home.

Some people are only interested in a cat that has a lot of a certain breed in it. Unique and rare cats tend to generate a lot of interest. Accurate representation is important for cats. Society, in general, is not very knowledgeable about cat breeds. People tend to be familiar with some of the very popular breeds, like Siamese or Persian cats. Maine Coons, Snowshoes, Himalayans, and Manx's are other popular breeds. It is not uncommon to find some of these cats in shelters or as strays.

Keep a cat breed book easily accessible. Offer to show adopters more information about a breed they are interested in adopting. Adopters like to look at the photos of the cats in the books. Be happy to take advantage of an opportunity to educate someone about cat breeds. In an advertisement present as much information as possible about a cat.

Devon is a Balinese and Snowshoe cross.

Jessica Barbazon

> **Advertising Alert**
> Know cat breeds well, to be a good feline advocate and to correctly represent cats for finding homes.

Newspaper

Newspapers can be a great source for reaching adopters. I usually would advertise using the word "kittens" first and then cats, so it would read, "kittens & cats." Most people are looking for kittens, so they come to get a kitten. Many times they will fall in love with an adult cat. The adult cat ends up getting a home.

In the ad include descriptive, impactful words such as;

- Rescued
- Spayed
- Neutered
- Vaccines
- De-wormed
- Friendly
- Many colors available

Use whichever descriptive and informative words apply for each ad placed. Newspaper ads can be very expensive. Inquire about any good deals that can be obtained. Don't take no for an answer from one person as the final decision. Call or go to the newspaper office. Ask to speak with someone else. It often depends on whom is spoken to as to what deals can be obtained.

Internet

The Internet has some great options available, most at no charge. There are some great animal adoption websites, put out by the ASPCA, for instance that allow non-profit organizations to have a web page all about their rescue operation. Another page displays photos and descriptions of pets available for adoption. Search the Internet to find more of these types of sites. All exposure can be beneficial, someone may want to donate or adopt a cat.

Other types of Internet sites are those of the classified advertisement type. Many of these are free. The downside to some of these is that there are so many free cats posted on them that the response rate is rather low. However, this all depends on location. This sort of site may work great in the shelter's region. Citizens may be glad to adopt a cat with all the medical necessities already completed for an adoption fee.

Local Media

Getting the cat haven recognized by the local media is a great way to create public awareness. Contact someone from the local newspaper and perhaps a television station to do a chronicle on exactly what the shelter is doing to help local cats. Citizens become aware that a local person(s) is on a mission to reduce the number of homeless cats by sterilization and through finding adoptive homes.

A good quality article can be very beneficial to the plight of homeless animals because the reporter can include statistics about local and/or national euthanasia numbers. The reporter can mention that every person can help in decreasing this number by doing something, like donating money or time to an organization. The best way to help cats, is to adopt a cat, whether one currently living on the streets or one from a shelter. This method of recognition can help spread word-of-mouth advertising.

Word-of-Mouth

Word-of-mouth advertising is a good way to attract more adopters. Having a good reputation is important to establish and maintain this type of publicity. Creating a good reputation includes displaying proper manners to adopters and adopting out healthy cats. Being helpful and courteous to people calling and visiting the shelter is the only way to be a successful shelter, in my opinion.

The staff needs to be passionate about the cause of cat rescue. People will respond to genuine passion. It creates cohesiveness within the community for getting others involved with the mission. People will tell their friends about the assistance and support they received when contacting or visiting your shelter. Now that the plan is in place for attracting potential adopters to the shelter, matching potential adopters and cats together is necessary.

Chapter 13

Adopting out the Cats

"I love cats because I enjoy my home; and little by little, they become its visible soul." Jean Cocteau

Finding homes for the rescued cats is a crucial element of running the retreat. Potential adopters need to be treated courteously. After all, they are the ones interested in giving a homeless cat a new home. It is important to try to assess what type of care someone is willing to provide for a new cat. Determine the adopter's level of commitment to a pet. Make sure the cat is going to a safe home. The people must love the cat.

A lot can be learned about someone, simply by his/her appearance. There are two types I fear the most, when someone is coming to meet the cats. One would be someone who is in a cult. The other would be a filthy, trashy person, the type who does not bathe himself. No, these kind are not the majority of the population, but they do exist and probably in nearly every community. They are more common than one would think, I assure you.

Adopters need to be given pertinent data about caring for their new family member. Written information is essential to provide to the adopter. Cats have requirements to receive proper care and the shelter needs to accept delivering this information to a cat's new guardian. A form that I gave to adopters with a new cat is included at the end of the book, in the Appendix.

Adoption Process

The adoption process is an integral part of operating an animal refuge. Permanent, loving homes must be found for the cats so that resources can now go towards helping another cat in need. A cat is taken from a bad situation and given a new chance at life with food, love, and medical care. Do it again for another cat in need of help.

Part of the adoption process involves speaking to potential adopters to determine if they have the cat's best interest at heart. This includes asking them many different questions about how they value cats. I will elaborate on questions to ask a bit later.

One other aspect to be aware of, regarding rules of adoption, is that adoption agencies can be too strict, as well. Each pet haven can determine what might be too strict for adoption rules. Just know that too many extreme rules can prevent placing cats into adoptive homes.

The most important factors for a good home are great levels of commitment, responsibility and love by the adopter to the cat. This indicates that consideration will always be given to the needs of the cat. Someone that can financially care for the cat properly is another crucial factor.

Adoption Counselors

All personnel must be knowledgeable about cat care data. Genuine passion promotes one's ability to learn and it enhances one's skills for teaching the subject matter. Hopefully, a shelter will have truly passionate people (about cats) educating and counseling potential adopters. I consider myself a cat connection specialist because I take great pride in trying to make a perfect match for the cat and the people involved. Someone should always be immediately available to answer questions about a specific cat or to extend any information about cat care.

Adoption Counselors need the following skills;

- Show adopters the proper method for carrying a cat.
- Demonstrate how to trim the claws.
- Explain about purchasing quality cat food.
- Define the facts about correct litter box care.
- Explicate what type of veterinary care is expected of a cat guardian and about parasites, including worms and fleas.
- Describe what the transition period will be like, once the cat is in his new environment.

Explaining what to expect in the new environment is a critical component of the adoption process. It is normal if a cat hides under a bed for a few days, only coming out when it is dark, since this is when an insecure cat feels most confident, to eat and use the litter box. People may become insulted or mad at the cat if the cat is not sitting on their lap immediately, once they all arrive home. Each cat adjusts in his own manner, based on his past life experiences and genetic makeup. Once this information is expressed to a new guardian, he or she is now more at ease with however his or her new cat behaves.

Understanding a Person's Character

Understanding an adopter's character is crucial. The shelter staff member who has very keen instincts and /or lots of experience interacting with all sorts of people would be ideal for this position. Most people will come just as themselves, but others perform quite an act to appear a certain way when in fact they are very different.

At times, you will surely have a renter come along pretending he or she can have a cat at the apartment when this is not true. The reason this becomes a topic that needs to be addressed is because when the landlord finds out about the cat, the cat will most likely need to find a new home very quickly.

A cat should always be allowed to come back to the facility at any time for any reason. This point needs to be expressed to new cat parents. However, if someone feels they were in the wrong regarding the adoption, they may still be hesitant to bring the cat back. A landlord may even call Animal Control to come pick up the cat. For these reasons, it becomes a valid topic to inquire about permission of pets at apartment complexes.

When someone arrives to meet the cats, work into the conversation whether the person rents or owns a home. When renting is the response, ask them if pets are allowed. Ask them the amount of the pet deposit required to have a cat. With a slow response to this question, they probably have no intention of telling the landlord about the cat.

Once a renter decides there is a cat that he or she would like to adopt, calling the apartment complex to verify information about the pet policy is one method that can be used to confirm permission of pets. Providing additional pet counseling for renters can be beneficial. This includes mentioning that when the person moves, it is important to find another apartment, when this is the case, which allows the cat to come. There are too many apartments available that welcome pets, so one should never settle for one that does not. I say to him or her, "you are renting, you have choices." There is no commitment to the cat to just get rid of him, like some old piece of furniture.

Certainly there are plenty of responsible pet guardians that rent. However, in this business what we must be prepared for, are the worst situations and worst case scenarios, so that we can act in the best manner for the cat's sake. Finding each cat a loving, committed, responsible home is the reason we do this labor of love, after all.

Components of a Good Adopter

A responsible, committed, and kind person should be the main ingredients for a good guardian. A responsible person is imperative. A person of this category will be sure the cat is properly fed, watered, and cared for in all ways. They are not likely to ever abandon the cat. Not abandoning the cat is very important because that is exactly the cause that puts most cats into a homeless situation.

Commitment to the cat is an important factor. When a person's own life presents some difficult challenges at some point, we want to know the cat is part of the family and will not just be tossed aside. The cat is definitely an important member of the household. Dedication to keeping the family together will be emphasized, with a committed person.

Kindness is important because the cat should never be mistreated. A person that is kind, but not responsible would not make a good guardian. They may never intentionally hurt the cat, but may not get proper medical care or may not be driven to keep the cat, should their own circumstances change. When keeping the cat becomes a challenge, a non-responsible person will get rid of the cat. Evaluating a person's character involves some intuition, but lots of valuable information will come by asking some pertinent questions. This information allows the agency to comprehend which particular cats will be best suited to the family's lifestyle.

The questions should include the following:

- Are you planning for the cat to live indoors, outdoors, or both?
- Do you have other pets?
- Are children present in the household?
- How old are the children?
- What do you expect from a cat, in other words, what are your intentions for the cat: to be a total companion, to be a mouser, to be entertainment for a child (not good), or to be a companion for another cat already in the home?
- How do you feel about declawing?

- Does anyone smoke tobacco or anything else in the house? If the answer is yes, then an indoor only cat should not be adopted into this household.

Being a cat connection specialist will involve matching a human family and a cat that are, best suited for one another. Both the cat and the family or adopter needs to be happy with each other. Cats in my care have clearly not liked someone so I never would let a cat go with someone that she, (the cat), did not like. After all, it is the cat that has to live with that person.

Never Adopt out a Cat to Someone the Cat Dislikes

Cats can accurately detect the energy field surrounding a person (we all have one). They do not need any words to be spoken to fully comprehend exactly what a person's purpose includes. However, with spoken words, the feline mind responds to the tone of a person's voice, whether there is kindness or anger in it. The cat detects the energy of intention from within the human. Cats do not understand the concept of sarcasm, either. To them sarcasm comes across as negative energy, which is what is in the tone of voice and frankly, the person's mind. The cat knows if they do not click with a particular person. I fully trust what the cat feels about someone. Some signs one can notice are described in the following two paragraphs that indicate a cat does not like someone.

A cat will cower from someone and place its ears in a defensive position, back and downward. The cat will keep a great distance from the person it does not like. The cat does not act this way towards most people. It will just be that one person that the cat does not like.

Often cats are the best judges of character, they know when someone is not genuinely nice, as the person may claim. Not every cat has the same level of intuitive ability (just like people), as some have fallen victim to abuse by those that are supposed to love them or strangers, but when one does tell you they don't like someone, you had better listen! Now back to formal components of adoption.

Indoor Smoker and Indoor Cat Do Not Mix

There is an important portion of information to be aware of for adopting a cat to an indoor only home. Anytime a household includes a smoker (that smokes inside the home) that wants an indoor cat, a cat should not be adopted into this environment ever. A cat will not be able to escape the toxic smoke which infiltrates and settles on everything it encompasses. Many cats develop oral cancer from living in this environment. The carcinogenic smoke lands on the cat's fur and when the cat grooms itself, it ingests all the poisons.

A cat does not have a choice about breathing such fumes in his habitat. This is a form of animal cruelty to force an animal to inhale such filthy air. Clean air to breathe is a right every pet should have. If a person chooses to live in a carcinogenic, hazy environment, then that is his or her conscious choice.

Do not inflict your toxic fumes on someone else, especially a cat who cannot verbally holler at you for such inconsiderate treatment. A rescue agency has to be the voice for the cat. One should look-out for the cat's best interest. A nocuous domain is not beneficial in any way to a cat.

Cat Connection Specialist Expertise; Knowing the Cats Well

A cat connection specialist must match the people with the cat. Many times what the person originally had in mind will be the correct match. In some cases, however, the stereotype of cat they were seeking is not best suited for their family. For instance, a young woman, with a child of about two years of age came to my organization seeking a kitten. I explained to her that very young children and young kittens are not the best-suited match.

Children can get rough, seriously harming a fragile kitten. She saw how gentle and friendly one of the adult cats was that needed a home. Adult cats are calmer and, in some cases, more tolerant than a young kitten. Certainly they are not as fragile as a tiny kitten either, but caution and supervision still must be maintained. Some adult cats have come from families with children. Cats with this prior experience make excellent family companions where young children are part of the household.

Other situations can be better suited with an adult cat, as well. For instance, a person with the desire to control rodent populations immediately would be best matched with an adult cat that is an experienced and skillful mouser. A young kitten will not be able to accomplish rat killing nearly to the magnitude of an adult that is a proven rodent removal service provider. It may not be known whether this kitten will be a good mouser ever.

Some cats are less skilled than others. People come to adopt, wanting mouse-killing cats for their barn. Some come, specifically wanting a kitten. I explain to them the benefit of getting established adult cats, known by me, to be mousers. I learn every trait possible about each cat that I rescue through caring for the cat. This helps me to be able to place this cat in the best home. Also, kittens less than four months old should never be left unattended outdoors, unless their mother was feral, having raised them in this environment.

The best way to get a rodent problem under control is to adopt two cats. Two cats that are compatible with each other is the most ideal situation. They will often work together on catching a particular rat or mouse. One may scare the mouse out of its hiding spot, while the other cat is readily waiting to grab the mouse when it gets corralled directly to him. This method ensures the rodent will not escape.

Does the gender or the color pattern of a cat make a difference in determining who will be a good hunter? A particular sex of cat is not superior to the other, with regards to hunting. There are males and females that are great hunters, but one is not more numerous, with enhanced skills, than the other. However, color does seem to matter. All colors of cats have some that are highly competent hunters. There is one color pattern that has a high number of talented predators. The black and white tuxedo cats are extremely proficient hunters, in general. They are most inclined to play fetch with a toy, with their guardians, as well. Black and white tuxedos are usually high-energy cats. They enjoy chasing and catching something, whether a toy or the real thing. Each breed has individuals that enjoy and are adept at hunting.

There are felines who prefer not to hunt. These cats are happy to rest and eat. Being concerned with a rodent is not an interesting concept to them. An individual cat's personality is the key component for its behavior pattern.

Adoption Fee

The adoption fee has many aspects to consider in deciding its amount. One very important thing to contemplate is the fee of other local adoption agencies. The fees need to be very similar to have a successful adoption program. For instance, if one local agency charges $50 and another charges $55, yours should be somewhere in that vicinity, if you truly want to place cats into adoptive homes.

Most adoption facilities offer the same procedures for a cat available for adoption such as: vaccines, de-worming, de-fleaing, FeLV/FIV test and sterilization. Some very rural areas do not perform sterilization before adoption, but the fee may include for the surgery. A voucher is given to the adopter to take to a veterinarian.

Spaying or neutering before adoption is the best method to use because people may procrastinate in getting the procedure performed, resulting in a litter being conceived and born. The person could have an accident or some unforeseen event that causes a delay in getting the operation done. That being said, let's get back to pricing the adoption fee.

Charging a fee that covers the entire cost of getting a cat ready for adoption is not always feasible. This depends on how much it costs for the medical care on each cat. Ideally, one would want to charge enough money to cover the cost of the medical care, but if this price is way off base with other adoption facilities in the area, adoption numbers will likely suffer.

Each cat does not cost exactly the same to care for because some will have injuries or be ill. These cats will need very extensive and expensive medical treatment. The length of time a cat resides at your facility will vary the food costs for each cat. My point is the adoption fee almost never covers all the expenses involved in caring for that particular cat.

Some cats pay the way for other cats. There will be cats that need placement, but are already spayed or neutered. Some cats will be current on all their vaccines with their guardian providing all of the veterinary paperwork to prove this fact. There will be cats that get adopted almost immediately after arriving. Consequently, they will not consume lots of food and litter during their stay. When a cat gets adopted, some data should be collected from the new guardian.

Adoption Form

An adoption form needs to be ready for the adopter to fill out. This form requires the person's contact information. It should have a place for the cat's name and description. The date of adoption should be included. This paper provides the shelter with the record of who adopted the cat and where she now resides.

It may be necessary to contact the person about the cat. After a kitten gets adopted, a vet may discover something the cat haven was not aware of and it could affect the entire litter. Calling others whom adopted a kitten from this litter to warn them to get the cat to the vets or to watch for certain symptoms would be possible.

Another feature this form should include is a disclaimer statement that requires the new guardian to read and write his or her signature. This statement needs to state your policy about refunds on adoption fees. I found it necessary to do this after years of never having any such statement, so I warn aspiring shelter founders in advance to simply do it.

Someone once adopted a cat, kept the cat for a month then no longer wanted to keep the cat. Not only did they bring him back, they wanted a full refund! One other lady did the same thing, except she claimed the cat urinated on her chair. Now, she needed to buy a new chair. She wanted her money back, to go towards the chair.

The audacity of these people was astounding to me, keeping the cat until it was inconvenient, then as if it is not enough that I will gladly take the cat back and it will be safe (not like dropping it off at the local Animal Control), they want their menial adoption fee back from a no-kill shelter struggling to bring in enough donations to keep operating. A statement was quickly added to my adoption form so that there will be no confusion about adoption fees. No issues of this nature ever arose from this point forward. The statement is as follows:

> "There are no refunds on adoption fees. Adoption fees are a donation toward the daily and medical care for maintaining a cat. This organization is a no-kill shelter. If your circumstances change and you can't keep your cat, it can always be brought back to the shelter, by appointment only. I have read the above statement and agree to it."
> **Adopter's Signature**

As you can see, I decided this is a perfect place to state that the cat can be brought back anytime. I always went over this portion of the form verbally with everyone. It is very important to tell people the cat can always come back. This ensures a great chance the cat will be returned to the organization, not abandoned or ditched at a kill shelter if someone feels great pressure in his or her life to relinquish the cat. Stating that no questions will be asked upon return of the cat could be listed or verbally mention this information if one chooses to handle a returned cat in this method.

Requests for Free Cats – Don't do it

Another topic, speaking of audacious people, is that of giving a cat away without charging any fee. Every organization will surely run across people that will ask to have a cat without paying any fee. At times, a decision may be made to temporarily reduce the adoption fee, like around kitten season, or offer a reduced rate on each cat if someone adopts a pair of kittens, but a cat should never be given away for free.

Someone may claim that he or she will provide a good home, but currently has no money for an adoption fee. Do not fall for this attempt at a free cat because if that is indeed the case, then how can the person afford food and proper medical care for the cat? Why would a cat be given to someone that can't feed it? Kind of a contradiction of your organization's mission, isn't it?

Other people might want a cat, but have the attitude of, why pay for a cat when I can get one for free someplace? These people often don't value the cat enough to pay an adoption fee. People that don't value a cat are very prone to "dispose" of the cat when it becomes inconvenient in some way.

Letting Go

One thing to know about performing adoptions is that your control of the cat's well being is truly out of your hands once the cat leaves. No matter how thoroughly a person is screened, the outcome of the cat's destiny cannot always be controlled or can the actions of his new family. The best indoor home in the world could lose the cat. He may escape through a window or door, never to be seen again. Some things in life we just cannot control. This is just the fact of the matter. An adoption specialist can only do the best screening possible and hope the cat does have a wonderful long life in his home.

Have Pet Carriers for Adopted Cats

A shelter must have a pet carrier available for the cat to ride to her new home. Cardboard carriers are good to have because they are cheap enough to be included in the adoption fee. They work well for most cats, but a feral cat or one that hates to be in a small, dark space probably will be able to escape these foldable boxes.

It is wise to have strong, plastic pet carriers available for adopters to borrow and/or purchase. A cat guardian needs to own a stable cat carrier to transport the cat to the vet and for emergency evacuations. Never allow a cat to leave the shelter wrapped in a towel, under the new guardian's arm. The friendliest, calm cat can become spooked.

Written Cat Care Information for Adopters

Written information is another aspect that is lacking at many organizations. It only makes sense to send someone away with information about what to expect upon arrival to the new home, information about vet care and parasites, and other general care information. What if this is someone's first pet? How can a completely inexperienced person be sent home, with a precious living being with many different needs, and know how to provide everything required?

The cat should not have to suffer due to ignorance. It is the adoption agency's duty to thoroughly educate every adopter on the needs of a cat. Adopters should be sent home with a resource. No one will remember every detail verbally explained, that's why combining written information is important. Telling someone to go call a vet is really not sufficient. Give them something tangible to immediately begin their lives together. A paper was created for the purpose of familiarizing a new guardian with what should be expected upon arriving home and general, yet essential cat care knowledge. I titled this paper "What to Expect and How to Care for Your New Cat." This documentation is in the Appendix, at the end of the book.

Declawing Pamphlet

Including a pamphlet about declawing is a good idea when giving information out after an adoption takes place. Mentioning the terrors of this procedure is imperative, but should someone ever feel compelled to think about this subject in the future, they should have some literature on the topic to review. Options include making one up oneself or find one through another organization that specializes in writing about this topic.

Chapter 14

Feline Lifestyles: Inside or Outside

"I've met many thinkers and many cats, but the wisdom of cats is infinitely superior." Hippolyte Taine

When performing adoptions, it is important to discuss where the cat will be living. Not one lifestyle fits every cat. Cats are individuals. Each cat has its own history. I think it is critical that a cat is adopted into a new home based on the cat's preferences. Some organizations will only adopt cats into indoor only homes. Their goal is to get the cat the safest lifestyle, but declaring such rules has a downside.

Outdoor-loving felines should not be forced to live in a cat rescue with many other cats, if they are not in bliss to live in this manner. Most cats prefer not to live with an extremely large number of other cats, becoming immensely stressed in this environment. Each cat should be given the opportunity to get adopted into a situation that best suits him or her. A cat deserves its own human family. In other words, a rescue shelter should not "stockpile" all the outdoor-suited cats, forcing them into whatever living quarters it has to offer. Some rescues force a group of cats, let's say, thirty to live together in a small shed forever. In many situations, they are not allowed outside ever, for the fear that something will happen to them. There are situations where hundreds of cats are kept, in these colonies, where conditions are not ideal them.

The cat's personality should be the deciding factor on his future. The rules of a rescue should not! If a particular cat is always quarreling with all the other cats, then clearly she should be adopted out into a home with no other cats or maybe one other cat.

Most people already have in mind what lifestyle their cat will be living. Often where a person lives can determine the lifestyle. For instance, if one lives in a city in a high-rise apartment building, an outside lifestyle of any type is not an option. It is critical to match the most suitable cats to that type of lifestyle. There are three types of lifestyles: inside only, inside and outside, and outside only.

Inside Only

An inside only way of living has several benefits. Safety is the most important reward. The fact is that cats face fewer dangers, by staying inside the home at all times. This lifestyle is the best one for allowing your cat to live out its life to old age. I recommend an indoor lifestyle whenever possible or necessary.

Any cat staying within the home at all times will need some specific items to make it content. A cat should be supplied with fresh grass to eat. Oat and wheat grass are favorite types to most cats. Grass from the yard is fine. Be sure there are no pesticides or any type of poison on the grass. Cats love to eat grass. Some prefer it more frequently than others. Toys that provide mental stimulation are necessary for a cat. Indoor cats can become bored. The cat needs objects to play with for entertainment. New trinkets should replace old ones periodically to provide interest in playing again. A scratching post or condo is required for indoor cats. Now that one knows the essentials for an indoor cat, there are possible dangers to be aware of inside.

Different objects in the home present dangers. Any age of cat could get inside the washer, dryer, or dishwasher. A feline could get its head caught in the back of a wooden chair, the kind with a wider opening between slats on the top, for instance, and strangle. A cat could get into a filing cabinet while the drawer is open and someone may slam hard to close it, not knowing the cat crawled inside, doing great harm to the cat. Most of these dangers I would not have thought of, except that most of these occurrences happened to people I have spoken with through my operation of the cat shelter.

Plastic bags are another huge danger. Ones with handles, like the kind from the grocery store are extremely dangerous. Cats put their head through the handle and the bag easily twists around, which can strangle the cat. A plastic bag with no handles poses a threat, also. Never leave bags out where the kitten or cat can access them. Beware of any loop handles, such as those on any bag or the end of a flashlight, as these can effortlessly become caught on a cat's neck.

Electrocution and fire are pertinent dangers to cats in the house. House fires are rare, but they do occur. Indoor cats can't escape. Very young cats are especially prone to chewing on objects, like electrical cords. Their toes or claws can get into electrical outlets. One should definitely put plastic outlet covers on all of the outlets. Be sure to buy cord covers for electrical cords to prevent chewing from occurring on dangerous wires.

All choking hazards should be kept out of reach at all times. Any small objects are of particular concern. The cat may put these items in her mouth, which can become lodged in the throat. Objects that can be swallowed are also a great concern. Items like ribbons, rubber bands, and string can all get stuck in a feline's body. These articles may get trapped in the stomach and intestines, which can present a life-threatening situation. Get professional veterinary care immediately, should ingestion of objects occur. Other ingested items can be deadly, too.

Poisons are a serious threat to a feline. Some houseplants are poisonous, so be sure to find out, from a vet or elsewhere, as to just which plants this includes. Toxic chemicals, like household cleaners, can kill your cat. Most individuals figure these substances smell bad, so a cat will not eat them. However, this is not always the case. Antifreeze is a lethal liquid and pets often enjoy its taste. So don't risk it, put these things way out of reach.

Windows can pose a risk to a cat's life. Be sure that screens are secured properly on the home. If a very young kitten, especially, escapes this could be certain death when confronted with outdoor dangers. When any windows are above ground level, this point can't be stressed enough. A good idea would be to attach a metal mesh, or something very strong, yet allows the breeze in, over the window so the cat does not fall out. High-rise dwellers take note of this, please. The truth is a cat could tear a screen if it so desired. A screen may have an existing rip, which could easily expand.

One must be extremely careful when raising a kitten. They are small, getting into the strangest places. Kittens just do not have the wisdom yet, that an older cat has acquired. They face the risk of being caught and squashed in a reclining chair. Toilet lids should always be kept down as the kitten may find her way in, but will not be strong enough to get out. The kitten could jump face in becoming stuck, so never leave the lids up.

Very young children do not mix well with very young kittens, as a general rule. When young children are present in the home, like ages one and one-half years to four years old, then the two beings should not be left together unattended. A young child just does not understand the damage it can inflict on a tiny, fragile kitten. A kitten can be harmed in no time at all.

A man once told me he recently had a kitten, but it was dead now. He proceeded to tell me the kids were playing with the kitten. The kids put the kitten in a Tupperware container (with lid on, I concluded by the results of this story). They were pulling it around in their wagon and then apparently, as kids do, went on to play elsewhere. When the kitten was discovered later, it was dead by suffocation! Kittens are not toys. This never should have happened.

Kittens are often hurt, by children chasing, grabbing or hitting them. Baby felines can easily suffer neurological injuries, broken bones, and head trauma. As one can decipher from my example of a true story, kittens and children should always be supervised.

Oleander can't wait for his daily serving of grass!

Options for Indoor Cats to Enjoy Outdoor Air

Indoor cats can enjoy outdoor rewards without being in any danger. There are fixtures one can purchase that attach to a window. It's like being in a safety cage that extends out the windowsill while the cat can't be harmed by outdoor dangers. Some are very small, but allow the cat to smell the air and feel the wind. Others can lead to an enclosure that is outside. A pet door in the window can be used for access. The cat is safe and can go back into the house when he wants.

There are different ways for a cat to experience the outdoors safely. Pet strollers are wonderful to safely push the cat around outside, to allow her the experience of new views and smells. I push my cats around in a pet stroller and people are thrilled and amazed to see a cat in a stroller. A stroller is especially great to have when traveling with your cat, too. This way the cat can easily go any place that you go. Carrying the cat in a pet bag, which is essentially a purse made for pets, with it securely fastened, the cat can encounter the outdoors in this capacity. There are backpacks made to carry a cat on your back. When being hands-free is necessary or when hiking on a rough trail where a stroller can't be pushed, this provides a convenient option. Some people have screened porches or pool areas the cat can get a fresh breeze.

Inside and Outside

Cats that come into the home, and are allowed to go out, get the best of both worlds. They still will face the risks that are outside. Always have your cat properly vaccinated before he goes outside. An unvaccinated cat could pass an illness to the cat, through any contact. The ideal way to manage this lifestyle would be to keep the cat inside at night, since predator dangers are most prominent at this time. Some cats enjoy going out to eliminate instead of using a litter box. Some kitties like to investigate what is happening on their property.

Great care must be given to kittens. After handling so many kittens, I don't think they should ever be left outside unattended when they are less than four months of age, as previously mentioned. An exception would be for a feral kitten that was reared by its mom in, an outdoor environment. A feral kitten had been shown by its mother, how to survive.

Domestic, socialized kittens are just too inexperienced with potential dangers. They are not mature enough to make decisions regarding life and death. A human comparison would be like putting a three-year old child outside unattended and expecting that it would know how to avoid danger. Kittens, like children, need to reach a certain level of maturity before having the wisdom to survive all of life's obstacles.

> **Baby Banter**
> **Never allow kittens less than four months old to remain outside unattended.**

Outside Only

Outdoor lifestyles have more inherent dangers. That being said, in most cases, not all of these risks are going to be present in every yard.

Some outdoor risks are:

- Coyotes
- Dogs
- Cars
- Fights with animals including other cats with a risk of disease through these fights
- Exposure to parasites
- Coming into contact with mean humans

As guardians, we must make the best decisions for our cats. We want them to be safe, but happy and given the opportunity to enjoy a quality life, as well. Keeping a cat in an outdoor lifestyle is sometimes the best situation for some cats.

An adult feral cat may never be content inside a home. The cat may feel as though it is being kept in a prison. This situation would cause severe stress to a cat of this type. The cat would be extremely scared and upset, either bouncing off the walls, injuring itself immensely in an effort to escape or cowering in a dark corner too fearful to even eat. A cat that was born feral, meaning it was born to a wild mother cat, is taught how to hunt for food and avoid predators.

Since this feral cat has survived to adulthood, one can assume it is quite smart. Once a cat survives to the age of about three years old, it is fair to say this cat is very savvy about all of the outdoor dangers. The mother cat teaches them to fear all large creatures that could do them harm, including humans. This is a survival strategy. Ferals are not the only cats best suited for living outdoors.

Cats have individual preferences, like any living being. A cat that is very happy outdoors and miserable inside of a home is a prime example of a very friendly cat that should, perhaps, stay outside. There are some cats that love to hunt rodents. Others appreciate complete freedom. Some want to choose their own litter box location. They do not appreciate a small box with some form of digging substance placed in the home. Yet, others may have unfixable behavior issues that are not acceptable for living inside the home. These preferences should be respected.

Ben, a DSH, enjoys an outdoor lifestyle.

Bird Enthusiasts

Many bird enthusiasts cite cats as being non-native, so this justifies to them, that no cat should be allowed to live outside ever. However, cats have been here at least since the European settlers came to America about four hundred years ago. This fact certainly qualifies them as native citizens.

Cats are often the scapegoat blamed for reducing bird populations. Extremists actually hold cats responsible for the fact that some bird species are endangered. Many of these bird worshippers would love for cats to be eradicated completely. The truth is cats are not to blame for bird species endangerment.

Humans are the sect most responsible for bird annihilation. We continually clear the land in volatile habitats. We drain natural marshlands, which provide the perfect ecosystem for many species of birds to nest and find food. We infect our land with pesticides and other pollutants. Consequently, countless birds are poisoned and deformed annually. Controlled burns kill numerous baby birds, as they are burned alive in their nests. Add up all the dead birds from "our" activities across the nation and the world. It should become clear who is really decimating bird populations! However, we are not the only creatures to blame.

Many animals include eggs, baby birds, and adult birds in their diets. Snakes, raccoons, foxes, opossums, hawks, owls (Oh, look other birds!), rats, even coyotes and other opportunistic feeders love to eat birds. Add up all the victims to these predators and the result is many dead birds. Condemn the correct creatures for predation. Keep in mind any cat trying to get a meal for survival wherever he may find it, the blame falls back on the human, for abandoning the cat in the first place. Yes, a cat will attempt to catch a bird when she is starving, but so will many other creatures.

Write your articles as you will, but you had better include all of the facts. Include humans and all of the other predators towards birds. Quit blaming cats. I don't ever want to see any article written on endangered birds with blame being directed solely at cats. I am so sick of the biased trash written on birds! Remember, bird numbers can't escalate if all the facts are not presented. Did you know that birds have wings? That means they can fly in the air. What an advantage. I have never met a cat with wings, apparently some bird aficionados have.

When a baby bird falls from a nest, unfortunately, his wings are not fully formed. Otherwise, he would fly away to not become a predator's dream come true. Sadly, for the chick survival is not much of an option in this situation. He can't climb back into his nest. Will it be a raccoon, a snake, a cat, or ants that will eat the baby?

I like birds. Many birds are beautiful. I have raised many chicks that have fallen from their nest. Extinction of any creature (other than fleas, mosquitoes, ticks, and coyotes) is not something I want to see, but when people are given incorrect information, then proper steps can't be utilized to address the real cause of the problem.

The propaganda that bird conservancy organizations put into the media is an injustice. The birds are not benefiting from the one-sided messages. The intellectually challenged citizens that believe the biased literature often will or intend to harm cats because of it.

Plenty of biased bird people have called my organization to tell me just that. They will say that a stray has arrived in the yard. They fear it will kill a bird, so if someone does not come to remove the cat, they are going to kill the cat.

Attention Avian Adorers
Cats do not have wings. They cannot fly. I hope this eases your concerns that cats have any advantage to inflict harm on a bird.

Chapter 15

Black Cat Persecution in Society

"A black cat crossing your path signifies that the animal is going somewhere."
Groucho Marx

It is necessary to include some current and relevant information about cults that harm cats. Cats have suffered throughout human history. Particularly, in the Middle Ages when many thousands of cats were killed because of superstitious beliefs, when people associated cats with witches. History cannot be changed, but one would think people will get smarter as the generations continue to be born.

Sadly, some individuals in our society in this very day and age are superstitious. Some of these ignorant individuals belong to "religions" that sacrifice cats to their God or gods. Killing other beings for any religion is absolutely wrong. Other persons believe superstitions, which say that a black cat crossing one's path will bring bad luck. This line of verbal garbage exists in the United States and a few other countries. In England, the belief is that a black cat crossing one's path will bring good luck. Superstitions have absolutely no relevance.

Superstitions come about by one person's experience and correlating two events together. Other non-thinking people, or followers, just believe the story as a fact, passing it along. It is puzzling to me how these ritualistic ways of thinking can go on and on! How difficult is it to find someone that actually questions a statement fed to them as fact?

Halloween, Cults, Superstition and Black Cats

Cult members are people that will kill cats, as part of their religion. One may think only teenagers would temporarily participate in such lunacy, but there are all ages of these followers. My first exposure to this type of group was when I was in high school. Awareness of such activities was beyond my scope of knowledge prior to this time.

While performing cat adoptions, more information came my way about what these cults really practice. Most cat shelters do not adopt out any black cats in October because of the high prevalence of these cults. These cults absolutely participate in animal sacrifice. Most of us have seen stories on the news about such practices, when someone makes a grim discovery.

This leads me into a very critical component about adoptions. Unfortunately, the majority of our society participates in Halloween, which is the Devil-worshippers most important holiday, as far as I know, and black cats suffer greatly. Halloween is the absolute worst day of the year for me! I totally dread its arrival every year.

Halloween celebrates evil judging from its origin and the way humans act today on this day. History traces Halloween back to the pagan religion of the Celtic people, from Ireland, the United Kingdom, and Gaul. This day was called Samhain, which was the beginning of the winter season.

This day held great significance to these people. The ancient Celts believed that on this day the spirits of the dead would come back to wander around the Earth. Evil spirits, like demons, are just as likely to wander about as any that may not be evil. The Druids, the priests of the Celts, performed rituals to try to appease the evil spirits from doing too much damage to people and property. Bonfires were the common ritual. This word comes from, "bone fire."

Sacrifices were offered to their many gods. Animals, humans, and crops were sacrificed to the gods. The fire was supposed to represent the sun. The sacrificed live beings, as well as, crops were thought to ensure less havoc on the community. It also helped the people feel secure in the belief that the sun will return after the winter. The practice of sacrificing humans was stopped, in mainstream, around the year 1600 A.D. Effigies were often burned instead.

Other cultures began to enter the scene. The Romans conquered much of the Celtic territory by the year 43 A.D. They combined their holiday of Feralia with the Celts holiday of Samhain. Sacrifices were still used in the rituals. Christianity started to become influential in this location. In the Seventh century, Pope Boniface IV, proposed All Saints Day. The intention was to honor saints and martyrs by replacing the traditional pagan holiday. In the year 834, Gregory the third moved the date of All Saints Day to November first (this is the day of Samhain, though their days began the evening before, hence

October 31). This day came to be known as All Hallows' Eve (All Saints Eve), and eventually Halloween. Through time, with the influence of additional religions, not much changed for this holiday, except its name.

Many people think it is totally innocent and fun to dress up in costumes. Masquerading oneself in a costume, originated from the scared, superstitious people dressing up as goblins, devils, and other demonic creatures. The goal was to blend in with the real evil spirits that were wandering around the area.

The spirits were looking for a body to in-habit or some such thing. Halloween today is considered by followers of evil cults to be the best day of the year to contact spirits. These followers of the occult, still offer sacrifices to their "supernatural leader," this being black cats on Halloween!

If people today even had a clue what was really happening, I'm sure most people would truly abandon any participation. Large corporations that simply take advantage of the masses' ignorance are very happy to sell lots of candy and costumes to them. These companies receive huge profits during this time of year.

Why won't more people question what they are participating in, instead of obliviously following along with the masses and what the media tells you? The fact that nasty pranks occur, such as throwing eggs and toilet paper onto other people's property should clue one in that this "holiday" is not a kind one. Come on people! Let me tell you what those who are very aware of what this "holiday" stands for, are doing on this very gruesome day in October.

Black cats are "sacrificed" on Halloween. Followers of these participating cults actively seek out to obtain a black cat for their Halloween ritual. So many people are not aware that this is happening. I so desperately fear for the cats! Many cats are given away without people having a clue about what some people would do to a black cat. Advertisements in October, especially "free to good home" ones in the newspapers or online can mean a horrible outcome for the innocent cat's life.

Attaining a cat for free is the most ideal for cult members. Individuals with an advertisement in the newspaper are most likely not aware of these kinds of death-minded people. These people would most likely not have any screening policies for getting the cat into a new home, either. But, these cult members are willing to pay for a cat if necessary. This is why cat rescues have rules about not adopting out black cats at this time of the year.

Most rescue organizations are very conscious of the cult problem. In fact, it is so enormous that nearly every cat adoption agency throughout the country will not adopt out any black cats in the entire month of October, for this reason. Some kill facilities often just euthanize the black cats, especially this time of the year. Therefore, they don't really need to be concerned about this problem and the other persecution that black cats suffer in our society.

Superstition is another ridiculous reason that black cats are tortured. The one that says if a black cat crosses someone's path that bad luck will follow, is the cause for more animosity towards black cats. Some citizens actually believe this verbal garbage. Derelicts will go out of their way to hurt or kill a black cat. After rescuing nearly six-hundred cats, the fact is more maimed black cats are commonplace.

> **Caution Cat Caretakers**
> Do NOT allow your cat outside anytime near Halloween, especially black cats!

Story of Hope

This cat was discovered in a parking lot, by a caring person. A woman called stating she found this skinny, black cat that was limping. The woman had all the cats she could care for and could not take it in herself. I named this cat Hope because I said to her, "I sure hope you make it (survive)."

A black cat was brought to me in terrible condition. Hope, an adult cat, weighed about three pounds. She was extremely emaciated. More than half of her tail had been chopped off and the end of it was burned. The fur was actually burned off leaving the skin exposed. One hind leg dangled. The leg did not hit the ground when she walked. It just swung around. The upper leg bone was broken completely in half.

Hope, a DSH, was a forgiving cat.

There was a band of white fur across a couple of her toes on that same leg, which indicated that perhaps something with great pressure was on her toes, scarring them. Hope's injuries indicated she had been intentionally abused, rather than hit by a car.

Hope made progress rapidly. She put weight on with the nourishing meals she consumed. The determined, gaunt cat did not seem to be in pain. Her friendly nature amazed me, after suffering such cruelty at the hands of humans.

After X-rays were taken, it was decided that it was best to leave her leg in the present condition. The break was not fresh. The leg had proceeded with the healing process. Amputation would not have benefited the cat in this case. A tight bandage wrapped on the leg was a consideration, but most likely would not have forced the bone to grow back together.

Screws and pins through surgery, which would essentially connect the bone, was an option. This procedure could only be performed at the University, the veterinary college. It would have been a few thousand dollars. Unfortunately, my budget did not permit this option. No, the University does not perform any pro-bono or even discounted work, according to the head of the department, with whom I communicated. Students could have gained valuable knowledge by treating such a unique case. The fur on her tail grew back for the most part.

Upon full recovery, Hope was available for adoption. It takes a special person to adopt a cat that has been injured or abused. Eventually, that person came along and adopted Hope.

Story of Orchid

Orchid's story begins when a newborn litter of kittens were discovered in the big straw barn at my familiar horse training center. My husband was informed by an employee. We set a trap near the kittens. To everyone's surprise, a gaunt, lanky black cat was in the trap a short time later. No one had ever seen this cat, prior to trapping her.

Orchid, named after a beautiful, black orchid flower, was a thin, black beauty who recently gave birth to five kittens. She was a very friendly cat. Orchid appeared ill, as one of her eyes was extremely watery.

I treated her for the eye problem, but it would not completely resolve. Soon I discovered her jaw was broken, as she ate in a peculiar manner. There is no way to know how this injury occurred. Orchid's broken jaw could have been caused by a couple of different options. An accident may have caused it or it could have been an intentional affliction by a human. The attentive mother did not appear to be in any pain. Now, it became evident why the eye would not heal. The eye and jaw were all related.

The black, lanky cat's jaw was X-rayed. An orthopedic specialist was shown the x-rays for review. The conclusion was that the jaw was not causing her any pain. She was getting along comfortably in her present condition.

Strong antibiotics were given to her. The troubling eye issue resolved. As you can see by Hope and Orchid's story, sometimes further bone repair is not always necessary. Each situation must be assessed individually.

Story of Jack

One case of the abuse of a black cat touched me even more personally. He is my own cat, Jack. My fiancé and I were standing in a straw barn when I found Jack on the floor, in the middle of the barn. This tiny kitten was only three weeks old.

My fiancé said we should name him Blackjack, so he was always called Jack. This young boy with dull, black fur was one of the first kittens that I raised and rescued. We were very close.

Jack, a DSH, was a very special cat.

Athletic Jack liked to hunt in the nearby barns. He always caught plenty of mice and rats. Most people that were stabled in the barns knew and liked Jack. After all, he provided rodent removal service. However, other people briefly come into the facility either to train their horse for one morning or for a few days during a horse sale.

One time upon speaking to someone stabled in the barn briefly for a sale, I learned some informative knowledge as to the way some people think about black cats. This ignorant rogue man made a comment about hating black cats because he was superstitious. This comment was shocking to me! I was naive to the fact that there really are people that believe this sort of semantic rubbish, in this day and time.

This is why such a point was made, to express what I now know about dangers to cats, by the vile people in the world. The reality of this situation was not in my scope of knowledge that some people adamantly feel that a black cat will give them bad luck. How can someone have the audacity to think that a cat would go out of his way to change some (insignificant) person's luck? Get a life people. The cat has better things to do with her day than to be concerned with some stranger. That incident enlightened me. When sales go on, Jack was kept well away from the barns.

One time when Jack was about five years old someone attacked him. A witness was not located, but the vet does not believe that he was kicked by a horse or injured by a vehicle, which are the only other options in his environment. Jack's injuries were life threatening.

This beauty sustained permanent injuries from the incident. My noble cat's head took on a slightly pointed appearance. Blood was draining from his nose. The skilled rodent-exterminator's abdomen was extremely sore. He had a fever of 106 degrees. Force feeding him was the only way to get any food in him, as he would not eat without any assistance. He developed a green discharge from one nostril. He was taken to numerous veterinarians, being X-rayed and put on nearly every antibiotic. The latest diagnosis is the belief there is a bone fragment in his head or within the sinus cavity, which continually causes aggravation.

At eight years of age, my aging cat developed tiny lesions along his belly. He would lick his abdomen. The fur was pretty much all gone there. A couple of his breasts were growing, which I found particularly odd. Originally, it was diagnosed as an allergy. Being prescribed a small dose of Prednisone, I brought him back to the vets for more testing when this problem did not resolve.

Jack needed a biopsy. The prognosis was narrowed down to two different bacterial suspects. Nocardia was one possibility. Actinomyces was the other possibility. These are both slow-growing bacterium that are difficult to eliminate. Jack was prescribed a course of Penicillin VK and Sulfamethoxazole & Trimethoprim (SMZ-TMP) antibiotics, both of which made him salivate intensely. After several weeks, hair began to grow back and the small lesions went away. How amazing it was that Jack conquered another very challenging predicament. Very little time had passed when a new problem emerged.

Just recently, at age nine and one-half years, Jack began to show signs of FIP, Feline Infectious Peritonitis. His abdomen became swollen with fluid within one week. As soon as it became visible that his abdomen was swollen, I took him to the vets with the fear that lethal FIP could be the culprit. After the vet examined my cooperative cat, he withdrew some of the fluid in his abdomen and blood from a vein. The diagnosis was that Jack probably did have FIP. My constantly challenged boy had a high fever at the exam.

This brave feline lived for two months after the diagnosis. The fluid increased in his abdomen, but he continued to eat, drink, and eliminate. He preferred to eat canned food predominantly, as his illness progressed. He had been consuming more water than usual, which is a sign of kidney failure. The day Jack died, he appeared to be uncomfortable. He was twitching the tip of his tail back and forth and refused to rest in his usual place. Canned food that he loved was given to him, but he did not want to eat. He was not feeling well. Three hours later, he was dead.

This cat is truly one of the most special cats I have ever known. He was a very intelligent green-eyed cat. Jack really seemed to understand English very well. My black beauty always knew what anyone told him.

This adorable cat loved people. He really enjoyed hanging out at the gatehouse where there is always a security guard. All the guards loved him. They brought him special treats. The guards all miss him greatly, as my family does, and his picture remains on the wall at the gatehouse. One of the guards keeps a video he shot with his cell phone, of Jack chasing down a big rat.

This short-hair black cat made a great impact on many lives. Jack represented his species well, showing many other people how friendly, smart and unique cats can be with his huge personality. He was a black cat, as well. Anyone that may have had stereotypical ideals of how a cat behaved or had any ridiculous superstitions about black cats in particular, after meeting Jack they could see that their preconceived notions were wrong. We love you always Jack! You will never be forgotten.

Story of a Black Stray at the Car Wash

Another situation of abuse of a black cat was brought to my attention. I agreed to take this cat, though space was lacking at the time. This cat was homeless. He was the victim of abuse. I could not even contemplate leaving him there to be further tormented! However, the person that found the cat figured out a way to keep the cat himself.

This friendly cat was found at a car wash. He had a tight noose on his tail. The concerned man that noticed the cat asked the attendant at the car wash if he knew anything about this cat. The attendant acknowledged that some people were hanging the cat from his tail. The man who found the cat was able to catch him. He soon discovered the noose was growing into his skin and could not be easily removed.

The victimized cat was taken to a vet clinic to receive the medical care he needed. The plan was that the cat would come to my shelter when he was ready to leave the vet clinic. The cat's rescuer lived in Texas. He and his family were moving to this area in about a month. He currently was the guardian for seven cats at his home, he explained to me.

The man from Texas visited the cat daily while in Florida, at the vet office. He did not think it was feasible to keep the cat, feeling that seven was enough.

I spoke to the man several times while the cat was being boarded. After nearly two weeks, it was time for the cat to come to my shelter. As plans were about to be made for the cat's arrival here, the man indicated he had become so attached to the cat he was going to keep him. Feelings of jubilation encompassed me with a happy ending for the cat.

Chapter 16

In the Event of Death; Feline or Human

"Until one has loved an animal, a part of one's soul remains unawakened."
Anatole France

Grieving pet guardians should be handled delicately. Guidelines should be in place on how to counsel people that have recently lost their cat to death or disappearance. Friends and family members will face this issue also, and the information on this topic is helpful for their needs. I faced this very topic with my own cats. Devastation swallowed every ounce of my being. I experienced lack of empathy from others in the loss of my cats. This is why I felt it is critical to have this entire chapter in the book. Perhaps persons lacking a complete understanding of the feelings a pet guardian, closely bonded with the pet, experiences will be enlightened. I hope so. I will share some of my most heart-felt losses.

Grief Counseling

At some point, all animal guardians will lose their pet to death or by becoming missing, which after time passes without the cat returning, one assumes death has occurred. This is a very difficult time for the guardian, not to mention the other animals that lived with this particular cat. They miss their friend, just like we (humans) miss the cat's presence. It is important to be very supportive to people who call or visit the shelter that have recently suffered the loss of a pet.

Most people want to adopt another cat, when they feel they are ready, after a special cat has died. Some people will come a day after their cat has died because they just cannot stand the void of not having a cat. They want another cat to love. The person also wants that precious relationship of feline companionship. Other people will wait weeks or months to get another cat. They need more time to grieve the cat that died. This person does not to want to rush when getting a new cat.

Everyone handles grief in one's own manner. Adopters know they are not replacing the cat that has passed on, as every cat is an individual. A grieving adopter knows he or she is saving the life of another cat, by adopting one. Someone whom is in one's daily life is greatly missed when he or she dies and is all the sudden just no longer there. This is true no matter what species this significant other is, providing there is a close bond. For instance, when a resident spouse dies, more devastation will result than when some relative that one talks to once a year or every decade dies.

The everyday loss of companionship will be missed. The one that slept in your bed every night is now gone. The one spoken to first thing in the morning is no longer there to listen and respond (whether in English or with a meow). Love between two beings is love. The bond of companionship is greatly missed when one being is no longer there. Life is now completely changed and lonely on a daily basis.

Depression and grief settle into one's life. These same feelings occur with the loss of a special pet. The deficit of the presence of that special someone is there, whether human or cat. When someone you know looses someone special, like a cat, be supportive of his or her feelings.

This is a horrible time for the person. He or she is constantly remembering what the day is like with that someone special. The person is feeling tremendous sadness by the loss of companionship. Shock is another issue to deal with because when death occurs very suddenly, it takes time to even come to terms with the loss. Never tell a person his or her feelings are ridiculous, by saying it is silly to be so upset about an animal dying. Don't say, "Just go get another one." Don't tell the person to just, "Snap out of it." Instead, offer your support.

Be thoughtful of a grieving person's feelings. Send a sympathy card about the death of the pet. Making a donation to a no-kill shelter, in memory of the deceased cat is a great action to perform. A donation of this nature can mean wonders to the person because he or she knows another cat is being helped. Call the person to see if he or she needs something.

Tell the person to call if a need arises, like to get something from the store or just to listen. The person will welcome another pet into his or her life if and when she feels it is the right time. Everyone grieves a little differently, but always try to be supportive of the choices the person makes for herself.

Many people want a cat that looks similar to a cat they once had. In so many instances, while doing adoptions, people will choose a cat because it reminds them of a previous cat that was in their life. I can say the same is true for me, as well. When I had lost one of my most special cats, one that has similar colors and markings, appeals to me. This story begins with my cat, Nolan. After he vanished, I was drawn to cats that resembled him in some way.

Sensitivity Sanction

A grieving pet guardian is extremely emotionally devastated. Be supportive any way you can.

Story of Nolan

Nolan came into my life by responding to an advertisement in the newspaper. He was born at a horse farm, being five weeks old when I brought him home. Nolan was predominantly white with peach colored patches on his body. I fell in love with him on the way home. A maternal bond was immediately sparked in me.

My new little bundle of joy was covered with fleas. Soon after arriving home, I gave him a bath. I manually removed every flea from his body.

When he was very young, sleep was rather sparse for me. Throughout the night I woke up to help him off the tall bed, into his litter box. He needed to go potty during the night. This action was performed until he was able to get down safely by himself.

Nolan was a unique little kitten. He made the cutest face, where he would turn one of his ears sideways. My growing boy did not like other cats very much because for the longest time, it was only he and I that lived in the house together. This peachy, spotted little man was my best friend. We did nearly everything together. He slept on my chest or by my side at night and rode in the truck with me. When Nolan got older, he wanted to go outside, so I let him. He came in and out as he pleased. The serious dangers that the outdoors presented was not information in my bank of knowledge. Nolan was in my life for more than a year.

Justice For Cats

Nolan, a DSH kitten, making his cute expression.

When my most special cat Nolan disappeared, I was beyond devastated. About two years would pass until the knowledge of exactly what had happened to him came to me. Wonder had absorbed me all this time about what happened to him. I missed him so much. I realized he was never coming back because a coyote killed him.

Nolan was one of the greatest joys and loves in my life.

Feelings of emptiness, despair, and loneliness compelled me to want to find that special bond again. I had other cats that I loved very much, but that same type of bond was not there. Much time would pass before meeting a special kitten that bonded strongly with me.

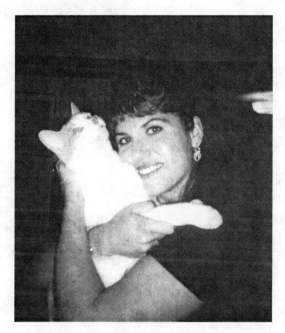

Jessica and Nolan

Story of Salmon

Several months later Salmon came along. I trapped Julie, Salmon's mom, in a straw barn. She had given birth to four kittens a few days prior. The kittens were; Salmon, Willow, Cimba, and Sambo. Julie was a semi-feral tortoiseshell cat. She and her kittens stayed in the house.

Salmon and I developed a very special bond. Salmon was orange, a darker hue of orange than Nolan. The bond we developed was just like the one that Nolan and I shared.

Salmon followed me everywhere. The soft, burnt-orange fur-ball always slept arched around my head, on my hair at night, while gently purring. Having this bond again ignited flames of euphoria in my very mournful heart. I thought of Nolan every day, but was thrilled to have Salmon in my life. He had so much love to give.

Jessica and Salmon

Salmon was in my life for a year and one-half. One morning he wanted to go outside at 4:30, so out he went. At 6:00 when I went to my barn, which was not near any other barns, to feed my horse, Salmon was nowhere to be found. This was so unusual! He was always right there when I hollered to him. Thoughts of wonder filled my mind as to where he could be that he would not come when I called him. Then at 3:30 that afternoon, a thunderstorm came. Still there was no sign of Salmon.

Panic consumed every molecule of my being at this point! I was looking everywhere for him. He never came home. The next day started the beginning of a huge search for him. I placed newspaper ads and looked at Animal Control. The newspaper ad produced a lead, but it turned out not to be him. I was beyond devastated. As each day went on, things got worse for me.

My mental state deteriorated with Salmon's absence. Salmon was like a child to me. A maternal bond blossomed within me towards him, just like with Nolan. No one in my life understood the immense devastation I was experiencing. Many people do not understand how a person can have a maternal bond with a cat. There are those of you that do understand, but the majority of the human population does not comprehend this issue. They have no clue about the suffering a person endures when losing a closely bonded pet.

Time was passing and Salmon did not return. During this time, some of my other cats vanished. I learned the hard way about the prominent existence of coyotes. Coyotes were seen on the racetrack, at night by the track crew. Footprints were evident in many places the next day, if only one looks for them. I became very observant and began to seek out knowledge about coyotes. In my very early days of rescuing cats, I was not endowed with the information that I now retain.

Salmon was killed by a coyote. Nolan was too. And the other cats were yet more victims. The coyotes had been here for years. Coyotes were the reason I lost my best friends, my children. My fight against these rogue canines began too late to save those already killed by them!

I mourned severely for many, many months, actually years, after Salmon was gone. I missed him so much. He disappeared on 6/6/2002.

After several months, this severe grief sure was taking a toll on me. The sadness is all-consuming. I would have done anything to bring this cat back to me. Knowing about coyotes, I decided my next cat would not go outside.

I tried to make the bond happen with a few different kittens that were rescued, but that special bond never occurred until Elijah came along. Elijah was truly like a combination of Nolan and Salmon. I previously described his entire story. Eli and his five other siblings were brought to me in a small, cardboard box by someone in the community. Immediately his color and markings caught my eye. He is white with orange spots, marked like Nolan but with spots the same color as Salmon's spots. As I mentioned above, it is often the looks of a cat that attracts someone to him, whom has lost a cat that looked similar to that cat.

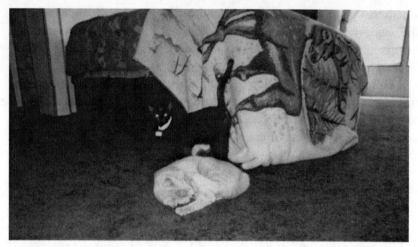

Salmon impacted my life tremendously. I never suffered through such grief as when this precious cat was taken from me! Willow was a wonderful cat. They were such special DSH brothers.

Story of Willow

I must tell Willow's story because he was truly a special kitten, though the bond was different. Willow, a shiny, short-hair black kitten, and I developed a special bond. This little guy was a special needs kitten.

This black, scrawny kitten was the runt of the litter. This vocal kitty had trouble remembering how to use the litter box. Exactly how old he was when he finally grasped the litter box concept escapes my memory, but probably he was three or four months old. Once he got that task engrained, he seemed completely normal and healthy. However, at eight months old he got a thrombo-embolism (a blood-clot) lodged in his pelvic area, where the artery splits to go down each hind leg.

Willow's hind legs were paralyzed. His paws were cold, like fresh-fallen snow on a winter's day. Immediately, I rushed him to the vets. The veterinarian put him on Prednisone. The vet did not say anything about a life-threatening condition. Willow died the next day. I was shocked and devastated. The fact that this ailing kitten was clearly in a possibly lethal situation was not in my mind. Willow was a wonderful cat.

Jessica Barbazon

Julie, a smart DSH, is 9 yrs. old.

Plan for the Cat after the Guardian Dies

"No one loves you unconditionally as your beloved pet."
Cynthia S. Dobesh

Cats are an integral part of the family. Plans should be made, by every guardian, for when the person dies as to where the pet will reside. A fortunate person will have a very trusted friend or family member that will take care of the pet for the rest of its life. Discuss this situation carefully with the selected person because knowing this person genuinely loves cats and wants to have this commitment is important.

In some situations, people assume someone will care for the cat when he or she dies. This topic might have only been addressed once very casually. The other person nonchalantly stated he or she will take the cat. This is certainly not enough discussion for the subject.

Caring for a pet for the rest of its life is a serious responsibility. Frequently, when someone dies, their relative relinquishes the cat to Animal Control. At times, the house door is opened for the cat to run out. This is a done deal for the trusted relative. Cats deserve better than this type of treatment. They are such wonderful, loyal and empathetic companions. Don't let abandonment or death happen to your best friend. Get an official and reliable plan in place.

As a shelter, taking in pets from guardians with a plan in place is a topic to think about. This gives people an option when they do not have a person in their life that can care for the cat for the rest of its life. Sometimes people just do not know how to have the cat cared for when they do not know someone personally that will do it.

A written paper could be given out on this topic to adopters or anyone, to raise awareness for a cat's care. People should plan to leave money to the person or organization that will take the cat in, to pay for veterinary care and food. The individual can use a trust company to manage and send stipends to the new guardian.

Using a trust company would prevent giving all the money out at once, with the fear that someone could discard the cat after receiving the money. Without this type of arrangement, no one would be checking on the cat's condition. By using a trust company, an employee of this company can verify the cat is visiting the vets. The trust company could require vet bills and photos of the cat.

Chapter 17

State and Federal Requirements to Operate a Shelter

"All the arguments to prove man's superiority cannot shatter this hard fact: in suffering, the animals are our equals." Peter Singer

Part of operating a shelter includes occupational decisions. As part of incorporating in your state, one needs to come up with a name for the shelter along with methods of operation. Who will be on your board of directors? Will a vote determine the directors of the shelter or will the President appoint them? How will money be raised to cover the costs of the shelter?

Next, one will get the big set of paperwork to apply for tax-exempt status through the IRS. All of this planning will be well worth it. It will help to prepare you for this grand endeavor. All the questions that one will encounter on the forms, force you to get a good foundation of methods and policies established.

Naming Your Shelter

Now that a plan is in place how the cat rescue will be operating, a name must be chosen. You may already have in mind what you want to call your operation, but there are a few pieces of information on this topic that one should know.

There are some very common names that are associated with animal rescue corporations. These well known terms can give recognition to a shelter. In other words, people will immediately understand the shelter's mission. However, many citizens wrongly assume any organization with these names are one entity or are a different chapter of the same parent organization.

Some of the familiar terms started out with one corporation at some point in time using this term in their name. These places of rescue became popular on a national level. The familiarity of the name just stuck in people's minds. For instance, S.P.C.A. is a very common term that the public associates with animal rescue. This acronym stands for society for the prevention of cruelty to animals. It first became popular because of one of the nation's first animal protection groups, the American Society for the Prevention of Cruelty to Animals. This local entity is in New York City.

The New York based corporation is talented in using outreach programs to gain members nationally. This affiliation uses the media to maintain public awareness. A coalition needs substantial funds to partake in national fundraising efforts. This large entity is not a parent organization, or umbrella organization, to other animal rescues throughout the United States that have this S.P.C.A. terminology in their name. Anyone can use this particular name as a part of the name of his or her organization.

Another very common name used by rescue groups is humane society. The Humane Society of the United States is the most familiar organization with these words in its name. This organization is nationally recognized amongst the public. Many people may think any rescue with humane society in its name is somehow associated with this large group. This is not true.

Each corporation is independent, having no association with any other affiliation that contains these words in its name. Every entity has its own independent mission and ideas. Fundraising is the responsibility of that particular organization. They will obtain their own board members, and are completely separate. Many rescue organizations prefer a completely unique name.

A name that reflects the type of rescue one will be doing is a good place to start. For example, a cat rescue could include the word "cat" or "feline." Since cats are companions and pets, these words are other possibilities for inclusion. I always knew what the name would be for my organization.

My style is formal and elegant, so I naturally would select a name that reflected these attributes. Cats in my care would live a classy lifestyle on a large property. The first word of the name, being feline, is the scientific name for cats. It sounds formal. The "estate" part of the name came from the idea that the cats will live on a large parcel of land. This is how Feline Estate, Inc. obtained its identity. Each of you will have your own method of reason as to how you will select the name for your affiliation.

Incorporating; Getting Non-Profit Status

Obtaining non-profit status is not difficult, but a solid plan for your enterprise must be in place. My organization was incorporated in Florida, so I am most knowledgeable about this state. I will describe the method of incorporating in Florida. However, I think most other states will have a very similar procedure. At the end of this book, there is a list of each state's division of corporations contact information for your assistance.

Non-profit status is acquired by contacting your state's government. The state capital is the official location from where each state's government is operated. The division of corporations is the department one will need to contact. That division will be further divided into for-profit and not-for-profit corporations. Obtaining the non-profit booklet is required. It can be mailed to you or downloaded from the Internet. In the not-for-profit brochure, one will find the articles of incorporation. This is where some decisions need to be made officially for the new organization.

The business's name should already be selected. One can search your state's database of corporation names, to avoid infringing on someone else's name choice. The best method to accomplish this task is to search your state's website for all corporate registrations.

Upon incorporation, a suffix must be added to the name of the conglomerate. The choices are either Corp., as in corporation, or Inc., as in incorporated. The next article to express is a fact, not a choice. This will be the business location and mailing address.

The following item which needs addressing is the purpose of the organization. This is really the mission statement. The mission statement is extremely important because this is the philosophy of the entire organization. This is the reason for the entity's existence. It explains what the intentions are for incorporating. Think about this one extensively before answering. Mission statements usually start with the word, "to." An example would be, "to rescue and provide for homeless felines."

Another choice to think about is the method of election of your directors.

- Will the incorporator appoint directors?
- Will directors be elected? Think about what will work the best for the corporation.

- Are there very wise people involved in the organization that will make competent choices?
- Or is it better to maintain the power oneself to ensure that the association will be run by only the most qualified personnel?
- Listing the directors' names and addresses is required. At least three are required.

The initial registered agent, the main person of the company, will need to provide his or her street address. The incorporator, the one that is filling out all the information, must provide his or her street address. Both must sign and date the form.

There will be a fee to apply to become a non-profit organization. Each state has a different fee, but they tend to be very nominal. The state will notify the incorporator of its decision within a few weeks. If a question was not answered to their satisfaction, just comply with their request and re-submit it. Upon satisfaction of the state's laws, this league will be issued a document number with the department of state.

A corporation is required to file a Uniform Business Report each year with the state. This form requires some factual information and an annual fee. It requires the name of the entity along with the state in which it was incorporated. Include the date of incorporation. The physical and mailing addresses should be written on the form. Names and addresses of the institution's directors are needed. The street address of its registered office in this state and the name of the registered officer will also be required. In Florida, the form must be received by May 1 of each year.

Should the report be returned stating more information is needed, it must be re-submitted within thirty days with the corrected information. The report needs to be filled out by the registered agent of the company. All information must be truthful and accurate at the time of its execution. If the report is not filed on time and with the correct fee, which at this particular time, in Florida is $61.25, the organization will be dissolved by the state. Another requirement of the form is that the affiliation must obtain a Federal Employer Identification number through the Internal Revenue Service.

The IRS issues EIN's to corporations. This number is the organization's identifying number for the IRS and the state. Form SS-4 needs to be completed. It can be acquired through the IRS. This form is quite simple. Now back to another portion of forms required by the state.

A charity must register with a separate division to be able to solicit donations from the public. In Florida, the Department of Agriculture and Consumer Services, Division of Consumer Services, is the entity in which one will need to file. The Solicitation of Contributions Act, chapter 496, Florida Statutes is the act in which the business will be complying.

The corporation will be assigned an identifying number within this division. Each year, you will be required to fill out a financial statement. It is very important to keep every receipt for all purchases throughout the year, for accurate reporting of the financial information. The charity's annual donation intake, as a whole, is required to be reported. Expenses are broken down into categories. By keeping all receipts in their own categories throughout the year, at the end of the year it is easy and time-saving to calculate all expenses in their proper place.

A cat shelter will have certain pertinent categories.

- Cat food
- Litter
- Supplies (like collars, beds, and toys) could be one category. One may choose to further separate these categories.
- Medical costs can be partitioned into veterinary charges and medical supplies.
- Office costs are the most specific, having their own categories on the form.
- Mailing expense
- Equipment, like repairs for the computer or purchasing an office chair will be its own classification.
- Advertising

With enough good fortune to generate $25,000 or more of revenue, one will be required to fill out form 990 from the IRS. This form can be substituted in place of the form from the Division of Consumer Services. These portions of operating the non-profit organization are required.

Benefits of Obtaining 501 © 3 Status

In the beginning days of my non-profit entity, I was not sure if filing for tax-exempt status would be necessary. I soon learned this would be a beneficial part of the alliance's existence, for it to become successful. Upon receiving the 501 © 3 designation, this will allow many doors to open for a corporation.

Nearly every business and most individuals that are potential donors require this classification before they are willing to help with your cause. Businesses especially want to see this paperwork before allowing any league a platform to collect donations.

The entryway of a busy store provides a great opportunity to solicit donations from citizens in the community. Management from stores will want to verify that the company is legitimate before allowing use of their property to further its mission. Donations made to an organization are only tax-deductible to any donor when the corporation has the 501 © 3 status. This matters very much, to nearly all, potential donors.

Business Benefit

Receiving a 501 © 3, tax-exempt status will be an immense advantage for a non-profit organization.

Federal Tax Exemption

Obtaining a tax-exempt status through the Internal Revenue Service will provide a non-profit company with many benefits. The organization will gain credibility. All donations will be tax-deductible for individuals and businesses. The institution will be exempt from certain state taxes, like sales tax. Non-profit mailing rates can be obtained through the United States Postal Service.

To apply for this status, the group must already be a corporation in your state. It must have an EIN (Employer Identification Number). Certain forms need to be filled out, which can be retrieved online or from an IRS office.

Forms Required

Form 1023, <u>Application for Recognition of Exemption</u>, and Publication 557, <u>Tax-Exempt Status for Your Organization</u>, which explains more details about Form 1023, from the Internal Revenue Service, are the materials one will need to obtain. There is more to fill out on this form than any other form you have filed thus far. Instructions are provided as to what information the IRS requires on each question.

Give careful consideration to all portions of operating the shelter before filling out this form. After completion of reading this book, having planned out all of the topics that I have discussed, you should have answers for all of the questions asked of the organization's methods on the IRS forms.

Some of the information that one needs to include is as follows:

- Who conducts the care of the cats?
- What activities are involved in caring for the cats?
- Where do you get your cats (from citizens or trapping, etc.)?
- What do you plan to do with them (adopt them out into new homes or provide them a permanent sanctuary to reside)?
- How much will you charge for an adoption fee?
- Where will the cats be housed?
- What percentage of the organization's time and resources are used for caring for and handling cats?
- How will funds be raised?

Public Charity or Private Foundation

The IRS wants to determine whether your organization is a private foundation or a public charity. A private foundation and a public charity have a main similarity, this being each wants to further the mission that the founding members felt strongly towards. For instance, a mission statement for a private or a public organization may include, "to provide assistance for homeless cats." On the other hand, there are distinct differences about an organization that make its status distinguishable as one from the other.

The main differences lie in the financial department. In order for a corporation to be established as a public charity there are two tests it must pass. The first requirement being that it must meet the one-third support test. This means it must receive at least one-third of its income from the general public or a governmental unit. Money can come from contributions, membership fees, gifts, and grants. Sales of merchandise and any money from a planned event, like admission fees, or a fee for a service can all be included.

The other test the corporation must pass is the not-more-than-one-third-support-test. This means that normally the organization will receive no more than one-third of its income from the following sources; "1) gross investment income, and 2) The excess (if any) of unrelated business taxable income from unrelated trades or businesses acquired after June 30, 1975 over the tax imposed on that income," according to Publication 557. Any net earnings of the charity must not benefit private shareholders or individuals. In other words, the purpose of the charity is to improve the cause, not make money for an individual.

A public charity cannot participate in a political campaign, either for or against a specific candidate. Acting as a lobbying group is not allowed, either. In other words, attempting to persuade legislation is not permitted if this type of activity is a rather large part of the organization's function.

Advance Ruling Period

Once one has satisfactorily completed form 1023, the IRS may decide that the company is eligible as a tax-exempt entity. If this is the case, the IRS will grant your organization an advance ruling. This is called a five year advance ruling period.

The year of incorporation is counted as the first tax year, even if this is only part of a year. The ending of the organization's first year will be the day after it became officially incorporated in the state. For example, if the organization was incorporated on May 1, 2007, then the first year of the accounting cycle will end on May 2, 2007. The first fiscal year would be from January 1, 2007 through May 2, 2007. Four more calendar or fiscal years will follow.

After these five years have passed, the IRS will determine whether the charity is indeed qualifying as a public charity. Through these years one had been filing the proper financial statement for the organization. This was either the state's annual financial form or the IRS Form 990. The amount of money that the business generates each year helps to determine which of these forms one should be filling out. Speaking of money, let's now discuss ways to generate some revenue.

Chapter 18

Fund-Raising Methods

"An idea that is developed into action is more important than an idea that exists only as an idea." Hindu Prince Gautama Siddharta, founder of Buddhism

Fundraising is a key factor for the operation of a shelter. The truth is that you have to ask for money to receive it. The cause of being able to help as many cats as possible should be the mission. It is a very important goal.

Hiring a professional fund-raiser will be an expensive deal. The fact is that money is required for all of the shelter's operating costs. A plan needs to be in place as to how funds will be generated to be able to buy the cats what they need.

As I previously mentioned, the people that bring cats to the shelter are the best source for regular income. The majority of these individuals care about cats. In most cases, these people are concerned about the particular cat he or she is bringing to the shelter. People relinquishing cats can be made to understand that donations from individuals, like themselves, are the reason the shelter is able to remain operating. Other methods need to be utilized, however, to bring in funds.

Mail Campaign

A mail campaign is a great way to get money, but it needs to be conducted wisely. To avoid wasting money on postage, especially if your budget is very small, targeting individuals known to care about animals is the best way to manage a mail-out. There are ways to establish a list of cat-caring people.

Persons that bring cats to the shelter and those whom adopt cats from the shelter are persons that could be sent a letter for fund-raising purposes. Another source of ailurophiles, or cat-lovers, can be found when your shelter gets media attention, such as when a reporter from the newspaper writes an article on the company. The article will contain contact information for your organization.

Some people in the community may send a donation to support your cause. Their names and addresses could be kept for future mailings. Another way to obtain names would be by purchasing a list of proven donors from other large animal welfare organizations.

This would be a very costly proposition though. One thing many people don't realize is that these types of affiliations, the ones that perform national mail-outs, have a lot of money, several million dollars in most cases. It is financially consumptive to execute a huge mailing campaign. Postage and other supplies add up quickly. That is why my recommendation is to mail to a targeted group of animal lovers.

In the shelter's very beginning, a specific list of ailurophiles may not be in one's possession yet. The phone book can become a valuable resource in this case. It lists addresses and phone numbers. A mailing could be conducted to as many individuals and/or businesses that the budget will allow.

Bulk mailing rates through the United States Postal Service offer a cheaper price per envelope, for mailing. To apply for non-profit status with the U.S.P.S., a form needs to be filled out. There is no fee for submission of this application. Once receiving non-profit status, it is not required that the corporation, obtain its own permit.

However, with the desire of a bulk-rate permit for the organization, there is a fee. It costs one-hundred seventy-five dollars to purchase the permit to receive a lower rate, when mailing through the post office. This fee must be paid annually. A lot of mailing would be required to make it worthwhile to purchase the bulk rate permit. The rate per envelope, in my local area at this time, in North Central Florida, is 15.5 cents.

Hiring a professional mailing service is an option. A low rate will be issued for mailing each envelope. These businesses usually operate on a quantity discount system. In other words, the more letters one mails, the cheaper the price will be for each one.

Create a Mailing List and Letter

Pestering people all year long for donations is not something I believe is ethical or wise. Some corporations like the wealthy ones that perform national mail campaigns, have letters going out about every couple of months. You know what I am talking about if you are on one of their lists, like I am. I don't like to be pestered constantly with requests for money, so I apply that sentiment towards my business's mailing pattern. This fact could even be mentioned in the mail-out, that this is the main mailing campaign of the year, if that is indeed the case.

The best time of the year to ask for donations is the main holiday time, being in the month of December. This applies to whichever fundraising method you are employing. People are in the mood for giving, this time of the year. For many, it is the only time of year that they consider giving to charity.

For those that donate for tax deductions, the end of the year is very appropriate for a charitable request letter to arrive. When most people think about tax deductions and they procrastinated all year in making a tax-deductible donation, now time is running out. Having that letter arrive at their home makes it convenient for them to write the check out to a good cause.

A decision needs to be made as to whether to perform additional mailings through the year. Late spring, kitten season, would be another great time for a mailing. The budget gets quite a strain when kitten season arrives (the main kitten season that is because in warm temperate climates kitten season is two times a year; spring and autumn). Kittens usually need all of the vaccinations (including the boosters), multiple de-wormings, and sterilization. Lots of kitten milk formula needs to be purchased, including many other items, specifically for rearing kittens. This seems like an appropriate time to request financial support.

A letter needs to be composed for the mail-out, consisting of the following;

- A letter should be kept to one page maximum to improve its odds of being read. Be concise in the letter, getting to the point of each topic one addresses.
- Telling the story of a particular cat is a great thing to include. A cat coming from extremely bad circumstances that the shelter rescued helps people to specifically know what their donation will be used for in the organization.
- State factually what the shelter has done for cats recently. This may be rescuing or sterilizing a certain number of cats. It could be providing assistance to pets in time of a natural disaster.
- Express appreciation for the support from the donors. The organization could not accomplish all that it does without the financial support of individuals in the community.
- Include a return envelope, with the address stamped on it. This makes it easy for someone to simply write out a check and put it in the

envelope. A short envelope inside the longer envelope works perfectly. Envelopes are very inexpensive.

- The law requires that you include certain information with every solicitation. Be sure to read all the legal paperwork carefully, or seek an attorney, so that you are complying with the law. For example, a statement that the affiliation is registered in the state, whichever one that is, but that the state does not endorse or support the organization in any way must be included, in all capital letters, is one type of requirement.

- Most donors want to know that their money will be put to good use, not stuck in a bank account or paying some lavish salary to a greedy person.

For instance, there are organizations that do not help any animals. They only "talk about" collecting enough money to "someday" build a shelter that will house animals. There are many of these types of conglomerates, unfortunately, that exist which have only formed a non-profit organization with the intention of lining their own pockets. These leagues hope that people will not question what they claim to be doing. They hope people will send them money because they "sound" good.

Donors should see some media coverage, at some point, to know the organization is legitimate in actually making a difference for the animals. When I speak of media coverage, I am referring to reporters or someone actually seeing animals being helped, not a story on simply bogus claims. Many great non-profit companies exist.

They are the ones who deserve support because they really are saving lives today. Homeless animals need food today, not in five years! They won't be alive in five years or whenever the group claims it can begin to spend money to help pets. Support active groups, not simply groups in existence. Groups with a true determination to save lives take action and find a way to make a difference today!

Putting pre-paid postage on the envelope is an action I would advise against. If someone is willing to send a contribution, then they are willing to provide a stamp. I never could waste money, like taking the chance that the person will not donate, therefore wasting a stamp. Mailing letters to individuals with the possibility of them becoming a donor, perhaps even for the long term is a risk that is necessary, but including an additional stamp within that letter is not good business.

All those stamps will add up quickly. Small amounts of wasted money will add up to large amounts of wasted money. I have always lived by this philosophy in my personal life. This is absolutely the truth with money management. Never waste money. Another way to generate funds is to ask local businesses, including large chain stores that are located in your town or city, to support your charity.

Local Business Support

Many businesses make donating to charities a part of their budgets. Giving back to the community is good for their public image. Some companies truly enjoy participating in making a difference for causes in which they believe. Businesses can be contacted in person, by mail, or a combination of both methods. One can go to the business and ask to speak with the manager. Calling the company may get some useful information for your group from the person answering the phone, as far as the way charities seeking financial support are handled by this company.

Keep in mind when someone from a charity calls, it is easier to just get them off the phone more quickly, perhaps making less of an impact than from physically coming to the business. With calling on the phone, one may find out the contact at the company that handles these affairs, giving one the ability to personally contact this person.

When dealing with a grocery store, one may benefit by coming in to see the manager. The manager may decide to donate a few bags of cat food right off the shelf. If that is not the case, do not fret. As I said, most of these large chain-store businesses have a plan in place about donating to charities, in their main corporate office. The store manager can provide the address and contact department to you. Often the department which handles charitable donations will send a gift certificate to an organization for use in their stores.

Stores and other businesses can provide another medium for your entity to collect funds. Placing donation cans any place that people will drop donations into is always helpful. My experience with donation cans is that they are helpful, but do not generate a lot of money. The more locations they are placed at, the more opportunity there will be to generate additional money.

Keep an extra can or cans so that a shelter representative can walk into the store, simply picking up one can and leave another in its place. This reassures employees that the person is affiliated with this organization, not some thief leaving with a donation can. I recommend having cans with a lock on them with a small hole for the money to go into, but cannot be shaken or picked out by thieves.

In one location where a donation can was placed, someone that worked at this animal feed store was stealing the donations. The donation box began to have almost no donations all of the sudden. To confirm my suspicion, I placed two dollar bills in it one time when I exchanged cans. The next time I checked it there was no money in it, other than a few coins. My thought that theft was occurring had confirmation.

Management was contacted about the theft situation. They felt bad about it. Since no cameras were in use at this store, I could not allow my donation box to remain there to be robbed. How awful that someone would steal from a charity providing for homeless cats! I certainly would not want people's donations to a good cause buying some drunken cashier more liquor, and not going to the good cause they intended their money to go to, either.

Another way that stores can help the conglomerate is by allowing it to set up a table at the entry or exit door to solicit donations. When one sets up a table, at a business, know that a large, prominent sign is needed with the organization's name with what it does stated clearly. This sign will get used many times for all fund-raising functions. Customers may drop money into the donation can or buy cat food for the cats in your care. Business cards are needed to give to people who want to bring you or adopt a cat in the future. This is also a good way to make contact with cat-lovers in your community. Keep in mind not everyone coming to the store likes cats.

Some people will tell you they hate cats, or some such rude comment. This is just part of fund-raising. I often tell this type of person that this organization works to get abandoned cats off the street and sterilized, so it is actually in their best interest to donate, so they don't have to see so many cats. They don't usually donate, but I want them to understand that the corporation's existence is beneficial to everyone in the community. It is not a cat's fault that it was abandoned. Cats are domestic companion animals that are just as much a part of society as any other segment of the population.

It is definitely not pleasant to deal with people with a bad attitude towards cats. I always say something geared directly for their particular mindset, or attitude, about cats to help them to see cats in a different light. My desire is to give someone a bit more of a positive attitude toward cats.

I feel that I am representing cats when I am out trying to raise community financial support. If people's attitudes don't start to change, then the plight of cats will not change as quickly as it needs to change. Use every opportunity to help cats. They deserve for every one of us that loves them dearly to do as much as possible to help them get more respect in our society.

Contacting as many businesses as possible can only benefit the cat shelter by increasing its support base. You have nothing to lose by asking them, other than some time and perhaps some postage. Think big! Don't hesitate to contact a car dealership, for instance. There are raffles held for vehicles that could raise lots of money for the cats. A dealership may donate a vehicle to your organization. They benefit from the tax deduction.

Businesses may want to donate some other item that can be sold to raise donations. For instance, a company may purchase potted flowering plants for a particular event they are holding. Once the event is finished, the business has no other use for the flowering plants. Tell businesses you will come to pick up their unwanted items that can be re-sold. There is another way a store may be able to help a pet haven.

Management at the store may allow you to set up a table at the doorway to sell your own products to raise money. Finding a busy store that allows one the opportunity to sell from their location is a tremendous benefit. I have tried selling on roadside corners, with the proper permits, and literally driving from business to business to try to sell to customers and staff. You will then realize how common the "no soliciting," sign is on the door of businesses. There are many businesses you cannot even enter. This method is so difficult!

Without a productive place to stay for the day, the alternative is financially and physically consumptive. One's time will be devoured. Gasoline will be exhausted, literally! This method of fund-raising requires a certain level of fitness because getting into and out of the vehicle while repetitively grabbing the item to carry in to sell is very redundant. With my previously broken back and current problems I have today, this was very physically tolling on my body.

There are some emotional considerations. Expect rejection, don't take it personal. It is not easy to get sales. People driving by don't usually stop. I have gone to flea markets, renting a booth for the day or weekend. All these methods are much more difficult than a store front.

If you find a business that allows the corporation a place to sell from with a large volume of potential buyers right at your table for the day, be ecstatic and grateful. As you can see, one must do whatever is necessary, to raise money. The cats must eat every day. Businesses can be a great asset to the shelter, so utilize the potential opportunity, but do not overstep any boundaries.

Do not become a nuisance to any business. Use good judgment on your level of persistence. The goal is to receive as much support as possible for the cats, in your community. Forming good relationships with the business community, as well as, individuals is important.

Representation Rule

Use every opportunity in life to represent cats in a positive light and improve other people's attitudes towards cats. Only those of us who care will be the ones to create change in the world.

Yard Sales

Individuals can donate unwanted items, for the shelter's use in a yard sale to raise money. This method has a potential downside, though. People may donate junk that is not even saleable. One way to counter the problem is to state requirements about what is acceptable, to avoid this problem. For instance, used clothing is not a fast mover. It does not sell for very much. People may bring torn, extremely worn clothing. Torn, wore-out clothes could be used for animal bedding, but not for sale. Another way to deal with items is to accept everything, going through it, discarding what is not useful.

Thrift Store

A thrift store is a means that many charities use to generate money. This will require an expenditure of money. One needs a building to receive and sell merchandise. Insurance will need to be purchased for the building and for personal liability purposes. Volunteers or paid staff will be needed to operate the store. Repetitive hours of operation will be required to establish a customer base.

Car Wash

A car wash is certainly a great way to earn cash. Many businesses are willing to allow charities to use their property for this purpose for a day or weekend. This activity will need several volunteers so that cars can be quickly washed. Have buckets, soap, sponges, towels, and hoses for this project.

Remember to bring money envelopes, the big plastic ones that banks give out, or something to put the cash into as it is collected through the day. In the summer, particularly when there has not been any rain for quite some time when cars are very dirty, is the best time to have a car wash. However, there are always dirty cars on the road, glad to find a quick wash.

Special Event Fundraiser

A formally organized event can draw a crowd to your endeavor. First, a place to hold the function is required. Then one can decide on the theme, like something held for Christmas, where children and parents can come to see Santa along with some cats needing a home. Perhaps an Easter egg search event could be held with a fee being charged to find the eggs or other hidden prizes.

Whatever type of event you organize, get the media to advertise it, to promote a large turnout of people. With these types of functions, it is important not to spend too much money for them. You cannot be sure how many people will attend the function. Generating more money than one spends is the goal. Some charities spend exorbitant amounts of money to put on an event, consequently defeating the entire purpose, by spending more than they make. Another type of fundraising involves more labor with a pen, than with people.

Grants

Many private foundations exist for the purpose of furthering philanthropic causes they believe in strongly. Tax-exempt charities can apply to receive money from these foundations to further their goals, like sterilizing cats. Many foundations have very specific guidelines in place for those who apply for money. One needs to obtain and fill-out a form from the foundation, in most cases.

Time frames are extremely specific. Some of these organizations allow only a few weeks of the entire year in which they accept applications. Others accept them from January through June of each year. Besides having certain time frames that applications are accepted, there are other requirements, such as location.

Many foundations want to make a difference, with their philanthropic cause, in a specific location. The requirement could be as broad as a regional area, like in the southeastern states of the United States. Quite often, however, you will find the area is much more limited.

The rules to apply for grants can be very specific. Grants sometimes are only given to charities within a certain state. Much of the time only charities within certain counties, within a particular state, qualify to be considered for the grant. The specifics on all of the rules that each particular foundation has in place is what makes applying for grants so challenging. A lot of time is required to research the foundations that give to animal based charities.

First establish that the foundation will donate to a cat welfare charity. Inquire exactly what the foundation will support. Determine whether this is a match for your charity. Only then will it be determined if you need to request an application for submission. For example, a foundation may give money only to charities that have their own spay and neuter program. Your charity may not. It may be required that the organization must wait six months before applying because the time of year is not correct for that foundation's period to read through applications. Good luck with your submissions.

Epilogue

Cats need all caring people to participate in improving their status in society. By working together with the common goal of respecting feline life, the situation will greatly improve for cats. All of us can play an instrumental role in this mission, by engaging with the cause in some way. We each have something to offer. Each person's contribution is his or her voice and actions.

Cat guardians have the information required when faced with behavior problems or simply training a kitty to use the scratching post. Understanding a cat's instincts is empowering. This knowledge can be utilized as a resource to solve cat care dilemmas. The new ideas presented give caretakers facts about options to consider when contemplating giving up your cat for circumstantial reasons, such as moving.

There are so many cats which have no safe options when they are faced with a homeless situation. With people taking the initiative to help a homeless feline when it crosses their path, many lives will be saved. Starting one's own shelter to help many cats is an awesome endeavor. It is not easy, but it is very rewarding. One needs lots of determination, plenty of love for cats, perseverance to face challenges, and financial management ability. Many more no-kill shelters are severely needed. If one decides to take on the monumental task of starting a refuge for cats, then decisions will need to be made.

Carefully think through how to conduct all elements of operating the shelter. There will be different forms to fill out to create a non-profit organization. These questions prepare one for issues that the haven will face through daily operations. All of the work will prove to be worth the effort. Know that by choosing this vocation, you are embarking into a journey of challenges, but with great rewards!

Appendix

A Hand-Out for Adopters

What to Expect and How to Care for Your New Cat

A cat will generally take a few days to adjust to a new environment. Remember that each cat is an individual. Some cats will take a couple of weeks to acclimate. This is perfectly normal. However, your cat may adjust almost immediately. Just know that each one is unique. A cat may be leery or standoffish toward its new guardian. Feeding the cat, especially something very tasty, will help the cat bond with its new caretaker. Letting all members of the household feed the cat will help the cat get used to them, also. Spending quiet time talking to the cat is a good way to create a bond.

If a cat does not bond right away with some members of the household, this is perfectly natural. It will just take a little time. Don't get discouraged or be offended. The cat's life experiences as well as his/her genetic makeup determine its present behavior and method of adjusting to new environments and people. When you adopt a cat, you are adding a new member to your family. This is a serious commitment. You must be willing to do whatever is necessary to adjust all of your family members to get along with one another and the surroundings. Don't expect the adjustment period to be any specific length of time because nothing is exact when you're dealing with individuals.

Any cat that will be primarily living outdoors will need to be confined in an area so that they get used to their new home before being allowed to go free. The cat will just run off if allowed to go completely free, before learning that this specific area is its new home. Cats usually will be frightened in a new environment, but the more time that is spent with them the quicker they will adjust.

What Your Cat Needs

Every cat needs:
1. Food and Water Bowl
2. Dry cat food
3. Canned cat food (not essential, but most cats love it)
4. Litter Box and litter
5. Scratching post and/or cat condo (with carpet, sisal rope, and/or wood and is not wobbly)
6. Cat toys (they especially love Wacky Mice, by Hartz)
7. Grass, a small handful daily, supplied to indoor cats who do not have access to it outdoors.

Cats should be fed dry food at free range, as they like to nibble many small meals throughout the day and night. Food should always be available to them. Kittens need to have a dry food that is made especially for kittens, until they are one-year old. They must have the extra protein that is in this food. This allows them to grow properly, having enough nutrition to develop strong bones and muscles.

Feeding bowls should be washed weekly, at a minimum. Canned cat food can be fed once or twice daily. Give them only what they will eat up in a few minutes time because it will spoil if left out for very long (most cats are glad to eat it very quickly). Bacteria could grow on the food, causing your kitty to become very ill. It may be necessary to try different flavors to see which ones the cat likes best. Water must be changed at least once daily.

The litter box should be placed in a quiet, non-busy portion of the house, if possible. Cats like to have some privacy. A closet, with the door open, would be an acceptable place for the box. The box needs to be scooped out daily. If more than one cat uses the box, then more often would certainly be required. Cats are extremely clean animals. With a box being filthy, they will find some other place to go potty. It is very important to keep it clean.

Whenever the box itself gets dirty, you will need to wash it. The litter box needs to be washed weekly, whether it appears soiled or not. Use bleach or another disinfecting cleaner to scrub the box with warm water. Do not use a cleaner that leaves a strong odor of any type. Many cats will have an aversion to the odor and may not use the box.

Keep in mind that cats have much better scent receptors than we, humans, do and they are only inches from the box itself. Only new fresh litter should be placed back in the box. Even if clumping litter is used, particles of it will fall off. Odors will remain in the box, maybe not detectable by you, but certainly by your cat. Consequently, every week the litter should be replaced. Pine pellet or corn litters are optimal choices.

Every cat needs a scratching post or a cat condo, which usually comes with carpet or sisal rope on it. A couple of lessons are usually all that will be necessary to teach the cat where to scratch. Pick the cat up and set him/her upright alongside the post. Gently place the front paws on the unit, performing the scratching motion with the paws. If you see the cat begin to scratch somewhere he/she should not, this is a perfect opportunity to pick the cat up and put him or her in the proper place for scratching. Even if the cat is declawed, getting a post or condo is recommended so the cat will have his/her own article of furniture to exercise the forearm muscles somewhat. These cats will still do the scratching motions. Declawed cats desire to strengthen their muscles and tendons, even though they are not able to grip anything.

All cats, young or old, should be given toys to entertain him or herself. Most cats really like Wacky Mice. They are similar in size, to a real mouse. Some of them rattle. Others do not. A homemade toy for the cat could be just as entertaining. Just be sure that the cat has something to play with, when he/she decides to play. Change the toys out for new ones once the cat becomes bored with the current toys. Be sure there is nothing the cat can get tangled in or swallow, for safety purposes.

Health Care

Each cat needs to have an annual exam by a veterinarian to assess the health of the cat and to identify any possible ailment the cat may be developing. A fecal exam, for parasites, should be done, at least annually. Some worms are not visible to the eye, but are very harmful to the cat's health. Worms will multiply and grow when left untreated. The tapeworm is one type of worm that is easy to see and recognize.

Portions of the worm break off, crawling out of the anus or can be seen on feces or in the cat's bedding. Fleas are the medium that transfers the worm to the cat. Fleas are the host of the tapeworm. When the cat ingests a flea, like when licking their fur, the cat becomes infected. Most fleas are carriers. All worms are devastating to a cat! This point can't be stressed enough! The good news is these parasites are very easy to eliminate, you just need the proper pill or oral liquid to kill that worm.

Fleas are a real nuisance. As I previously mentioned, they can bring more than an annoying itch to your cat. There are some great flea products available for purchase that need to be applied only once per month between the cat's shoulder blades. Some kill ticks, too. Ticks can be a serious pest and vector of disease, in some areas. For a cat that will be going outside, use of a flea-killing product is recommended.

Be very aware of your cat's behavior patterns. A change in behavior could certainly indicate the cat is not feeling well. For instance, if the cat does not eat the same amount of food as usual, the cat may have an illness, infection or dental problem. By feeling the cat's ear temperature, you can mildly reconfirm your thoughts that the cat may be ill.

Very hot or cold ears could indicate a fever is present. This is just a simple way to monitor the cat's health, but is certainly no replacement for visiting a vet. A cat should be taken right away to a vet upon suspicion of illness. There may be a serious problem that needs professional medical attention.

Enjoy your new family member, and be sure to treat him or her as part of the family!

State Contact Information for Incorporating

Alabama
Secretary of State, Land & Trademarks Division
P.O. Box 5616
Montgomery, AL 36103-5616
Phone: (334) 242-5325

Alaska
Secretary of State, Division of Banking Securities & Corporations
P.O. Box 110808
Juneau, AK 91891
Phone: (907) 465-2530

Arizona
Secretary of State
1700 W. Washington, 7th Fl.
Phoenix, AZ 85007
Phone: (602) 542-6187

Arkansas
Secretary of State, Aegon Building
501 Wood Lane, Suite 310
Little Rock, AR 72201
Phone: (501) 682-3409

California
Secretary of State, Trademarks/ Service Marks
1500 11th St.
Sacramento, CA 95814
Phone: (916) 653-7244

Colorado
Secretary of State, Business Division
1560 Broadway, Suite 200
Denver, CO 80202
Phone: (303) 894-2251

Connecticut
Secretary of State
30 Trinity St.
P.O. Box 150470
Hartford, CT 06106
Phone: (860) 509-6004

Delaware
Secretary of State, Division of Corporations
P.O. Box 898
Dover, DE 19903
Phone: (302) 739-3073

Florida
Secretary of State, Division of Corporations
P.O. Box 6327
Tallahassee, FL 32314
Phone: (850) 487-6051

Georgia
Secretary of state, Corporations Division
315 West Tower
#2 Martin Luther King Jr. Dr.
Atlanta, GA 30334
Phone: (404) 656-2861

Hawaii
Secretary of State, Business Registration
P.O. Box 40
Honolulu, HI 96810
Phone: (808) 586-2727

Idaho
Secretary of State
700 W. Jefferson St., Room 203
Boise, ID 83720-0080
Phone: (208) 334-2300

Illinois
Secretary of State, Business Services
69 W. Washington, suite 1240
Chicago, IL 60602
Phone: (800) 252-8980

Indiana
Secretary of State, Business services
302 W. Washington, Room E-108
Indianapolis, IN 46204
Phone: (317) 232-6540

Iowa
Secretary of State, State House
Des Moines, IA 50319
Phone: (515) 281-5865

Kansas
Secretary of State, Memorial Hall
120 SW 10th Ave
Topeka, KS 66612-1594
Phone: (785) 296-4564

Kentucky
Secretary of State, Trademarks/ Service Marks
Room 86, State Capitol
Frankfort, KY 40601
Phone: (502) 564-2848

Louisiana
Secretary of State, Corporation Division
P.O. Box 94125
Baton Rouge, LA 70804-9125
Phone: (225) 925-4704

Maine
Secretary of State, Bureau of Corporations
Elections & Commissions
101 State House Station
Augusta, ME 04333-0101
Phone: (207) 624-7740

Maryland
Charitable Organizations Division
Office of the Secretary of State
State House
Annapolis, MD 21401
Phone: (410) 974-5534

Massachusetts
Secretary of the Commonwealth, Corporations Division
1 Ashburton Pl., 17th Fl.
Boston, MA 02108
Phone: (617) 727-9640

Michigan
Bureau of Commercial Service, Corporations Division
7510 Harris Drive
Lansing, MI 48910
Phone: (517) 241-6400

Minnesota
Secretary of State
180 State Office Building
St. Paul, MN 55155
Phone: (651) 296-2803

Mississippi
Secretary of State
P.O. Box 136
Jackson, MS 39205
Phone: (601) 359-1633

Missouri
Secretary of State
600 W. Main & 208, State Capitol
P.O. Box 778
Jefferson City, MO 65102
Phone: (314) 863-5545

Montana
Secretary of State
P.O. Box 202801
Helena, MT 59620-2801
Phone: (406) 444-2034

Nebraska
Secretary of State, Corporations Division
Room 1305, State Capitol
P.O. Box 94608
Lincoln, NE 68509-4608
Phone: (402) 471-4079

Nevada
Secretary of State – Annex Commercial Recordings
202 N. Carson St.
Carson City, NV 89701-4271
Phone: (775) 684-5708

New Hampshire

Department of State, Corporation Division
State House, Room 204
Concord, NH 03301
Phone: (603) 271-3244

New Jersey
Division of Revenue, TM/SM Unit
P.O. Box 453
Trenton, NJ 08625
Phone: (609) 292-9292

New Mexico
Secretary of State, Operations Division
State Capitol, N. Annex, Suite 300
Santa Fe, NM 87503
Phone: (505) 827-3600

New York
Secretary of State, Division of Corporations
State Records & Uniform Commercial Co.
41 State St.
Albany, NY 12231-0001
Phone: (518) 473-2492

North Carolina
Secretary of State, Trademarks Section
P.O. Box 29622
Raleigh, NC 27626-0622
Phone: (919) 807-2162

North Dakota
Secretary of State
600 E. Blvd. Ave., Dept. 108
Bismarck, ND 58505-0500
Phone: (701) 328-4284

Ohio
Secretary of State
P.O. Box 1028
Columbus, OH 43216
Phone: (614) 466-3910

Oklahoma
Secretary of State, Business Services Division
2300 N. Blvd., Room 101
Oklahoma City, OK 73105-4897
Phone: (405) 522-3043

Oregon
Secretary of State, Corporation Division
Business Registry Section Public Service Bldg.
255 Capitol St. NE
Salem, OR 97310-1327
Phone: (503) 986-2200

Pennsylvania
Department of State
P.O. Box 8721
Harrisburg, PA 17015-8722
Phone: (717) 787-1057

Rhode Island
Secretary of State, Trademark Section
100 N. Main St.
Providence, RI 02903-1335
Phone: (401) 222-1487

South Carolina
Secretary of State
P.O. Box 11350
Columbia, SC 29211
Phone: (803) 734-1728

South Dakota
Secretary of State
Capitol Bldg.
500 E. Capitol Ave., Suite 204
Pierre, SD 57501-5070
Phone: (605) 773-5666

Tennessee
Dept. of State, Division of Business Service
312 8th Ave. N., 6th Fl.
William R. Sondgrass Tower
Nashville, TN 37243
Phone: (615) 741-0531

Texas
Secretary of State, Corporations Division
P.O. Box 13697
Austin, TX 78711
Phone: (512) 463-5600

Utah
Dept. of Commerce
Division of Corp. & Commercial Code
160 E. 300 S.
Salt Lake City, UT 84111
Phone: (801) 530-4849

Vermont
Secretary of State, Corporations Division
81 St. Drawer 09
Montpelier, VT 05609-1104
Phone: (802) 828-2386

Virginia
State Corp. Comm. Securities Division
P.O. Box 1197
Richmond, VA 23218
Phone: (804) 371-9187

Washington
Secretary of State, Corporations Division
801 Capitol Way S.
P.O. Box 40234
Olympia, WA 98504-0234
Phone: (360) 753-7115

West Virginia
Secretary of state, Corporations Division
Bldg. 1, Suite 157-K
1900 Kanawha Blvd. East
Charleston, WV 25305-0770
Phone: (304) 558-8000

Wisconsin
Secretary of State
P.O. Box 7848
Madison, WI 53707-7848
Phone: (608) 266-5653

Wyoming
Secretary of State
State Capitol Bldg.
Cheyenne, WY 82002
Phone: (307) 777-7378

References

Baker, Rex O.; Bennett, Joe R.; Coolahan, Craig c.; Timm, Robert M. "Coyote Attacks: An Increasing Suburban Problem". 2004. Agriculture & Natural Resources Research & Extension Centers; Hopland Research & Extension Center (University of CA, Davis). (accessed May 23, 2008). <http://repositories.cdlib.org/cgi/viewcontent.cgi?article=1004&context=anrrec/hrec>

Conrad, Jennifer. "Twenty Paws Repaired in 2005". The Paw Project No. 4 (Winter 2006): 1ff.

Department of the Treasury: Internal Revenue Service. "Application for Recognition of Exemption. Package 1023"(10/2004): 1-29.

Department of the Treasury: Internal Revenue Service. "Tax-Exempt Status for Your Organization. Publication 557". (11/1999): 1-55.

Division of Corporations. Florida Not For Profit Corporation Act. (3/2000): 1-62.

"Eight Strikes Against Fishy Feeding". Sept 22, 2007. catnutrition.org. (accessed Mar 16, 2008). <http://catnutrition.wordpress.com/2007/09/>.

Fogle, Bruce. The Encyclopedia of the Cat. First American Edition. New York, NY: DK Publishing, Inc., 1997.

Hofve, Jean & Galaxy, Jackson. "Catswalk". Catswalk 5.6. 8/2007. (accessed Feb 18, 2008). <http://www.littlebigcat.com/index.php?action=nlarchive&show=volume5no6>.

Judd, Bob. "Ban on Declawing Cats". *Texas Vet News*. Sept 15, 2006. Texas Farm Bureau Radio Network. <http://www.veterinarypartner.com/context.plx?P=A&A=2387&S=O&SourceID=69>.

"Norfolk Puts Ban on Declawing Cats". April 2007. CBS. (accessed Feb 16, 2008). <http://www.wtvr.com/Global/story.asp?S=6432471>.

"Onychectomy". Feb.17, 2008. Wikimedia Foundation, Inc. (accessed Feb 18, 2008). <http://en.wikipedia.org/wiki/Onychectomy>.

"Origin of Halloween". 1996-2007. A&E Television Networks. (accessed Mar1, 2008). <http://www.history.com/minisites/halloween/viewPage?pageId=713>

Pavia, Audrey. "Help for Moody Cats". Catnip 15.12 (12/2007): 3-6.

Reitman, Judith. "One Way Ticket to Ground Zero". AV Magazine: This is Vivisection CVIII.2 (2000): 14-17.

Rizer, George; Ryan, Andrew; May 23, 2007. "Coyotes and People Collide in West Roxbury". Globe Staff. The Globe. (accessed May 25, 2008). <http://www.boston.com/news/globe/city_region/breaking_news/2007/05/coyotes_andpeo.html>

Schelling, Christianne. "Outlawed Countries". (accessed Feb 15, 2008). <www.declawing.com>.

"Scientists Investigate Recent Coyote Attacks on Children in Southern California". May 12, 2008. Fox News. (accessed May 20, 2008). <http://www.foxnews.com/story/0,2933,354988,00.html>

Speigel, Crystal. "Cat Madness Human Research Using Cats". AV Magazine: Focus on Felines CXI.1 (2003): 3-7.

Thornton, Kim Campbell. "Spotlight on Feline Research". Catnip 15.11 (11/2007): 13-16.

CPSIA information can be obtained at www.ICGtesting.com
Printed in the USA
LVOW121430201012

303743LV00002B/33/P